To Make the Deaf Hear

To Make the Deaf Hear

Ideology and Programme of Bhagat Singh and His Comrades

S. Irfan Habib

First Edition September 2007
Second reprint January 2010
Third reprint 2017

ISBN 978-81-88789-61-0

Three Essays
COLLECTIVE

B-957 Palam Vihar, GURGAON (Haryana) 122 017 India
Phone: 91-124 2369023, +91 98681 26587, +91 98683 44843
info@threeessays.com   Website: www.threeessays.com
Printed and bound at Glorious Printers, New Delhi

Dedicated to the memory of my father
Dr. M.A. Zaidi

CONTENTS

PREFACE TO THE NEW REPRINT

I am happy and also surprised that a large number of people want to know and comprehend Bhagat Singh as an ideologue and do not want to venerate him merely as a martyr and nationalist. My book *To Make the Deaf Hear* was the first major attempt to understand the evolution of Bhagat Singh as a revolutionary thinker. It appeared first in 2007 and was soon translated into different Indian languages like Hindi, Tamil, Malayalam, Bengali and Punjabi. It is gratifying that I am writing a fresh preface for the new reprint of this book.

Bhagat Singh is one of the only national heroes, may be after Mahatma Gandhi, who is revered across India. This could happen because his appeal as a martyr cuts across political ideologies. I only wish that the same was true for his intellectual legacy as well. Most of us just lap him up as a martyr but seldom care to ponder about his intellectual legacy. We hardly take note of his hard hitting journalistic writings on issues of social and political concern, the issues that remain unresolved even today. I did not deal with them in this edition but will surely take it up as a fresh new chapter in yet another version next year. You may find a little flavor of that in this short preface.

We need to remember that the 1920s was Bhagat Singh's active revolutionary phase. This decade was crucial for our freedom struggle on various counts. It began with Mahatma Gandhi's first mass movement, which also initiated most of our young revolutionaries of this period into anti-colonial struggle. It ended with the Chauri Chaura fiasco, leading to widespread frustration among the youth, including Bhagat Singh and his comrades. This decade also saw the birth of *Rashtriya Swayamsevak Sangh* (RSS) in 1925. Thus we could see the institutionalization of identity politics around religion and culture, while in the midst of all this Bhagat Singh and his associates set up Naujawan Bharat Sabha in Lahore in 1926 with secular and socialistic commitments. Incidentally, this decade also saw the birth of the Communist Party of India.

Bhagat Singh wrote a series of articles in the late 1920s on vital issues like untouchability, communalism and role of the press. In the first piece in June 1928, writing for *Kirti*, a paper published from Amritsar, he spoke against untouchability saying that "our country is unique where six crore citizens are called untouchables and their mere touch defiles upper castes. Gods get enraged if they enter the temples." He spoke against the raging communalism of the 1920s when he castigated certain politicians and the press for being irresponsible. He went to the extent of saying that "there are few leaders, but their voice is easily swept away by the rising wave of communalism. In terms of political leadership, India had gone totally bankrupt". His views on both the issues sound so contemporaneous. It seems we did precious little to rise above these divisive issues.

I look forward to engaging with these concerns of Bhagat Singh in some detail soon. Hope the ideas of Bhagat Singh, as documented in this book, will continue to inspire the coming generations. They were always relevant but more so in the times we live in today.

S. Irfan Habib

New Delhi

August 25, 2017

Preface

The most attractive and convenient way to remember Bhagat Singh and his comrades has been to simply commemorate their martyrdom for the cause of India's freedom. We see this happen every year on March 23, when all political parties, cutting across ideological positions, get euphoric in appropriating this legacy of patriotism and self-sacrifice. Surely, we should all cherish and revere this inheritance but this is not the end of the revolutionary bequest. These revolutionaries were not merely trigger-happy adventurous patriots who sacrificed their lives for the country; more importantly, they espoused a revolutionary vision to transform independent India into a secular, socialist, and egalitarian society. We did not lose merely individuals, however valuable, in the hanging of Bhagat Singh and his associates; we lost rather an alternative framework of governance for post-independent India. Justice Medilton, who transported Bhagat Singh and BK Dutt for life in the Assembly Bomb Case, testified to their mature political understanding in the judgment itself saying that "These persons used to enter the court with the cries of 'Long Live Revolution' and 'Long Live the Proletariat' which shows clearly what sort of political ideology they cherish. In order to put a check in propagating these ideas I transport them for life." It has not been adequately realized that for the national revolutionaries national liberation meant political freedom as well as end to economic exploitation. Their vision of nation building was qualitatively different from the mainstream Congress model and was far removed from the right reactionary programme of the present day BJP and its cohorts, who leave no opportunity to appropriate their martyrdom.

The present volume is a modest attempt to delineate the sources of inspiration, and the ideology and programme of the national revolutionaries during the 1920s and early 1930s. Bhagat Singh and his associates were passionate about two vital issues, which have contemporary national and international relevance: one is secularism and ascientific temper, and second, the reorganization of society on a socialistic basis. We will find in the following pages how these ideological commitments evolved and matured in their short and eventful political lives. We will also locate their activities and ideological positions in the broader context of the Indian freedom struggle, which was dominated by the Congress and the Mahatma.

Most of the revolutionary groups in India agreed to suspend their activities to support Mahatma Gandhi's Non-Cooperation Movement and had pinned great hopes on the outcome of this struggle. However, the sudden recoiling of the movement in 1922 led to utter disillusionment among the people across India and the revolutionary groups in particular felt cheated by this turn of events. They felt that the national bourgeois leadership was terrified at the revolutionary outbreak of the peasantry and it had betrayed the workers, the peasants and the youth. The impact of the Bolshevik revolution was being felt more and more and this led to a widening of horizons in their outlook. "Socialism, though not clearly understood, was attracting their minds and the ideals of social justice which were in a nebulous form in the earlier period were turning towards taking a distinct shape."

The Hindustan Republican Association (HRA) was formed in the aftermath of their disillusionment with the Congress leadership in 1924 and its manifesto *The Revolutionary* in 1925 spelt out its ideological commitments. The manifesto did not use the word socialism even once though it talked about class struggle, of making exploitation of man by man impossible, of nationalization of major public works and industries, and preferred cooperative unions to private and unorganized business. They were clear on the issue of secularism as well and the position of HRA can be discerned clearly from the views of Shaheed Ashfaqullah Khan and Mahavir Singh, both involved in the Kakori Case. Ashfaqullah Khan wrote an open letter to his countrymen just three days before his execution in 1927, expressing his anguish at the political developments and communal mobilization. He condemned both the movements – *tabligh* as well as *shuddhi* – and warned his countrymen that such divisions were weakening the struggle for independence. He wrote: "It is impossible to purify seven crore Muslims and similarly it is absurd to think that twenty five crore Hindus can be converted to Islam. But yes, it is easy that we all put the chains of slavery around our necks." Mahavir Singh, facing life imprisonment in the Andamans wrote to his father: "By *Samaj* (Society) I do not mean *Arya Samaj* or any other narrow *Samaj* but a society of common people. This is because these religious societies mean nothing to me due to their myopism. Moreover I want to keep away from all religions because they are narrow, self centred and based on injustice and want others also to do the same. What I believe to be of greatest benefit to man and society is the following principle: the human relations should not be based on any distinction of caste, colour, religion or money." Ashfaqullah's another extraordinary statement on the socio-political set up of India to which he and his revolutionary group aspired is as follows:

> I consider the alien rule an evil, and at the same time I hate any democratic Indian rule where the weak are denied the rights, or if it is the creation of the rich and landlords, or there is no equal participation of the farmers and workers, or if the laws of the government are made on the basis of inequality and disparity. If India becomes free and our brother countrymen take the reins of government from the white masters, and if the inequality persists between the rich and the poor and the landlord and the tenant, I pray to God not to give me such freedom till equality is established in His Creation. Let me be dubbed a Communist for these ideas. I damn care.

Several films have been made on the lives and sacrifices of these revolutionaries in recent years but, unfortunately, most of them did not care to highlight the key role Ashfaqullah played in the Kakori case. While talking of celluloid experience, let me also mention an instance, which should have been highlighted in all the films on Bhagat Singh but is missing. Justice Agha Haider was the only Indian judge who resigned from the tribunal in protest against the brutal treatment being meted out to Bhagat Singh and his comrades in the Lahore Conspiracy Case. It is important to mention this selective amnesia as it conforms to the current trend of religion based nationalism.

The Hindustan Republican Association (HRA) was changed into Hindustan Socialist Republican Association (HSRA) after Bhagat Singh joined the revolutionary group. The word 'socialist' was added to its name after detailed deliberations among the revolutionaries from UP and Punjab in 1928 at Delhi's Feroz Shah Kotla. This was an ideological departure for the revolutionary group as the involvement of Bhagat Singh broadened its outlook by making HSRA more internationalist. They also envisaged the creation of a World Order which will free humanity from the scourge of capitalism and imperial wars. They proclaimed:

> Unless…Imperialism is brought to an end, the suffering and carnage with which humanity is threatened today cannot be prevented and all talk of ending wars and ushering in an era of universal peace is undisguised hypocrisy…a World Federation should redeem humanity from the bondage of capitalism and the misery of imperial wars.

One can see the relevance of the above yearning of Bhagat Singh and his comrades today when imperialist wars have spread terror and bloodshed from Afghanistan and Iraq to Palestine and other parts of West Asia.

When the RSS was being organized in 1925 in Nagpur, Bhagat Singh and his associates were busy founding the Naujawan Bharat Sabha in Lahore in 1926, which was actually the public platform for the otherwise secret group of revolutionaries. The Sabha was above all petty religious politics of the times and stood for secularism. "Before enrolment each member was made to sign a pledge that he would place the interests of his country above those of his community." Even Lala Lajpat Rai, the eminent pillar of extremist nationalism in India could not escape scathing criticism from the Sabha when he joined hands with the Hindu Mahasabha leaders. Rai was dubbed a traitor by Kedar Nath Sehgal in a pamphlet, *An Appeal to the Young Punjab,* while Lajpat Rai responded by accusing Bhagat Singh of being a Russian agent 'who wanted to make me into a Lenin'. In an attempt to check the rising communalism of the 1920s, the Sabha organized a series of public lectures to discuss socio-political matters. It regarded communal amity as an important part of the political programme; it raised two new slogans, *Inquilab Zindabad* and *Hindustan Zindabad,* hailing the revolution and the country.

Bhagat Singh was acutely conscious of the growing menace of communalism in the 1920s – the decade which saw the emergence of the Hindu Mahasabha and the Rashtriya Swayamsevak Sangh (RSS) – and specific movements of the Muslims like *Tablighi Jamaat.* These are hydra headed today with several political and cultural fronts, posing a serious threat to the socio-political fabric of Indian society. Bhagat Singh questioned the policy of encouraging competing communalisms, which ultimately led to the partition of the country in 1947. He stands out in bold relief as a modern national leader and thinker, emphasizing the separation of religion from politics and state as true secularism. All those who revel in the name of Bhagat Singh but talk of a hierarchical society should know that Bhagat Singh stood for a "social revolution", envisaging the dissolution of all social and economic disparities, an ideal which appears even more far-fetched today amidst the shrieks of communal rabble rousers.

Today, in the days of WTO and globalization, we are reminded of Bhagat Singh and his passionate involvement with the lives of workers and peasants. He could go with Batukeshwar Dutt and bomb the Delhi Assembly to make the deaf hear the plight of the workers. They threw a bundle of red leaflets saying, "we dropped the bomb in the Assembly Chamber to register our protest on behalf of those who had no other option left to give expression to their heart rending agony." As his own study and self development progressed during incarceration, Bhagat Singh's thoughts further crystallized and he could succinctly explain his notion of socialism before the Court on June 6 1929: "Producers or labourers, in spite of being the most necessary element of society, are robbed by their exploiters of the fruits of their labour and deprived of their elementary rights...and on the other hand, capitalist exploiters, parasites of society, squander millions on their whims... Radical change, therefore, is necessary and it is the duty of those who realize this to reorganize society on a socialistic basis." Today, socialism may be anathema to some, but it was undoubtedly a great inspiration to most of the oppressed colonial societies. Bhagat Singh's jail diary gives us deep insights into his rapidly growing maturity as a Marxist. It contains elaborate quotations from the works of Marx, Engels, Lenin, Trotsky, Bakunin, Prince Kropotkin, and even Darwin, Bertrand Russell and several others. In his June 6 statement again, Bhagat Singh categorically explained the meaning of revolution saying: "Revolution is not a culture of bomb and pistol. Our meaning of revolution is to change the present conditions, which are based on manifest injustice." Bhagat Singh agreed with Karl Marx that a radical revolution is not utopian, "What is utopian is the idea of a partial, an exclusively political revolution, which would leave the pillars of the house standing."

One of the chapters in the book is dedicated to the revolutionary nationalists' relationship with the Congress party and with some of its leaders as well as lay workers. Most of us are familiar with the discomfort in this relationship but the inner nuances of it are not so well known. For instance, Gandhi described the Saunders murder in December 1928 as a "dastardly act" while Jawaharlal Nehru could write to the Naujawan Bharat Sabha that many in India are "full of sympathy for them and are prepared to help them as much as they can". Even the hunger strike of the revolutionaries, which claimed Jatin Das' life, was dubbed by Mahatma as an "irrelevant performance" while Subhas Bose frankly admitted that Jatin Das' "martyrdom acted as a profound inspiration to the youth of India..." and Jawaharlal Nehru exhorted the people to follow in their (revolutionaries) footsteps and "free the country from foreign bondage by similar sacrifices". Quite a few revolutionaries like Sukhdev, and Bhagwati Charan Vohra, entered into polemical arguments with the Mahatma through an exchange of letters and circulation of pamphlets. One such exchange was Gandhi's 'The Cult of the Bomb' which prompted Vohra to retort with the HSRA manifesto called 'The Philosophy of the Bomb' defending the revolutionary ideology and programme, including the use of selective violence against the imperialist state.

I am beholden to a large number of people and it is time now to acknowledge the debt. I must begin by expressing deep gratutude to Professor Bipan Chandra, whose insightful article in 1972 encouraged me to take up the subject of ideology and programme of the national revolutionaries in greater detail. In the 1980s I had the benefit of consultations, interviews and correspondence with the survivors of the revolutionary struggle, most of whom are no more with us. I must begin with Shri Kultar Singh, younger brother of Bhagat Singh, who shared his memories and experiences through meetings and correspondence. Shri Vishnu Sharan Dublish and Manmath Nath Gupta were kind enough to discuss their exploits with me more than once. I had some memorable evenings with Comrade Shiv Verma in Kanpur and also Shri Rajendra Pal Singh 'Warrior', who was the HSRA commander for the Meerut region. I also had an interesting meeting with Shri Mathra Das Thapar, younger brother of the revolutionary martyr Sukhdev, who lived in Hapur. I will always cherish the time I spent with Comrade Ramchandra in the Teen Murti Library as well as few evenings at his old Daryaganj house, during the days he was writing his own account of the revolutionary struggle. Though in his eighties, Ramchandra still had the fire of a revolutionary, the fire I could corroborate from his speeches as a Naujawan Bharat Sabha activist in the 1920s, available in the National Archives of India.

I must acknowledge the help and support I received from the staff of the various institutions like the National Archives of India, the Central Secretariat Library, New Delhi, Sapru House Library, New Delhi, Dwarka Das Library, Chandigarh, and Meerut College Library, Meerut. The friends at Nehru Memorial Museum and Library at Teen Murti House, New Delhi deserve a special mention, as it was always more than a work place for me and all due to the extraordinary care of the staff at all levels.

I thank Kapil Kumar, GR Malik and BD Yadav, my friends and fellow researchers in the 1980s and my teacher SK Mittal, for their encouragement and interaction during the early days of my work. I am grateful to Professors Amba Prasad and Sumit Sarkar for their insightful comments and suggestions. Biswamoy Pati and Amit Gupta egged me for years to publish this book. I thank them for their tenacity. My deepest thanks are due to Asad Zaidi and Nalini Taneja, my old friends and now publishers of this book, who found the little manuscript worth taking up as one of their many interesting projects.

Finally, I owe a lot to my family, particularly my father, who is unfortunately no more. He would have been very happy to see this book published. He was always a great source of strength and inspiration for me during the formative stages of this work. And of course this book would not have been possible without Atiya's loving care and support.

S. Irfan Habib

New Delhi
May 22, 2007

ABBREVIATIONS

AICC	All India Congress Committee
BPCC	Bombay Pradesh Congress Committee
CWMG	Collected Works of Mahatma Gandhi
GOI	Government of India
HRA	Hindustan Republican Association
HSRA	Hindustan Socialist Republican Association/Army
NAI	National Archives of India
NMML	Nehru Memorial Museum and Library
SWJN	Selected Works of Jawaharlal Nehru

CHAPTER ONE

PROGRAMME AND IDEOLOGY OF THE EARLY REVOLUTIONARIES

Imperialism and Nationalism

The rising of 1857 marked the beginning of India's struggle for independence. Its suppression and the ensuing bureaucratic repression failed in putting out the fire of revolt which continued to smoulder beneath the surface. The suppressed feelings of the people found vent in the sporadic incidents of revolt accompanied by organised movements till the attainment of freedom in 1947. The ruthless repression, no doubt, made some people realise the futility of armed revolt. The activities of such people resulted in the growth of a number of political associations and also in the spurt of journalistic enterprise. But the feelings of revolt and the faith in revolution never died in the hearts of the people.[1] The issue for all the nationalists was freedom, and not really the methods to be employed to achieve this objective. We may debate on the methods and techniques now, but, if looked at in retrospect, no such issue was at stake. The course of Indian freedom was marked by a variety of methods and techniques. Each of them had, however, its genesis in the national life, and, to look deeper, in the very complexities of that life.[2] To distinguish any section of the national force merely by

---

1   NAI, Home Pol. F.No.19/1908.

2   AC Gupta (ed.), *Studies in the Bengal Renaissance*, Calcutta, 1958, p.225.

its apparent technique and method is to confuse largely the means with the end; and, secondly, to lose sight of the inner connection among the different nationalist forces.

The revolutionary armed resistance, as a useful nationalist activity, was pursued for about thirty years, from 1904 to 1934. We realise now the role nationalist revolutionaries played in the development and transformation of Indian politics as a whole. We also need to put their ideology and programme in its proper perspective. In the past, it had mostly been ignored or at best trivialised. No meaningful exercise was undertaken to analyse the evolution of the revolutionary ideology and programme, locating it in its proper national and international perspective.

The ideology of revolutionary armed resistance was enmeshed with people's yearning for freedom from political, social and economic bondage. Any proper understanding of their ideological development calls for an examination of the contemporary politico-economic and social system. We should keep in mind that a large section of the emerging bourgeoisie and around 300 million inhabitants were increasingly resentful of economic exploitation, political impotence and social inferiority.

By 1871, Dadabhai Naoroji was referring to the 'continuous impoverishment and exhaustion of the country.'[3] In 1901, RC Dutt wrote: "I do not think there is a question of graver importance connected with any part of the British Empire than the present condition of India",[4] while Bipin Chandra Pal, one of the spokesmen of the extremist party, wrote in the same year, in the very first issue of his militant weekly *New India*, the economic problems seem to our mind, the most pressing and important.[5]

3　Dadabhai Naoroji, *Essays, Speeches and Writings*, edited by CL Parekh, Bombay, 1887, pp.134-35.

4　RC Dutt, *Speeches and Papers on Indian Question*, 1901 and 1902, Calcutta, 1904, p.86.

5　*New India*, Calcutta, August 12 1901, cited in Bipan Chandra, *The Rise and Growth of Economic Nationalism in India*, New Delhi, 1969, pp.5-6.

Ever since the British occupation of India, the Indians had to live under economic subjugation. The relationship of the rulers with the ruled emanated from that law of the jungle which catered for the maximisation of imperial profit at the cost and utter neglect of the colonised. A liberal economic historian of India lamented:

> Amidst signs of progress and prosperity from all parts of the Empire, India alone presented a scene of poverty and distress.[6]

India's colossal poverty and consequent deepening depression was the result of the politico-economic structure created by the British. The vast expenses incurred on numerous costly wars waged to pander to the expansionist designs of the British were debited to India. Every section of the Indian populace was made to pay for the boast of the British, that 'England is the mistress of the seven seas', and for the growth of *Pax Britannica*.

The peasantry, constituting the bulk of the population, presented a sight of grim poverty. The introduction of British systems of land holding in India, through Lord Cornawallis' Permanent Settlement in 1793 in the Bengal and the subsequent other systems of land revenue settlements in other parts of India, provided for the inroads of imperial, capitalistic and bureaucratic elements into the rural scene further throwing the agricultural classes into the clutches of poverty bordering on chill penury.[7] Describing the condition of these classes, an Englishman observed:

> The condition of the Bengal peasantry is almost as wretched and degraded as it is possible to conceive, living in the most miserable hovels, scarcely fit for a dog kennel, covered with tattered rags, and unable, in too many instances, to procure more than a single meal a day for himself and family.[8]

The lot of the working classes was no better. There can be no doubt that "the wealth of the nation is founded on its labour, and that this

---

6   RC Dutt, *The Economic History of India*, Vol.II, New Delhi, 1963, p.xiii.

7   Kapil Kumar, *Peasants in Revolt*, New Delhi, 1984.

8   *Friend of India*, April 1, 1852 cited in G Subramania Iyer, *Some Economic Aspects of the British Rule in India*, Madras, 1903, p.9.

labour should be efficient in every way, must be strong, healthy and intelligent, is the first condition of the nation's prosperity."[9] But the Indian labour was starving due to the unprecedented low wages and inhuman attitude of the imperial rulers. According to Lord Curzon's own calculations, the annual income per head of the people of India did not exceed thirty rupees a year. It means an income of one anna and four paisa a day – exactly the wage earned by a famine coolie in the Government relief camp.[10]

The colonial government held India's rising population responsible for her economic plight and even claimed an upward swing in the national income. But the liberal politicians and economists like Dadabhai Naoroji, Romesh Dutt, GS Iyer, GV Joshi, GK Gokhale and DE Wacha etc. exposed the hollowness of the British pretensions before the people of the country by detailing the causes of poverty.

Dadabhai declared in 1876 that "India is suffering seriously in several ways and is sinking in poverty", and that "the masses of India do not get enough to provide the bare necessities of life."[11] Again in 1900, he observed, "the fact was that Indian Natives were helots. They were worse than American slaves, for the latter were at least taken care of by their masters whose property they were".[12] RC Dutt exposed the revenue policy of the Government which bled the peasantry and caused extreme penury leading to recurrent famines. The main point of the economic ideas of these leaders was the theory of drain, which in simple words implied the constant flow of wealth from India to Great Britain in the form of excess of exports over imports.

Influenced by these ideas, the emerging native press published articles, and reports, highlighting the economic degradation of

---

9   GS Iyer, op.cit., p.175.

10   Ibid, p.28.

11   Cited in B Chandra, op.cit., pp.7-8.

12   Naoroji, D, *Poverty and Un-British Rule in India*, London, 1901, p.652.

India. For instance, the Bengali paper, *Sulabha Dainik*, depicted the man in India thus:

> He has lost his vitality, he has lost his substance, his very life blood has been sucked dry, and he is bones. He is half-fed, he is half-clad.[13]

Similarly, another nationalist paper *Mahratta* wrote that India is not governed for India's sake but in the interests of England.[14] The early Indian economists and the nationalist press succeeded partially in unveiling the colonial character of the British rule, and demolished the facade of a welfare state which the British had toiled hard to show in order to hide the reality of the situation. The delineation of the economic aspect stirred the people from their stupor. It roused them from inertia to beat the Government with a heavy club. This late 19th and early 20th century nationalism can be characterised as "the period of economic nationalism". Most of the issues in this period were centred around economic deprivation and/or poverty, and most of the leaders were convinced that if the country was not economically progressing it was because of 'the presence and the policy of the foreigner'.[15] They were not hopeful of national economic regeneration 'except by their getting rid in the first instance of their European rulers.'

Moreover, the post 1857 India saw a change in British attitude, which was marked by aggressiveness and racial arrogance. The relative tolerance of the first half of the 19th century was replaced by positive contempt and condescension for anything native – its religion, knowledge, values, and including people. The exchange of ideas between the two was considerably lessened and almost a caste barrier was raised between them.[16] After the traumatic experience of 1857, the imperialist policies of the various Governor-Generals

---

13 *Sulabha Dainik*, November 2 1895. Report on the Native Press for Bengal, November 9 1895.

14 *The Mahratta*, March 13 1881.

15 B Chandra, op.cit., p.746.

16 Lajpat Rai, *Unhappy India*, Calcutta, 1928, p.431.

only served to exasperate the Indian sentiments. We can, in particular, mention Lords Lytton and Curzon, who created profound indignation, enough to push a large number of youth to the path of armed revolution.

Birth of Revolutionary Ideology

The emergence of revolutionary ideology in the late 19th and early 20th century was not alien to India but was the result of several internal and external influences working on the minds of the youth. The most vital factor was the growth of religious revivalism of the late 19th century. Besides this, there were several foreign influences, like the impact of the American War of Independence, the Irish struggle for freedom, the unification of Italy, the lives of Mazzini and Garibaldi, the Japanese victory over Russia and last but not the least, the revolution against the Tzarist regime in Russia. All these factors together changed the colour of national struggle from moderation to revolution.

The Indian National Congress was founded in 1885 by the Indo-British liberal politicians, and succeeded in bringing together educated, upper class Indians on a common political platform. Launched on a modest programme of politico-economic reforms, with so called constitutional methods, couched in the 'pray, please, petition mode', the Congress failed to achieve anything substantial from the haughty, imperialist officialdom. Even the emergent younger section within the Congress decried its policy of 'political mendicancy' and raised the banner of revolt. The Congress party, although representing the most progressive sections of Indian society, failed to keep pace with the wave of nationalism sweeping over India during the closing years of the 19th century.[17] This nationalism assumed varied forms.

The renaissance had led to a rediscovery of India of the ages past. The spirit of militancy came in the wake of religious awakening,

---

17   RC Majumdar, *Three Phases of India's Struggle for Freedom*, Bombay, 1961, p.21.

which lent its support to Hindu revivalism and strengthened the feelings of respect for national traditions but was also divisive. There was a curious blending of religion with politics. Many of the revolutionary leaders of this period were deeply religious men. There was contempt for alien rule and alien things, Western education, Western thought and Western ways of living. "It would not be incorrect to state that their nationalism had taken large draught from the fountain of Hindu religion."[18]

Maharashtra and Bengal emerged as the two powerful centres of the revolutionary activities tinged with religious revivalism. Bal Gangadhar Tilak provided the ideas, organisation and leadership in Maharashtra, while Aurobindo Ghosh and Swami Vivekanand did the same in Bengal. Tilak, like Bankim Chandra in Bengal, developed a faith that Hinduism was capable of becoming a powerful force of regeneration and union. He thought of giving a deep-rooted cultural basis to the political movement, with imagery taken exclusively from Hinduism. It was given to Tilak to offer a revolutionary and political interpretation of *Gita*. In one of his speeches he emphasised, "The most practical teaching of the *Gita*, and one for which it is of abiding interest and value to men of the world, with whom life is a series of struggles, is not to give way to morbid sentimentality when duty demands sternness and boldness to face terrible things."[19] Tilak was deeply inspired by *Bhagwat Gita's* clarion call to duty and Krishna's exhortation to Arjun. Besides this Tilak re-oriented the Shivaji and *Ganpati Utsav* for political purpose and militant dreams.[20] Tilak's speeches, writings and activities inspired the young Chaphekar brothers to form *Hindu Dharam Sanrakshini Sabha*, which was responsible for the murder of several hated British officers.

---

18 VPS Raghuvanshi, *Indian Nationalist Movement and Thought,* Agra, 1951, p.115.

19 JC Kerr, *Political Trouble India,* Delhi, 1973, p.49.

20 AC Gupta, op.cit., p.233.

VD Savarkar swore before goddess *Durga* to "raise the banner of an armed revolution." He started an association called the *Mitra Mela* at Nasik in 1900. It was changed into *Abhinav Bharat Society* in 1904 and shifted to Poona. The title was taken from *Young Italy* of Mazzini. This society actively took part in organising meetings, bringing out publications and celebrating Ganpati and Shivaji fesivals.[21]

The revolutionary movement in Bengal derived its inspiration from the works of Bankim Chandra Chatterji and the exhortations of Swami Vivekanand. The other notable contributor to the revolutionary creed was Aurobindo Ghosh. P Mitra launched an organisation in 1901, called *Anushilan Samiti*, a name taken from Bankim's writings. It was joined by Aurobindo, CR Das, Barindra Ghosh and Jatin Bannerjee. *Bhagwat Gita* was used in different ways in several publications. A scene with Arjun in his chariot and the God holding the reins beside him adorned the front page of Aurobindo Ghosh's paper, the *Karmyogin*. The motto printed on the front page of *Yugantar* was also taken from the *Gita*. Barindra Kumar Ghosh, in his paper *The Yugantar* quoted extensively from the *Gita* and assured the people that the nasty British rule was bound to end.[22]

Bankim Chandra Chatterji's cult of Mother India and Vivekanand's Vedantism caught the imagination of the young revolutionaries. Both of them reawakened a sense of pride in the Hindu past. They helped to kindle a sort of militant courage and feeling of service for the *daridranarayan* and for the motherland.[23] Bankim's novel *Anandmath* (The Abbey of Bliss) exercised tremendous influence on the Bengali revolutionaries. The greeting *Bande Mataram* (Hail Mother) of *Anandmath* became a war cry of the extremist party in Bengal. Bankim gave a religious significance to the idea of motherland by declaring that

---

21 *Sedition Committee Report*, 1918, p.1.

22 NK Guha, *Banglay Biplavavada*, Home Political, File No.64, 1924, p.23.

23 AC Gupta, op.cit., p.232.

in the image of the benign goddess *Durga* could be seen the future greatness of the Motherland. The papers, the *Yugantar* of Barindra Ghosh and *Sandhya* of Bhupendranath Dutt, further gave a new revolutionary interpretation to the worship of mother *Durga*. The new revolutionary gospel or cult of *Shakti* called upon the Bengalis to shed the blood of their oppressors:

> Will the Bengali worshipper of *Shakti* shrink from the shedding of blood? The number of Englishmen in this country is not above one lakh and a half, and what is the number of English officials in each district? If you are firm in your resolution you can in a single day bring British rule to an end. Lay down your life, but first take a life. The worship of the Goddess will not be consummated if you sacrifice your lives at the shrines of Independence without shedding blood.[24]

The rationale for shedding blood was provided thus:

> A handful of alien robbers are ruining the crores of people of India by robbing the wealth of India through the hard grinding of their servitude, the ribs of this countless people are being broken to pieces...[25]

In the words of Gopal Haldar, "*Yugantar* breathed revolution in every line and pointed out how revolution can be effected by collection of arms, by terrorism of Russian type armed rising, guerilla warfare and so on."[26] Aurobindo, who inspired the young revolutionaries of Bengal has been called by Valentine Chirol as one of the most remarkable figures that Indian unrest has produced, "the high-priest of a religious revival which has taken a profound hold on the imagination of the emotional youth of Bengal."[27] In his pamphlet *Bhawani Mandir* Aurobindo presented *Bhawani* as one of the manifestations of the goddess *Durga*, who was the tutelary goddess of Shivaji, and his celebrated sword was called after her, *Bhawani*.

---

24 Valentine Chirol, *Indian Unrest*, New Delhi, 1979, p.94.

25 Ibid, pp.90-91.

26 AC Gupta, op.cit., p.238.

27 Chirol, op.cit., p.89.

Books like *Bartman Rananiti, Mukti Kon Pathe, Sikher Balidan, Desher Katha*, and *Manual of Explosives* exercised a powerful impact on the revolutionaries. The *Bartman Rananiti* was written by Aurobindo's friend Abinash Chandra Bhattacharya in October 1907. It declared:

> Destruction is natural and war is, therefore, also natural. When any part of the body is rotten it should be cut off with the help of surgical instruments, otherwise the gangrenous wound would expand and cause destruction to the body. Vice, persecution, the dependence are but gangrenous sores in the body of the nation. War is inevitable when oppression cannot be stopped by any other means...[28]

Mukti Kon Pathe meaning 'Which way lies salvation?' was a collection of articles from *Yugantar*. This book emphasised the utility of secret societies and followed Russian revolutionaries. It bitterly denounced the narrowness and shallowness of the Congress ideals.[29] At another place, the book revealed the feeling of class consciousness, which existed, somewhat vaguely among the revolutionaries of the pre-World War era. It said:

> We must loot only the houses of the anti-nationalists, opponents of the *Swadeshi* movement, government approvers, drunkards, debauches, oppressors of the poor and the weak, economic exploiters of the race and nation, usurers and the miser money lenders... We take a pledge that we must never hurt the women, the children, the weak and the helpless people at the time of committing dacoities.[30]

The *Sikher Balidan* was by Miss Kumudini Mither and dealt with the sacrifices of Sikhs against their oppressors. *Desher Katha* was a book by Sakharam Ganesh Deuskar, and was described in an advertisement as "the only resort for worshippers of the Motherland".[31] The *Manual of Explosives* describes its purpose in these words: "The aim of the present work is to place in the hands

---

28   JC Kerr, op.cit., p.52.

29   *Mukti*–2, July 1972, (in Hindi), p.27.

30   Ibid, p.28.

31   JC Kerr, op.cit., p.60.

of a revolutionary people such a powerful weapon as explosive matter is."[32]

This religious revivalism generated a contempt for the British and instilled a hatred for foreign rule, but it also alienated a sizable section of population, particularly Muslims from its ranks, because of its strong accent on Hinduism. The ideologues of this period articulated their nationalist appeal in such a tightly structured manner that there was little possibility for any 'outsider' to share their vision of 'Hindu nationalism'.

As mentioned before, the Indian revolutionary movement was also influenced by the lives of Mazzini, Garibaldi, several Irish revolutionaries, the victory of Japan over Russia in 1905 and the revolutionary principles of France, America and Russia. BC Pal held Mazzini to be one of the principal sources of the birth of new nationalism in India.[33] Annie Besant also compared Mazzini and Aurobindo and described them as men of the same type. VD Savarkar had translated Mazzini's Autobiography into Marathi.[34]

When the revolutionary ideas were gaining ground under these influences, the partition of Bengal in 1905, came as a bomb shell. The revolutionary forces discerned the old game of 'counterpoise of native against native' and the *Divide et Impera* in the disguise of administrative efficiency. People began to emulate Russian methods and an attempt was made to kill an ex-Magistrate of Dacca on December 23, 1907. The next target was Kingsford who had ordered several young men to be flogged. At Muzaffarpur, Khudi Ram Bose and Prafulla Chaki threw a bomb on two innocent British ladies by mistake as they were in the same colour carriage as that of Mr Kinsford.[35] On the upshot of the Muzaffarpur case, Tilak remarked that 'the appearance of the bomb in India had changed the outlook of

---

32 Ibid, p.61.

33 BC Pal, *Birth of Our New Nationalism, Memoirs of My Life and Times,* Vol.1, pp.245–49.

34 Earlier SN Bannerjee and Lajpat Rai had also translated Mazzini's life.

35 *Sedition Committee Report,* p.31.

Indian politics.' He urged the Government of India that 'the answer to the bomb was political reform and not repression.'[36] Writing in the same vein *The Punjabee* commented:

> The growth of the so-called anarchism in India is a thing which no one could even dream of ten years before. It shows the depth and intensity of discontent which has brought about the existing state of things and converted even a timid, docile, westernized Bengali into an anarchist...[37]

Sachindranath Sanyal founded the *Anushilan Samiti* in Benares in 1908, which was later rechristened as Young Men's Association. Hardayal, alongwith Amir Chand and Dinanath, became active in Delhi. But Hardayal left for U.S.A. in 1911 so till the arrival of Rash Behari Bose, the Delhi group remained languid. Bose activated the group and started a magazine called *Liberty* which taught people to make bombs. Soon an attempt was made on the life of Viceroy Lord Hardinge on December 23, 1912 in which he escaped unhurt. The organisers issued a bulletin and invoked the authority of religious scriptures to justify their actions:

> The *Gita*, the *Vedas* and the *Koran* all enjoin us to kill all the enemies of our Motherland irrespective of caste, creed or colour...[38]

Rash Behari escaped arrest while four persons were hanged in this Delhi Conspiracy Case.Rash Behari Bose and his associates next made an attempt for a simultaneous uprising with the help of Indian soldiers. The plan leaked out before the appointed date of February 21, 1915 and all prominent revolutionaries were rounded up.[39] Rash Behari again evaded arrest and reached Japan to continue the revolutionary struggle.

The British policy of repression led to the Banaras and Lahore Conspiracy cases in which several revolutionaries were eliminated.

---

36 Ram Gopal, *Lokmanya Tilak*, Bombay, 1965, p.290.

37 *The Punjabee*, May 6 1908.

38 *Sedition Committee Report*, p.144.

39 SN Sanyal, *Bandi Jiwan*, Part I, Allahabad, 1922, p.10. Also *Chand* (Hindi Magazine), Allahabad, November, 1928.

There was a lull in the revolutionary activities but one Gendalal Dixit of Mainpuri kept the torch of revolution burning for some time. He was soon arrested in the Mainpuri Conspiracy Case and after his release died in tragic circumstances.

The leaders who evaded arrest and secretly left the country continued their struggle from the land of their exile. Many of them chose America because the Indian revolutionaries thought of America as being 'the land of freedom and opportunity.' Hardayal started a paper called *Ghadar* in May 1913 from San Francisco. Later *Ghadar* party was named after this paper. The party was strictly secular and the aim of the *Ghadar* party was the overthrow of the British *Raj* in India and the establishment of *Panchayat Raj* (Republican State) based on freedom and equality.[40]

The *Ghadar* spirit also travelled to the Far East and a branch was established by Barkatullah Khan in Japan, and some others did the same in Hong Kong and Shanghai. With the outbreak of the Great War, Kabul also became a rendevous of some leading rebels. It was here that a provisional Government of India was established by Raja Mahendra Pratap, who became its President, and Barkatullah, it's Prime Minister.

Ideology of the Early Revolutionaries

The early revolutionaries did not articulate their ideology and programme categorically. Yet most of them were well read people who were receptive to new ideas. Their thirst for knowledge was evident from Lajpat Rai's request to Shyamji Krishnavarma, the doyen of revolutionaries in England, "to employ a little of his money in sending out a number of books containing true ideas on politics to the student community here."[41] *The Calcutta Anushilan Samiti* is said to have had a library of 4000 books, a list of 230 titles in the collection of the *Mymensing Suhrid Samiti* has been preserved in

---

40 BB Majumdar, *Indian Political Associations and Reform of Legislature*, Calcutta, 1965, p.315.

41 *Sedition Committee Report*, p.143.

the home political files,[42] and most of the revolutionary societies had a system of regular classes. The *Sedition Committee Report* stated that the revolutionaries drew up a remarkable series of text books for their colleagues. They organised libraries and reading rooms to gather political education. These books in the first place aroused feelings of patriotism, spirit of self-sacrifice and hatred of servitude. Secondly, these books delineated the experiences and lessons of previous revolutions and liberation struggles. In the third place, some of these books dealt with economic misery and ruin wrought by the British occupation of India.[43] The reading list of the revolutionaries made it explicit that they discovered from these books the moral, philosophical and economic rationale for their deeds, while the revolutionary experiences of mankind stirred them into action.

The activities, writings and the speeches of the revolutionaries of this period reveal a strong religious bias, romanticism and emotionalism. Many of them were convinced that "a purely political propaganda would not do for the country, and that people must be trained up spiritually to face dangers." But their religion was different from the one practised by the majority of the people of the country. They were puritans to a certain extent. This was so because they thought it indispensable for the life of a revolutionary. At the same time they were against all sorts of narrow mindedness and prejudices which erect barriers between man and man. Despite the dominance of religiosity in their mental make up, the revolutionary groups were not totally devoid of the influence of secular or even anti religious trends. Bhupendra Nath Dutta refused to take a vow on Hindu

---

42   The list includes titles like *Condemned as a Nihilist, Self-Help, Free Trade and Protection, Lives of Cromwell, Washington and Napoleon, Life and Teachings of Vivekananda, Nabya Japan, Palashir Yuddha* and *Maharaj Nand Kukar Chant*, D.O. No.936, J.R. Blackwood to R. Nathan, 28 Jan, 1909 – Home. Pol. Deposit; April 1909, n. 2, quoted in Sumit Sarkar, *The Swadeshi Movement in Bengal, 1903–1908*, New Delhi, 1973. p.483.

43   Dr Jadugopal Mukherjee gives a long list of such books in his *Biplabi Jiboner Smriti*.

shastras alone.[44] Some of the early revolutionaries complained that the Hindu rituals were alienating possible Muslim and Brahmin sympathisers. Hemchandra Kanungo and his comrades at Midnapore provided further strength to an emerging anti-religious stance of a number of revolutionaries.[45] Interestingly, three out of four early martyrs including Satyendranath Basu, Kanailal Dutta, Khudiram Bose were among the sceptics.

The stalwarts of India's awakening, the inspirers of the national revolutionary ideology resisted European attempts at cultural conquest of India. But they did not stand for indifference. On the contrary they advocated assimilation of the best in European culture with the best in Indian traditions. Swami Vivekananda declared :

> I am thoroughly convinced that no nation or individual can live by holding itself apart from the community of others and whenever such an attempt has been made under false ideas of greatness, policy or holiness – the result has always been disastrous to the secluding one. To my mind, the one great cause of the downfall or degeneration of India was the building of a wall of custom, whose foundation has been hatred of others...[46]

At another place he said:

> No man, no nation can hate others and live, India's doom was sealed the very day they invented the word *mleccha* and stopped from communion with others.[47]

One of the best representatives of the radical intelligentsia, Bipin Chandra Pal wrote in *New India* :

> The Swaraj of ours is not merely the Hindu, nor merely the Mahomedan, not merely the Christian *Swaraj*, but the *Swaraj* of every

---

44 An assortment of the sacred books of different religions had to be provided for him eventually, in Sumit Sarkar, op.cit., p.486.

45 Sumit Sarkar, op.cit., p.487.

46 *Swami Vivekanand on India and Her Problems*, Advaita Ashram, Calcutta, pp.17-18.

47 Ibid, p.25.

> child of India, Hindu, Christian or Mahomedan, the *Swaraj* will be
> the *Swaraj* of the Indian people not of any section of it.[48]

He called upon the people to turn their eyes from the leaders and the Government Houses at Calcutta or Simla. He told them:

> The heroes of the nation live in its hamlets. To these hamlets we must go. If we cannot, the sooner we give up playing at politics the better for us all... That is the cornerstone of our movement, namely, faith in the people, faith in our movement, namely, faith in the people, faith in the genius of the nation, faith in God who has been building the genius of the nation through the ages, by historical evolution, faith in the eternal destiny of the people.[49]

Inspired by these ideas the revolutionaries had shed all personal respect for social privilege and family biases for the good of their country. Untouchability and the casteism prevalent in Hindu society had no place in the mental make-up of the revolutionaries.[50] They did not embark upon a campaign of social reform, yet among the ranks of the revolutionaries, in their mode of living, work and thinking, prejudices like untouchability, casteism and other superstitions, which went by the name of religion, were discarded as early as 1905.[51] No doubt, there were weaknesses in the ideology of the early revolutionaries, particularly in their reliance on religious teachings for advancing the cause of revolution. Yet it is also clear that to these revolutionaries the emancipation of India through armed struggle was the supreme goal and that unlike the mainstream Hindu intelligentsia they looked upon religion only as a means to serve this end. This aspect should not be lost sight of or under-estimated while making an assessment of the early phase of the revolutionary movement.

---

48 IM Reisner and NM Goldberg (eds.), *Tilak and the Struggle for Indian Freedom*, New Delhi, 1966, p.312.

49 Ibid, p.274.

50 SN Mazumdar, *In Search of a Revolutionary Ideology and a Revolutionary Programme*, PPH (Delhi), 1979, p.47.

51 Ibid.

Occasionally the writings and speeches of the early revolutionaries of the pre-War period breathed a spirit of class consciousness. But it had nothing to do with Marxian concept of class war. The colonial subjugation dominated the minds of the thoughtful leaders, not so much the feudal oppression and exploitation. They sympathised with the exploited peasantry but attributed all this to the foreign domination. The feeling of hatred, natural in the minds of enslaved against their enslavers overshadowed everything else in the conscious thought and activities of the revolutionaries. Sometimes they did touch upon the socio-economic exploitation of the Indian masses. Aurobindo once declared: "the proletariat is the real key."[52] This key, however, remained beyond his reach and he came to accept the middle class as the source of rebel strength. In Punjab also, Lala Lajpat Rai and Ajit Singh took up the demands of the peasantry along with other demands of *Swaraj* and *Swadeshi*.

Ajit Singh, particularly, toured the villages from time to time and in his speeches linked the agitation on economic demands with the political struggle for *swaraj*. The weekly *Ghadar* appealed to the masses and highlighted the economic exploitation of India, the drain of wealth, ruin of Indian home industries by British rulers and also called for communal harmony. "But there was no fundamental difference in approach between the *Ghadar* and other Indian revolutionaries. Their approach and outlook were dominated by the main contradiction i.e. the contradiction between the British rule and the Indian people as a whole."[53] Satish Pakrashi has summed up their line of thinking in these words:

> They had seen before their eyes the nature of oppression and exploitation of the people by the landlords and money lenders and desired that an end should be put to the same. How and by what method, about that they did not have any clear idea. They were inspired by the simplified subjective belief that once independence

---

52 *Indu Prakash*, March 5 1894, quoted in AC Gupta, p.232.

53 SN Mazumdar, op.cit., p.71.

> is won all these corruptions, exploitations and oppression, poverty and misery would be automatically eradicated.[54]

If we draw a balance sheet keeping in mind the prevailing conditions, we will find that the positive contributions made by the national revolutionaries outweigh their failures, weaknesses and mistakes. It must be kept in mind that the mass national struggle was itself in an embryonic stage. The masses had just begun to participate in political action consciously. In this atmosphere, the revolutionaries proclaimed a fight for complete independence through armed struggle. This by itself was a creditable contribution. They sacrificed their burning youths and lost no opportunity to die for the motherland. Most of them left the world unheard of. In this way, they instilled among the people a dare-devil spirit to rise against the mightiest of empires of the world.

They initiated the search for a revolutionary ideology and revolutionary programme by drawing lessons from our own history as well as from the histories of the revolutions in other countries. They could not always draw correct lessons but at that stage the very beginning of the search for lessons was an outstanding achievement. They did not preach social reform but broke down the barriers of age-old revered customs. They revolted against anything that was an obstacle in the path of the revolutionary movement.[55] Their undue emotionalism and romaticism could only be overcome by the realisation that revolution is a social process. This realisation came with the impact of the Bolshevik Revolution in Russia.

Birth of a New Revolutionary Spirit

The world economic situation worsened during the War. The peacetime industries and agriculture were in a miserable shape in all the belligerent countries. This was accompanied by direct and indirect taxes, which were levied on workers and peasants to

---

54 *Agnidiner Katha*, Nalajatak Prakashan, pp.134-135 cited in Ibid, p.63.

55 SN Mazumdar, op.cit., p.98.

replenish the empty treasury. The war revealed the crisis of capitalism everywhere and provided tremendous boost to revolutionary forces. The material conditions became ripe for national and revolutionary explosions. The proletarian revolution succeeded in Russia while the black colonies of the white races experienced tremors and new awakening of the revolutionary forces.

The British government was aware of the storm of political feeling in India during the period of the First World War. The commercial classes, after making profits during the War were disillusioned by the policy of the British government and were avid to snatch more power. On the other hand, the miseries of the toiling masses had increased due to the rise in the prices of necessary commodities. There was acute unemployment among the educated middle class. The optimism generated by the Wilsonian sentiments, the solemn pledges during the war and the Montague Declaration of August 1917 were not enough to contain either the masses or the classes. They wanted these declarations to be matched by concrete actions.

But all illusions about British promises were shattered with the introduction of the Rowlatt Bill, calculated to smother free expression and political activities. The provisions of the Defence of India Act were to expire six months after the end of the war. The threat of revolutionary "terrorism" and Bolshevism goaded the British to arm its Indian administration with powers of preventive detention. The Secretary of State for India, Edwin Montague, observed in the House of Commons:

> There are dangers that justify this emergent and exceptional power at a period of the close of the war, with all the difficulties of peace, and when Bolshevism, even though its attractions are waning, is still a force to be reckoned with.[56]

There was a chorus of universal condemnation joined even by the sophisticated elements of Indian polity like the moderates and the

---

56 Cited in David M Laushey, *Bengal Terrorism and the Marxist Left*, Calcutta, 1975, p.18.

Congress. Gandhiji gave a call to organise protests and *hartals* all over the country. In the wake of this agitation, on 13th April 1919, the Jalianwala Bagh massacres took place at Amritsar. Its impact was the tremendous growth of national consciousness in India. Gandhiji wrote to the Duke of Connaught in February 1921, "We are determined to battle with all our might against that un-English nature which has made Dyerism possible."[57] Mahatma Gandhi launched the Non-cooperation Movement and the boycott of British goods. He assured freedom by the midnight of December 31, 1921 and appealed to the revolutionaries to desist from their activities for one year. It should be remembered that the revolutionaries as a class were averse to Congress methods owing to ideological differences. CR Das arranged a conference between Gandhi and the revolutionaries in September 1921 (1920) in order to win the latter's active support for the campaign of non-co-operation.[58] The revolutionaries assured Gandhi that they would suspend their violent activities for one year. Many of the students, in enthusiasm, gave up their studies at the Mahatma's call and devoted themselves whole-heartedly to the struggle for freedom. The economic and labour crisis of the time added fuel to the fire.[59] Settling down quietly seemed a difficult proposition and not even Gandhiji's advice could make sense to the people.[60] But the Mahatma retracted his movement at the first glow of revolution at Chauri Chaura on February 5, 1922. This led to utter frustration among his young cadres. The country was plunged into the deepest gloom; the mountain, many felt, had brought forth a mouse. Subhas Bose said it

---

57 Blanche Watson (ed.), *Gandhi and Non-Violent Resistance*, Madras, 1923, p.445.

58 SC Bose, *The Indian Struggle 1920–42*, Calcutta, 1967, p.60. The meeting appears to have taken place in 1920 and not in 1921 as Gandhi was away in South India in September 1921.

59 Hiren Mukherjee, *India's Struggle for Freedom*, Bombay, 1948, p.111.

60 Rajni Palme Dutt, *India Today*, Bombay, 1949, pp.302–305.

"was nothing short of a national calamity".[61] Jawaharlal Nehru went to the extent of saying that if this was the inevitable consequence of a sporadic act of violence, then there was something lacking in the philosophy and technique of non-violent struggle.[62] Many young men like Chandrashekhar Azad, Vishnu Sharan Dublish and Manmathnath Gupta could not appreciate Gandhi's concept of combining politics with such morality which dealt a fatal blow to the popular movement. They were drawn towards the militant creed and thus the sudden bottling up of a great movement brought a revival of the revolutionary activities in India.

Birth of Hindustan Republican Association (HRA)

Sachindranath Sanyal, who was sentenced to transportation for life was released in February1920 as a consequence of general amnesty. Sanyal had addressed an open letter to Gandhi promising to suspend the revolutionary activities for one year. But when the Non Co-operation movement grounded to a premature halt, Sanyal began to have restless nights. He contacted his old associates and attracted several like-minded youth to study his book *Bandi Jiwan* which was published in Hindi and Punjabi, and had become a bible for the revolutionary youth of the time. Moreover, the youth felt that the national bourgeois leadership had become terrified at the revolutionary outbreak of the peasantry, and it was betraying the workers, the peasants and the youth. The impact of the Bolshevik revolution was becoming widespread and this led to a widening of horizons. "Socialism, though not clearly understood, was attracting their minds and the ideals of social justice which were in a nebulous form in the earlier period were turning towards taking a distinct shape."[63] It was not only the young generation of revolutionaries which was exposed to the new ideas but the elders had "also started

---

61 SC Bose, op.cit., p.90.

62 Manmath Nath Gupta, *They Lived Dangerously*, Delhi, 1969, p.56.

63 SN Mazumdar, op.cit., p.100.

discussing Soviet Revolution and Communism in 1924."[64] The upsurge of the working class after the Great War greatly influenced all of them. They watched this new social force carefully. They could see the revolutionary potentialities of the new class and desired to harness it to the nationalist revolution.[65]

With this objective, the revolutionaries of U.P. and Punjab set in motion an organisation called the Hindustan Republican Association (HRA) in 1924. The Constitution of the HRA declared its objective "to establish a Federated Republic of the United States of India by an organised and armed revolution."[66] The Association envisaged that the "basic principle of the republic shall be universal suffrage and the abolition of all systems which make any kind of exploitation of man by man possible."[67] It was committed to "the organisation of labour and *kisans*" as this was necessary for the successful struggle against capitalism and feudalism.

The programme of the HRA reveals that its members and founders had travelled some distance. They were not inspired by the *Bhagwat Gita, Anandmath*, Aurobindo, Vivekanand and the militant nationalists; they had also read about the Russian, the French and the Irish revolutions. Jogesh Chandra Chatterji, its principal founder, was exposed to socialist thought in jail during 1916 and 1920. There he read *Nineteenth Century and After*, and Werner Sombart's *Socialism and the Social Movement in the 19th Century*. It's another prominent pillar, SN Sanyal, read Bukharin's *ABC of Communism* and several works by Lenin.[68]

---

64 Jogesh Chandra Chatterji, *In Search of Freedom*, Calcutta, 1967.

65 SN Sanyal, op.cit., pp.237–9. V Sandhu, *Yugdrishta Bhagat Singh,*, Delhi, 1968, p.138; Yashpal, *Sinhavalocan*, Lucknow, 1951, Vol.I, p.138; Ajoy Ghosh, *Articles and Speeches,* Moscow, 1962, p.15.

66 NAI, Home Pol. F. No.375 of 1925. *The Constitution of the HRA.*

67 Ibid.

68 David M Laushey, op.cit., pp.37-38.

Ideology and Programme of HRA

The Hindustan Republican Association shifted ideologically from a narrow selfless patriotism towards socialism – and even internationalism. This came out clearly in its pamplet *The Revolutionary* published on January 1, 1925, and which was said to be the manifesto of the revolutionary party of India.[69] This pamphlet revealed to a very large public that the revolutionaries were committed to certain lofty social ideals. They were not fumbling and knew what they were after.[70] A secret document of the U.P. Provincial Committee of the HRA reveals that the organisation had decided to send chosen members to Russia for training and had also resolved to secure help from MN Roy and others for the purpose.[71] This document further indicates the ideological shift of the HRA revolutionaries during this period.

The pamphlet *The Revolutionary* began with the words of Neitzsche: "Chaos is necessary to the birth of a new star" and the birth of life is accompanied by agony and pain. "India is also taking a new birth, and is passing through that inevitable phase, when chaos, and agony shall play their destined role, when all calculations shall prove futile, when the wise and mighty shall be bewildered by the simple and weak, when great empires shall crumble down, and new nations shall arise and surprise humanity with the splendour and glory which shall be all its own."[72] The HRA, crossing the barriers of narrow nationalism, proclaimed in its manifesto:

> The revolutionary party is not national but international in the sense that its ultimate object is to bring harmony in the world by respecting and guaranteeing the diverse interests of the different nations; it aims not at competition but at co-operation between the different nations and states.[73]

---

69 For full text of the manifesto see Appendex C-1.

70 MN Gupta, op.cit., p.69.

71 NAI, Home Political File No.253 of 1925.

72 *The Revolutionary*, January 1 1925.

73 Ibid.

The HRA did believe and act in accordance with the methods of older revolutionaries. It also believed in the armed overthrow of the imperialist government. The manifesto categorically declared that the foreigners "have no justification to rule over India except the justification of the sword, and therefore the revolutionary party has taken to the sword."[74] However, the advance made by the HRA was spelt out clearly in the next sentence: "But the sword of the revolutionary party bears ideas at its edge."

The HRA recognised the utility and significance of nationalisation of large industries, e.g. the railways and other means of communication and transportation, the mines and other kinds of very great industries, such as the manufacture of steel and ships, and many more. While, on the other hand, most of the political parties, including the Congress, were still far away from this ideal. It believed in furthering the spirit of co-operation in the domain of economic and social welfare. Instead of private and unorganised business enterprises, the revolutionary party preferred co-operative unions. It aimed at the establishment of the Federal Republic of India on the principle of universal suffrage. In this republic of HRA, the electors would have the right to recall their representatives if so desired; otherwise, they felt, the democracy would become a mockery. The HRA was the first Indian party which envisaged a society where exploitation of man by man was to be made impossible.[75] The constitution or the manifesto *The Revolutionary* did not use the word socialism even once, nor did it talk of class struggle. "Of course socialism was implicit in a system in which exploitation of man by man was to be abolished."[76]

Given the faith in their respective religions, the revolutionaries of the HRA could not conceive of a neutral role for the state, or de-link politics from religion in their proposed manifesto. Instead, on the communal question, the revolutionary party contemplated

---

74 Ibid.

75 MN Gupta, op.cit., p.68.

76 Ibid.

granting whatever rights the different communities may demand, provided they did not clash with the interests of other communities, and lead ultimately to a hearty and organic union of the people in the near future. They keenly observed the rising communal tension in India in the 1920s and castigated both the Hindu as well as Muslim communalists for weakening the fight for freedom. Ashfaqullah Khan, a prominent member of the HRA, wrote an open letter to his countrymen just three days before his execution in the Kakori case in 1927, expressing his anguish at the political developments and communal mobilisation. He condemned both the movements – *tabligh* as well as *shuddhi* – and warned his countrymen that such divisions are weakening the struggle for independence. He wrote: "It is impossible to purify seven crore Muslims and similarly it is absurd to think that twenty five crore Hindus can be converted to Islam. But yes, it is easy that we all put the chains of slavery around our necks."

Though the HRA revolutionaries did not formally proclaim themselves as socialists, yet they visualised a society based on the progressive and socialist principles. Mahavir Singh, a Kakori case accused facing life imprisonment in the Andamans wrote to his father:

> By Samaj (Society) I do not mean Arya Samaj or any other narrow *Samaj* but a society of common people. This is because these religious societies mean nothing to me due to their myopism. Moreover I want to keep away from all religions because they are narrow, self centred and based on injustice, and want others also to do the same. What I believe to be of greatest benefit to man and society is the following principle: The human relation should not be based on any distinction of caste, colour, religion or money.

The manifesto of the HRA tried to condemn the mischievous propaganda against the revolutionaries for being terrorists and anarchists. It said:

> The Indian revolutionaries are neither terrorists nor anarchists. They never aim at spreading anarchy in the land, and therefore they can never properly be called anarchists. Terrorism is never their

object and they cannot be called terrorists. They do not believe that terrorism alone can bring Independence and they do not want terrorism for terrorism sake, although they may at times resort to this method as a very effective means of retaliation. The present Government solely exists because the foreigners have successfully been able to terrorise the Indian people.[77]

It further proceeds:

This official terrorism is surely to be met by counter terrorism… Moreover the English masters and their hired lackeys can never be allowed to do whatever they like, unhampered, unmolested. Every possible difficulty and resistance must be thrown in their way.

The manifesto concludes with the expression of faith in mass organisation as an objective of the revolutionary party. It says:

….the party will never forget that terrorism is not their object, and they will try incessantly to organise a band of selfless and devoted workers who will devote their best energies towards the political and social emancipation of their country.

"All these together reveal that the HRA wanted to cut itself asunder from the old revolutionary ideology of religious nationalism, but under a leader of Sanyal's eminence and calibre, it could not make much progress."[78] Sanyal was a man of deep spiritual and religious convictions. At the same time he was not so blind as not to see the possibilities of the new ideas that were coming from Russia and fast infecting the younger revolutionaries. But in a self-complacent manner he fondly liked to believe that "these new values and ideas and much more were included in the ideas of the seers."[79] In the manifesto of the HRA, *The Revolutionary*, Sanyal declared that the revolutionary party "follows in the footsteps of the great Indian *Rishis* of the glorious past and of Bolshevik Russia in the modern age." He was closer to Vivekanand and Aurobindo than to Marx and Lenin.[80] Yet, as referred to earlier, both Sanyal and Chatterji

---

77   *The Revolutionary*, January 1 1925.

78   MN Gupta, op.cit., p.70.

79   Ibid.

80   Ibid.

were in correspondence with MN Roy and made personal contacts with some of his agents. They regularly received copies of *Vanguard* and other communist publications. Sanyal was initially very much impressed with Marxian economics and the economic interpretation of history. But he could not accept a thorough going materialist philosophy of life.[81] He was apparently much influenced by *Vedantist* thought, and he could not overcome his faith in God or his belief that there was much of value in traditonal Hindu philosophy.[82] Sanyal believed that India wants a Krishna who can give a worthy ideal, to be followed not by India alone, but by all humanity, by all the members of this humanity with diverse temperaments and capacities.[83]

Ashfaqullah, a prominent member of the HRA and a hero of the Kakori case was a staunch Muslim himself. But he did not shut his mind to the new ideas coming from Russia. While criticizing the Communists on certain grounds, he accepted their ideology to a great extent. In his memoirs Ashfaq entreats the Communist group:

> As you have brought in an alien movement to India, you consider yourselves as aliens, you hate the *desi* things, you are great admirers of foreign-dress and ways of living; it will not work. I do agree with you to a great extent and I shall say that I have always been perturbed about the poor farmers and wretched workers. More than often, I have wept to see their condition during my period of exile.[84]

Jogesh Chandra Chatterjee has also referred to a letter written by *Shaheed* Ashfaqullah to his friend where he says that, "I got Lenin's address from your letter and today I am thinking of writing a letter to him."[85] This clearly indicates the leanings of Ashfaqullah towards

---

81 SN Sanyal, op.cit., pp.314-315.

82 David M Laushey, op.cit., p.38.

83 *Young India*, February 12 1925. Sanyal's letter to Gandhi published anonymously.

84 *Memoirs of Ashfaquallan Khan*, quoted in the *Souvenir* on the occasion of Chandrashekhar Azad's *Balidan Diwas*, New Delhi, Feb. 26-27, 1979.

85 Ibid.

socialism and its leader Lenin. He had planned to visit Russia but was arrested in the Kakori case. Another extraordinary statement of Ashfaq refers to the future socio-economic and political set up of India to which he and his party HRA aspired. Despite his faith in Islam, Ashfaqullah was ready to be branded a Communist for the truth he spoke. He said:

> I consider the alien rule an evil and at the same time, I hate any democratic Indian rule where the weak are denied their rights, or if it is the creation of the rich and landlords, or there is no equal participation of the farmers and workers, or if the laws of the Government are made on the basis of inequality and disparity. If India becomes free and our brother countrymen take the reins of Government from the white masters and if the inequality persists between the rich and the poor and the landlord and the tenant, I pray to God not to give me such freedom till equality is established in His Creation. Let me be dubbed a Communist for these ideas. I damn care.[86]

It appears from the views of Sanyal and Ashfaqullah Khan that at this point of time religious influence on them was too strong to allow for an atheistic, materialist philosophy of life. But, there is no doubt that the HRA was greatly influenced by the Russian Revolution and the socialist experiment. There was a definite inclination towards socialism in their attempts to chalk out a social and economic order for independent India. They began to accept the indispensability of the role of workers and peasants for the socio-economic and political transformation of India. Moreover, there was a hazy beginning in the understanding of the international character of the national struggle. The influence of petty bourgeois romantic revolutionism prevented the leaders of HRA from giving primacy to the above principles. Nevertheless, the HRA was the first revolutionary organisation in India to begin the transformation from terrorism to communism.[87]

---

86 *Memoirs of Ashfaqullah Khan*, op.cit.
87 David M Laushey, op.cit., p.39.

Chapter Two

Towards a Revolutionary Programme And Socialist Outlook

The late 1920s saw severe economic depression followed by intense labour upsurge. The Indian working class was increasingly coming under radical left influence leading to the formation of a number of labour unions with distinct communist leanings. Besides, there were youth movements in 1928 and 1929, raising the demand for complete independence and radical social and economic changes. Jawaharlal Nehru and Subhas Bose were kept occupied during these two years addressing youth conferences in many parts of the country. For instance, Jawaharlal Nehru presided over a Socialist Youth Congress in Calcutta in December 1928, which called for independence as 'a necessary preliminary to communistic society.' Both Nehru and Bose organised the Independence for India League as a pressure group within the Congress to carry forward the campaign for acceptance of the goals of complete independence and what the U.P. branch of the League in April 1929 described as a 'socialist democractic state in which every person has the fullest opportunities for development... (with) state control of the means of production and distribution.' But once again, this left theoretical radicalism of the Congress could not find adequate expression in concrete action or organization. Jawaharlal Nehru, when questioned by Gandhi, went back to the liberal, bourgeois politics of the Congress, leaving the youth charged but frustrated.

Disillusioned by such verbal radicalism of the Congress, the members of the HRA, which was rendered weak and powerless after the Kakori Conspiracy Case, decided to rebuild the organisation. Most of the experienced revolutionaries were behind the bars and the rest were underground to escape arrest. In these circumstances, the young members of the HRA led by Bhagat Singh, Sukhdev, Shiv Verma, Chandrashekhar Azad and Vijay Kumar Sinha, undertook the task of reorganizing the party. A meeting of the important members was held in 1927 at Kanpur, primarily for this purpose. Bhagat Singh and VK Sinha made extensive tours of Punjab, Bihar and U.P. to mobilise support. An important meeting for the formation of the Central Committee of HRA was held on September 8 and 9, 1928 in the romantic surroundings of the ruins of the *Ferozshah Kotla* at Delhi. This was a crucial meeting which was attended by ten participants from U.P., Bihar, Punjab and Rajasthan. The meeting resulted in the adoption of a revolutionary programme with an advanced revolutionary socialist outlook for their organisation. Finally Bhagat Singh and his friends succeeded in convincing their critics who agreed to rechristen the association by including socialism as one of the main goals.[88] In this, Bhagat Singh was ably assisted by Sukhdev, who had a sharp mind and had a good study of communism. The truth is that Sukhdev and VK Sinha were the chief thinkers and men to lay down the principles of the party.[89] Thus, the name of the Hindustan Republican Association was finally changed to Hindustan Socialist Republican Association.

The HRA aimed at the establishment of a Federal Republic of the United States of India where the basic principle would be adult suffrage, while the HSRA, as indicated by its name, proclaimed the

---

88 The opposition of members from U.P. was not to the adoption of socialist creed but to changing the name. They argued that HRA was quite popular and is associated with such august personalities as Ram Prasad Bismil, SN Sanyal and JC Chatterjee.

89 JN Sanyal, op.cit.

goal of establishing a socialist republic. Long before this, Bhagat Singh and his comrades formed *Naujawan Bharat Sabha* in Lahore with a distinct goal of establising a socialist republic in India. Bhagat Singh was convinced that the salvation of India lay not merely in political independence but in economic freedom.[90]

The newly formed HSRA was divided into two departments – the military and the organisational wings. The organisational wing was to have two types of members, the active workers and the sympathetic supporters. The active wing was entrusted with the responsibility of collecting arms, and conducting the propaganda and organisational work for the party.[91] The supporters and sympathisers of the party were assigned the duty of contributing and collecting funds for the party, giving shelter to the active workers and propagating the ideals of the party.[92] Chandrashekhar Azad was, in absentia, appointed the commander of the military wing called the Hindustan Socialist Republican Army. He could not attend the September meeting but gave his consent to all the suggestions of Bhagat Singh.[93] Chandrashekhar Azad was not merely a military leader, though uneducated, he made others read and explain to him books in English.[94] A Central Committee was formed with two members each from U.P., Bihar, the Punjab and one from Rajasthan. Jhansi was to be the central office of the party. It was also decided that the soldiers of the HSRA will leave their homes, keep no contact with their families and devote full time and energy for the party work. Religious communalism and ritualism were banned so Bhagat Singh had to do away with his beard and hair.[95]

---

90 Ibid.

91 Vaishampayan, *Amar Shaheed Chandrashekhar Azad*, Vol.II, Varanasi, 1967, p.65.

92 JN Sanyal, op.cit., p.44.

93 Shiv Verma, *Memoirs*, Kanpur, 1974, p.27.

94 Yashpal, op.cit., Vol.I, pp.148-49.

95 JN Sanyal, op.cit., p.46. However, some other sources reveal that Bhagat Singh had to do away with his beard and turban when he disguised to escape arrest after Saunders' murder in 1928.

"The year 1928 was, politically, a full year," writes Pandit Jawaharlal, "with plenty of activity all over the country."[96] The trade union movement was pushing itself steadily and its militant ideology was fostering class consciousness among the workers. The labour associations were rending the air of industrial centres with cries of "Down with Motilal and Mahatma" as useless bourgeoisie and "Long live Revolution".[97] In this electrified atmosphere, the Simon Commission landed in Bombay on February 3, 1928. It was an all white commission appointed to report and review the political situation of India. No Indian was given a berth in the Commission which was considered an affront to national respect by all the political parties of the country. The major segments of the country unanimously decided to boycott the Commission. It was greeted with *hartal* in Bombay and slogans like 'Simon Go Back' were raised.

There were clashes between the police and the people at various places but Lahore brought matters to a head. The anti-Simon Commission demonstration was led by Lala Lajpat Rai in Lahore and as he stood by the roadside he was assaulted and hit on his chest with a baton by a young English police officer. For Lalaji, being a heart patient, a severe blow on the chest proved fatal. His death sent a wave of indignation and the young of the country saw it as an insult to the nation. The HSRA decided to kill Scott, the Chief police executive, who was present on the spot. The revolutionaries had two things in mind; first they wanted to convert the popular movement into a violent one, and secondly to show to the world that India has not taken the death of Lalaji silently. They also wanted to confirm by this action the existence of an active revolutionary party in India.[98] A meeting of the revolutionaries was held on December 8 and 9, 1928 in Mozang House at Lahore to chalk out the plan of action.

---

96 Jawaharlal Nehru, *An Autobiography*, New Delhi, 1962, p.170.

97 VPS Raghuvanshi, op.cit., p.191.

98 JN Sanyal, op.cit., p.51.

Apprehending threat to his life Scott took shelter in the police training school from where he seldom ventured out. Later on Saunders, his deputy was chosen as the target and his movements were watched for several days. December 17, 1928, was fixed for Saunders' murder and Rajguru, Bhagat Singh and Chandrashekhar Azad were entrusted with the responsibility. A great sensation spread in Lahore at the murder of the Deputy Superintendent of Police. The next day, red leaflets written in English were distributed by the HSRA men saying "Bureaucracy alerted. Lala Lajpat Rai's death is avenged by the murder of JP Saunders." The revolutionaries repeated their objective in the leaflet saying, "We are sorry for shedding the blood of a man but it is necessary to shed blood on the altar of revolution. We aim at such a revolution which would end exploitation of man by man."[99]

Though it became known that the Saunders murder was an act of revolutionaries, the police failed to arrest them. Bhagat Singh escaped from Lahore in the guise of a westernised young man with Durga bhabhi and Shachi acting as wife and child. Rajguru travelled as his servant in the first class compartment of the train. Azad sneaked out in the guise of a sadhu.

Bhagat Singh reached Calcutta during the Congress Session week where he came in contact with Bengal revolutionaries.[100] Bhagat Singh met Trailokya Chakravarti, Pratul Ganguli, Prof. Jyotish Ghosh and other important leaders and renewed contacts with Jatindra Nath Das, who was a member of the HRA in 1924-25. He requested Jatin Das to teach few of his comrades the art of bomb making. Jatin Das readily agreed and so a factory was started at Agra. Two houses were hired, one at *Nai-ki-Mandi* and another one at *Hing-ki-Mandi*. They prepared some explosives which were used in the Assembly Bomb Case of 1929.[101]

---

99 Yashpal, op.cit., Vol.I, p.161.

100 NAI, Home Pol. File No.192/1929.

101 Yashpal, op.cit., Vol.I, 170.

The revolutionaries stayed at Agra for sometime. They got an opportunity to read many books connected with the revolutionary movement. Bhagat Singh soon established a small library by collecting books from his friends and supporters. Though small, the library was rich in literature, mainly comprising books on economics. There were some books regarding trade union movement, explosives and bomb-making, and a few life-sketches of Russian revolutionaries.[102] The revolutionaries in Agra, while studying this literature, also had intense ideological debates within the group.

The HSRA planned to bomb the Assembly Hall if the Public Safety Bill and the Trade Disputes Bill were passed by the special powers of the Governor-General. They wanted to show that if the Government can ignore the voice of the majority and rush through the passage of the bills by resorting to Governor-General's powers, then the HSRA can also pay back in the same coin. After the Saunders murder, a meeting of the Central Council of HSRA was held in Agra to discuss the two bills. These bills were brought by the Indian Government to suppress the struggle being waged against the establishment by the workers and revolutionaries.[103] Bhagat Singh, while commenting on these bills said:

> There is no place for justice in British imperialism. They do not want to give even a breathing space to the slaves and instead, want to suppress them. They want to rob them and kill them. More and more oppressive laws will be passed and the dissenting voices will be put down. Let us see what happens. Only sacrifice can save us from this repression. The eyes of Indian and British members of the Assembly will have to be opened.[104]

He felt that the awakening of the working class indicated a new turn in the political life of the country.[105] Thus, he wanted the HSRA to

---

102 JN Sanyal, op.cit., p.47.

103 *Mukti*, July 1972, Delhi, p.39.

104 Ibid.

105 Shiv Verma, op.cit., pp.32-33.

do an 'action' which should express the solidarity of the party with the labour and peasant movement.[106]

The Central Committee of HSRA at first decided to send Jaidev Kapoor and BK Dutt to throw the bombs, but on Sukhdev's exhortation and friendly advice, Bhagat Singh accompanied BK Dutt. On April 8, 1929, the deafening sound of the bomb explosion in the Assembly shook the Empire to its foundations. Members of the Assembly ran helter skelter. Both the bombs exploded without doing serious harm to anyone.[107] The young men could have escaped under the cover of smoke but they held their ground and shouted slogans at the top of their voice:

"Long Live Revolution"

"Down with Imperialism"

"Workers of the World Unite"

They threw bundles of red leaflets on behalf of HSRA and gave its message to the whole world. The message began with the quotation of the French revolutionary Valliant, "It takes a loud voice to make the deaf hear." It was further stated on behalf of the helpless Indian masses that "it is easy to kill individuals but you cannot kill ideas. Great Empires crumbled while ideas survive. Bourbons and Czars fell while revolutionaries marched triumphantly ahead."[108] Both of them were arrested on the spot. Thus occurred the great event, which sent a chill down the spine of British imperialism and gladdened the hearts of freedom fighters throughout the world. Bhagat Singh used the Court as a platform to popularise the idea of socialism and a few months later in December 1929, Jawaharlal Nehru raised this slogan of socialism inside the Congress at Lahore. Bhagat Singh's statement made it clear that the HSRA was, in the true sense, fighting for the masses and also specified that it intended to work for a classless

106 JN Sanyal, op.cit., p.72.

107 NAI, Home Pol. F.No.192/1929.

108 Yashpal, op.cit., Vol.II, pp.185-86. Also Sukhdeoraj, *Jab Jyoti Jagi*, Mirzapur, 1971, pp.63–68.

society.[109] The British press traced the link of bomb explosions to Russia and the *Daily News* attributed the explosions to "the mischief of Moscow and its master criminals."[110] Bhagat Singh and Dutt filed a written statement in the Court on June 8, 1929, in which they made clear the motive and circumstances leading to the event. They agreed with Lord Irwin's statement in the Parliament, where he described their action as an attack on the Constitution itself.[111]

Yashpal, who had remained in the background till now, came to the scene with Bhagwati Charan Vohra and Inderpal. They planned to blow up the Viceregal Special, the train carrying Lord Irwin. The action took place near Purana Qila in Delhi on December 23, 1929. One man was killed but the Viceroy escaped unhurt with some damage to the dining car. However, the incident created a sensation all over India. A special meeting of the British cabinet was summoned on December 23, 1929, to discuss the incident. The Lahore Congress in December 1929, expressed mixed feelings of appreciation and condemnation of the act. Gandhi moved a resolution in the Congress describing the act as dastardly and cowardly and thanked Almighty for the escape of the Viceroy.[112] The resolution became controversial and could be passed only after Gandhi's pathetic appeals and his supporters' threat that if the resolution was not passed, Gandhi might leave the Congress. It was passed, finally, by a margin of just 81 votes in a house of 1713. The extent of support revolutionaries received must have been an eye-opener to Gandhiji.[113] The Government was also led to conclude after the Lahore Congress deliberations that there was some measure of sympathy in the Congress for the revolutionaries

---

109 MN Gupta, *The History of Indian Revolutionary Movement*, p.121.

110 *The Tribune*, April 11 1929.

111 Joint Statement of Bhagat Singh and Dutt in the Sessions Court, Delhi, June 6 1929.

112 *Collected Works of Mahatma Gandhi* (CWMG), Vol.42, p.341.

113 *The Times of India*, December 30 1929.

and some disposition to encourage them.[114] This was no doubt a moral victory for the revolutionaries.[115]

Mahatma Gandhi was so angered by the bomb explosion and the circulated manifesto of the HSRA at the Lahore Congress that he publicly denounced the revolutionaries in an article entitled 'The Cult of the Bomb', in his *Young India*. Azad wanted that a befitting reply should be given on behalf of the HSRA, and so Bhagwati Charan wrote 'The Philosophy of the Bomb' at the instance of Azad and after a full discussion with him in January 1930.[116] The aim of the manifesto was to put forward the correct position of the revolutionaries who were maligned by the Anglo-Indian lobby as enemies of peace, order and humanity. The manifesto declared that 'the revolutionaries believe that the deliverance of their country will come through revolution. The revolution will ring the death knell of capitalism, class distinction and privileges.[117] Further, it was stated that revolution, "will establish the dictatorship of the proletariat and will for ever banish parasites from the seat of political power." The pamphlet clearly stated that in sacrifice the revolutionaries were in no way lagging behind the followers of the Mahatma. As usual, the pamphlet ended with the popular slogan 'Long Live Revolution'.

Though the main organisers were in hiding or behind the bars in U.P. and the Punjab, there were some enthusiasts who kept the revolutionary activities going. Hansraj 'Wireless' and Inderpal organised a party named *Aatishi Chakkar* or 'Fire Ring Party' in the Punjab so that it may not be identified with the HSRA.[118] Hansraj conceived a plan of exploding bombs simultaneously in various cities of the Punjab. He masterminded the plan and the explosions

---

114 NAI, Home Pol. F.No.4/13/1930.

115 Yashpal, op.cit., p.139.

116 Yashpal, op.cit., Vol.III, pp.66-67; MN Gupta, *The History of the Revolutionary Movement*, p.142.

117 *The Philosophy of the Bomb.*

118 *Terrorism in India 1917–36*, Home Dept. Government of India, S.No.1338, p.90.

were successfully carried out at six places on July 19, 1930. A day before the explosions, a manifesto was distributed on behalf of *Aatishi Chakkar* in which it was said:

> We will not get freedom by killing and weakening ourselves. It is highly essential to break the chains of slavery to attain freedom. It is imperative to throw away the rule based on oppression and injustice. We will have to organise ourselves into a strong army to win the war. It will be a decisive war 'Independence or death'.[119]

This pamphlet was prepared by Indrapal and his comrades and was distributed on behalf of the HSRA. The police were alerted throughout the Punjab but failed to make any immediate arrest. Later, on August 26, 1930, the Lahore police arrested several people in connection with the July bomb explosions. Inderpal was also arrested and he disclosed many revolutionary activities to the police including the Viceregal train blowing attempt of December 23, 1929.[120] Many others were arrested and were sentenced to various terms of imprisonment.

The HSRA was in dire straits. Its hard core was thrown out of action due to imprisonment and death. Those who evaded the ubiquitous police were in dire need of money to reorganise the scattered workers of the party. Besides, the problem of following up the court cases of the fellow revolutionaries constantly haunted them. These difficulties appeared to be insurmountable. But the daredevils of the HSRA remained obdurate and their faith in revolution remained unshakable.

In these circumstances, Azad masterminded a dacoity in Delhi on July 6 which came to be known as the Gadodia Stores Dacoity Case. Vidya Bhushan and Bhawani Sahai participated in this dacoity. The revolutionaries gained Rs 13,000 by this action. Within a few months, almost all participants of this dacoity were arrested but Azad was again declared an absconder. A case known as Delhi

---

119 Sukhdeoraj, op.cit., p.164.

120 NAI, Home Pol. F.No.4/13/1930.

Conspiracy Case was instituted after a lengthy investigation, with Kailashpati as an approver.

Azad was now amidst difficulties and dangers which he had to face alone in the absence of his trusted comrades. The HSRA was weakened because the more energetic and imaginative leaders were now either in jail, under trial or in hiding.[121] It could not make a concerted revolutionary effort against the alien rule in this period and the movement now was confined to small local conspiracies and numerous but isolated cases of bomb throwing.

Chandrashekhar Azad, who was basically a soldier and the C-in-C of the HSRA, badly felt the need of thinkers like Bhagat Singh, Sukhdev, VK Sinha and BC Vohra. Azad was fond of Bhagat Singh and treated him as a younger brother. Though he deputed him to throw the bombs in the Assembly, he was much grieved at the thought of losing him in this action.[122] He tried to rescue Bhagat Singh and Dutt from jail but the plan had to be dropped owing to the death of BC Vohra. When Bhagat Singh and his two comrades were sentenced to death in the Lahore Conspiracy Case, Azad tried for the commutation of their sentences through some Congress leaders like Ganesh Shankar Vidyarthi and Motilal Nehru.[123] Azad later met Jawaharlal Nehru to seek the release of his fellow revolutionaries through the Gandhi–Irwin Pact, but despite prolonged discussion he failed to convince Nehru, and came back disgusted and dejected.[124]

The arrest of Vaishampayan on February 12, 1931 was another telling blow to the party and individually for Azad. Chandrashekhar Azad, now, planned to send some of the young men to the Soviet Union to learn and study Soviet techniques and methods of struggle. Azad was now convinced that the HSRA had moved far ahead

121 *Terrorism in India, 1917–36*, p.82.

122 Shiv Verma, op.cit., p.65.

123 NK Nigam, op.cit., p.104.

124 Sukhdeoraj, op.cit., pp.206–209. Jawaharlal Nehru refers to his meeting with Azad in his *Autobiography*, pp.261-62.

and that individual armed actions will serve no purpose. A mass revolutionary upsurge is required for a socialist revolution and this is possible only after a thorough study of the method of Bolsheviks in Russia, he said. Bhagat Singh too wanted that a few revolutonary young men should go to Russia. While in jail, he had deeply and minutely studied Marx's and Lenin's communistic philosophy.[125] He was convinced that a new socio-economic order can be established after the study of Bolshevik methods in Russia.[126] Prithvi Singh Azad went to Russia in 1931 at the behest of Bhagat Singh and Chandrashekher Azad. Chandrashekhar Azad also tried to send Yashpal and Surendra Pandey to Moscow.[127]

On February 27, 1931, Azad and his associate Sukhdeo Raj were discussing a plan of sending some revolutionaries to Russia via Burma or Afghanistan in Alfred Park at Allahabad. It is believed that Azad was betrayed by one of his associates Virbhadra Tiwari, who informed the police of Azad's presence at Alfred Park. A strong police force under the command of Superintendent Nott Bower reached the spot immediately. A revolver duel took place between Azad, Sukhdeoraj and the police. Sukhdeoraj escaped at the instance of Azad and in this unequal fight Azad shot Bisheshwar Singh in the jaw. Azad was hit by a bullet and he died instantaneously. Some believe that seeing the hopelessness of the situation he shot himself as he had taken a vow never to be arrested alive. Azad's indomitable courage, his dedicated life and ultimately his death made him one of the immortals in India's fight for freedom.[128]

When the people around came to know that a well known revolutionary Chandrashekhar Azad had been killed by police, a large crowd assembled in the Park. Loud national cries were raised

---

125 Baba Prithvi Singh Azad, *Lenin ke Desh Mein*, Delhi, 1978, p.19.

126 Ibid, p.21.

127 *Vaishampayan*, op.cit., p.230; also SP Sen (ed.), *Dictionary of National Biography*, p.265.

128 Bhagwan Das Mahour in BD Chaturvedi (ed.), *Yash Ka Dharohar*, Delhi, 1968, pp.126-127.

as the vehicle started off with the dead body of Azad.[129] The people rushed immediately to pick up the earth stained by his blood.[130] The cremation was secretly arranged by the police at Rasulabad.

While the HSRA worked as an underground secret organisation of the revolutionaries, the Naujawan Bharat Sabha worked openly to realise their objectives. It is, therefore, in the fitness of things to sketch briefly the activities of the Sabha.

Formation of Naujawan Bharat Sabha

The Naujawan Bharat Sabha was formed to channelise the militant nationalist movement on ideological lines in March 1926, by Bhagat Singh, a spirited youth and ex-student of National College, Lahore.[131] In this task, he was ably assisted by Bhagwati Charan Vohra, Dhanwantri, Ehsan Elahi and others. Ram Krishna and Bhagat Singh became its first President and Secretary respectively. Bhagwati Charan Vohra was appointed as its Propaganda Secretary.[132] The leftist Congressmen like Dr Saifuddin Kichlew, Dr Satyapal, Kedar Nath Sehgal, Lala Pindi Das and Lala Lal Chand Falak extended their sympathies and co-operation to the Sabha.

Objectives and Programme

The Sabha had two-fold objectives – social and political. The social objectives comprised the popularization of swadeshi goods, plain living, physical fitness, inculcation of the sense of brotherhood and

---

129 *The Leader*, Allahabad, March 1 1931.

130 *Abhudaya*, Allahabad, March 4 1931.

131 JN Sanyal, op.cit., p.25; NAI, Home Pol. File No.27/5/1931, p.1, speech delivered by Ramchandra, Vice-President of the Provincial Naujawan Bharat Sabha, Punjab at Ganj Mandi, Rawalpindi city on May 17 1931; also NAI, Home Pol. File No.130 and KW/1930, p.5. The same file on page 36 says that the Sabha was founded at the suggestion of Dr Satyapal. But a CID Report on page 5 confirms that Dr Satyapal had nothing to do with its founding. The Sabha owes its inception and existence to Bhagat Singh.

132 Yashpal, op.cit., Vol.I, Lucknow, 1964, p.91.

the stimulation of interest in Indian languages and civilization.[133] The Sabha also had a definite political programme and soon these "social objects of the Sabha" became "merely a cloak for the dissemination of revolutionary ideas."[134] The political programme of the Naujawan Bharat Sabha included the following :

> a. To establish a complete independent republic of the labourers and peasants of the whole of India;

> b. to infuse a spirit of patriotism into the hearts of the youth of the country in order to establish a united Indian nation;

> c. to express sympathy with and to assist the economic, industrial and social movements which, while being free from communal sentiment are intended to take us nearer to our ideal; namely the establishment of a complete independent republic of labourers and peasants;

> d. to organise the labourers and peasants.[135]

It is significant about the Sabha that along with English imperialism, it wanted to see the end of other imperialisms also. The Naujawan Bharat Sabha movement had a wider perspective...it believed in freedom of enslaved nations, i.e. China; Kabul etc.[136]

Thus, it is clear that unlike the Congress, the Sabha had a definite aim and a clear ideology to offer, i.e., the establishment of an independent socialist republic, and to stop the imperialist onslaught on other countries.[137]

---

133 NAI, Home Pol. File No.130 & KW/1930, p.36.

134 Ibid.

135 NAI Home Pol. File No.130 & KW/1930, p.36.

136 NAI, Home Pol. F. No.27/5/1931, speech delivered by BN Sanyal of Allahabad on 22 May, 1931, at Muttra in the Naujawan Bharat Sabha Conference. In his speech he said, "If any atrocities are perpetrated on them (China, Kabul, etc.) and the army of our country goes there to fire at and annhilate the people, it is a matter of great shame that we cannot check it. We shall have to check it and ask the people of our country, not to go to other countries which have no conflict with our country, to fire at and kill them and enslave the innocent people there..."

137 What the Congress had to offer was only *swaraj* to the masses. It stood for political liberty only and had always side-tracked the peasants and workers demands of economic emancipation. Whenever the peasantry attempted to

The Sabha was above all petty religious politics of the times and stood for secularism. "Before enrolment each member was made to sign a pledge that he would place the interests of his country above those of his community."[138] Even Lala Lajpat Rai, the eminent pillar of extremist nationalism in India, could not escape scathing criticism from the Naujawan Bharat Sabha when he joined hands with the Hindu Mahasabha.[139] The Sabha often organised social dinners with the object of developing healthy secular nationalist feelings among the people of the country. People of all castes and creeds were invited at meals where they served each other. On one such occasion, some over-enthusiastic young men cooked *halal* and *jhatka* meat (either of which was considered repugnant or taboo by one community or another) in the same pot and it was consumed by all present – Hindus, Muslims and Sikhs.[140] With the object of eradicating dogmatic communal feelings, the members of the Naujawan Bharat Sabha also organised a series of public lectures and discussed socio-political matters. The Sabha went to the extent of issuing a leaflet discarding Buddha and Christ and praising Karl Marx and Frederick Engels as the greatest men of the world.[141] It regarded communal amity as an important part of the political programme, but unlike the Congress it did not believe either in the appeasement of various religious faiths or in raising such slogans as *Allah-o Akbar*, *Sat Sri Akal* and *Bande Mataram* as a means of demonstrating its commitment to secularism. On the contrary it raised two slogans, *Inquilab Zindabad* and *Hindustan*

---

throw away the yoke of feudalism, it was checked by the Congress. (See SK Mittal and Kapil Kumar, 'Baba Ram Chandra and Peasant Upsurge in Oudh, 1920-21' in *Social Scientist*, Vol.6, No.11, June, 1978.

138 NAI, Home Pol. File No.130 & KW/1930, p.36.

139 Ibid. In September 1926, a pamphlet entitled 'An Appeal to the Young Punjab' was issued by Kidar Nath Sehgal and others on behalf of the Sabha attacking Lala Lajpat Rai as traitor.

140 Yashpal, op.cit., Vol.I, pp.92-93.

141 Sukhdeoraj, op.cit., p.27.

Zindabad, hailing the revolution and the country.[142] The objectives of the Naujawan Bharat Sabha revealed the firm faith of its founders and members in the ideals of a socialist republic. It placed before the country the triple objectives of independence, secularism and socialism or economic emancipation of the masses. The objectives could be achieved, they believed, by freeing people from divisive caste, creed and communal sentiments; by infusing the spirit of patriotism into the hearts of the youth who, as the vanguard of the revolution, shall guide and take the masses to the cherished destination.

Activities and Modus Operandi

Once the objectives and ideology of the Naujawan Bharat Sabha were outlined, its activists launched a programme designed to further their goals. Soon after the establishment of the Sabha its members commemorated the death anniversary of a young revolutionary, Kartar Singh Sarabha, who sacrificed his life in the Lahore Conspiracy Case of 1914-15. Bhagat Singh searched out a picture of Sarabha which Bhagwati Charan got enlarged at his own expense. The portrait was covered with a milky white cloth and kept in the Bradlaugh Hall in Lahore. The function began with a very heart-touching scene. Both Mrs. Durga Devi (wife of Bhagwati Charan Vohra) and Sushila Devi paid their homage to the martyr by sprinkling the blood of their fingers on the white cloth cover of the portrait. This function of the Sabha "was an open manifestation of calling upon the young men to devote themselves to the revolutionary activities."[143] In March 1927, the Sabha invited a revolutionary leader of Bengal, Dr Bhupendranath Dutt, who lectured on the Youth Movement in the west.[144] The Naujawan Bharat Sabha with its headquarters at Lahore, soon became a nucleus

---

142 Yashpal, op.cit., p.93.

143 Yashpal, op.cit., p.92.

144 NAI, Home Pol. File No.130 & KW/1930, pp.36-37.

to rally round the patriotic youth. Its activities, from March 1926 to April 1927, were confined to Lahore. Sohan Singh Josh writes:

> The Lahore Naujawan Sabha did some good work from March 1926 to April 1927 among students to politicise them. But outside Lahore nobody was aware of its existence at all. And then "the Sabha's activities came to an end. The Sabha during this period had accomplished nothing." In the British government's view, its open programme was only a cloak for the secret propaganda of extreme political doctrines of communism and violence.[145]

Soon after, the Sabha had to bear a severe blow when Bhagat Singh, its moving spirit, was implicated in the Dussehra Bomb Case in July 1927. The Sabha or its members had nothing to do with the bomb outrage in which about twelve innocent people were killed; it was merely an attempt on the part of the Government to malign it in public. The Government failed in its mission and Bhagat Singh had to be released, although on a very high amount of bail of Rs 60,000.[146] The Naujawan Bharat Sabha in its very first year of existence, became the *bete noire* of the imperialists who came to regard it as a very potential menace to the imperial structure.

Collaboration with Kirti Kisans

The Naujawan Bharat Sabha organised a "national week" in the end of March 1928 at Lahore.[147] During this week, public meetings were held, the most important one being on March 28 where SA Dange, a Bombay Communist leader and Philip Spratt of the British Communist Party spoke on the meaning of Indian Independence.[148] In the same month, a poster was brought out by Kirti[149] management with the signatures of Bhagat Singh Canadian and Sohan Singh

---

145 Sohan Singh Josh, *My Meetings with Bhagat Singh and Other Early Revolutionaries*, New Delhi, 1976, p.13.

146 Virendra Sindhu, *Yugdrishta Bhagat Singh*, p.159.

147 NAI, Home Pol. File No., 130 & KW/1930, p.37.

148 Ibid.

149 Kirti Kisan Party was a peasants and workers party with communist leanings and had its headquarters in Amritsar.

Josh, in which it was decided to hold a Youth Conference in the Jalianwala Bagh on April 11–13, 1928.[150] A few days before the Conference, Bhagat Singh went to meet one of the signatories of the poster, Sohan Singh Josh at Amritsar in the Kirti office. Bhagat Singh told him about the Naujawan Bharat Sabha, its programme and activities at Lahore and also expressed his desire to participate in the Youth Conference. Sohan Singh Josh welcomed the participation of the Naujawan Bharat Sabha in the conference. The Conference was held under the presidentship of Kidar Nath Sehgal, who was an associate of the Ghadr Revolutionaries and was also a member of the Naujawan Bharat Sabha, Lahore.[151] It was decided in this Conference that the youth of Punjab should be organised in a central body called the Naujawan Bharat Sabha of Punjab, with headquarters at Amritsar instead of Lahore.[152] With this decision, the policy of the Sabha was definitely enlarged, "to work in association with the Kirti group at Amritsar and thus to include a programme of devolution of power by revolution or other methods to the peasants and workers."[153] In this conference, it was also decided that the Sabha will have a provincial organisation with a branch in each district, tehsil, thana and village, and special emphasis was laid on work in the rural areas.[154]

Sabha and the Peasants

Only a month after this decision, the Sabha tried to stir up an agrarian agitation over the failure of the wheat harvest. A meeting was organised at Village Jahman in Lahore district on May 23, 1928 to discuss the failure of the crop. The meeting was addressed by prominent extremist leaders like Dr Satyapal, MA Majid and

---

150 Sohan Singh Josh, op.cit., p.11.

151 Ibid, p.15. Josh says that they were then not aware that KN Sehgal was also a member of Naujawan Bharat Sabha at Lahore.

152 NAI, Home Pol. File No.130 & KW/1930, p.100.

153 Ibid.

154 Ibid.

Kidar Nath Sehgal.[155] This meeting was advertised as a Congress meeting but was actually inspired by the Naujawan Bharat Sabha.[156] The Sabha collaborated with the Congress party whenever it fought for the betterment of the peasants and workers. In June 1928 the Sabha supported the Congress in its agitation over the Bardoli re-assessment because it considered the Satyagraha Campaign of Bardoli as an economic protest against the high-handed policy of the Bombay Government. Even before the collaboration with the Kirti group, the Naujawan Bharat Sabha had emphasised the role of peasants and workers in the freedom struggle but the association with the Kirti group brought this aspect into greater prominence. Now the activities of the Sabha centred around the organisation of workers and peasants, the most numerous and oppressed class of the Indian people. It took up the class demands of the peasantry, fought for their agrarian and economic grievances, and inculcated in them a passionate love for freedom. It made them conscious of their political role in the freedom struggle and emphasized that the problem of winning freedom was also their problem because they were the most oppressed and brutally exploited classes in the British regime and hence they must get organised and prepare for the popular revolution.[157]

To infuse a spirit of struggle and to make the peasantry and workers conscious of their rights, the Sabha took a very keen interest in organising a workers' and peasants' conference at Lyallpur at the end of September 1928.[158] Among the prominent participants were Spratt, Bradley and Dange, who were extra provincial communist leaders, Kidar Nath Sehgal, president of Naujawan Bharat Sabha and Chhabil Das, Secretary of the Tract Society of the Sabha. Ram Chandra, in his address, as Chairman of the Reception Committee, made quite clear the views of the Sabha on the different problems

---

155 Ibid, p.38.

156 Ibid.

157 Josh, op.cit., p.17.

158 NAI, Home Pol. File No.130 & KW/1930, p.41.

of the country. He lauded the revolutionaries and denounced imperialism, capitalism and the present system of society. He recommended the nationalisation of wealth, a social revolution, the organisation of workers and peasants to resist exploitation by capitalists.[159] When the nation was charged with anti-British feelings and the Congress party was meeting for its historic session at Lahore in December 1929, the All India Peasants' and Workers' conference was organised there which was attended by 25,000 people.[160] The Naujawan Bharat Sabha, on February 1, 1930, held a conference with the peasants of the surrounding villages at Shahdara.[161]

The bond between the Kirti Party and the Naujawan Bharat Sabha was further strengthened when Sohan Singh Josh, leader of the Kirti Party, was elected Chairman of the Amritsar branch of the Sabha in July, 1928. Supported by the Congress leftists, they celebrated the "Friends of Russia Week" in August 1928.[162] During the celebration, several resolutions were passed to the effect that no Indian would render assistance to the British in any future war; expressing friendship with Russia and sympathy with the anti-imperialist Soviet policy.[163] The resolutions decreed the Sabha's policy that in future England's difficulty shall be India's opportunity to free her from foreign rule. It was further stated that the destruction of capitalism and the establishment of labourers' and peasants' Government were the only road to freedom and prosperity.[164] In the Punjab the low prices of wheat had depressed

---

159 NAI, Home Pol. F. No.130 & KW/1930, p.42. The programme of the Sabha as laid down by Ram Chandra was severely condemned by Choudhry Chotu Ram, who was presiding over an important annual meeting of the Provincial Zamindar League at the same place. He openly advocated the cause of Zamindars.

160 *The Tribune*, 28 Dec. 1929. The Conference was marked by slogans of "Long Live Revolution" and "Long Live Bhagat Singh".

161 NAI, Home Pol. File No.18/3/1930, p.17.

162 NAI, Home Pol. File No.130 & KW/1930, p.40.

163 Ibid.

164 Ibid.

the peasantry. The Governor of the province admitted that there was "undoubtedly a difficulty in paying the last Kharif demand... Genuine economic distress is being felt and is exercising the mind of the rural population. The Naujawan Bharat Sabha and the Kirti Kisan Party mobilised the peasants on the issue of land revenue and demanded its complete remission. In the villages of Delhi, the workers made extensive tours in order "to obstruct collection of revenue." They asked the tenants to apply for remissions, and printed forms were issued in this connection.[165]

The Sabha along with the Kirti Party, tried to spread its influence among the workers as well, when it made an attempt to capture various unions in Amritsar in August 1928.[166] The Sabha resisted almost all anti-working class policies of the Government. It opposed the Trade Disputes Bill which appeared in the Assembly in August 1928. At Amritsar, a meeting was organised on August 18, to discuss the question of "war between Capital and Labour", the meeting was addressed by Sohan Singh Josh, MA Majid, Ram Chandra and KN Sehgal who condemned the Bill and eulogised the Russian Revolution.[167]

Tract Society

They quoted Voltaire, one of the philosophers of the French Revolution, to explain the need of cheap and small booklets. He said:

> What is the use of writing books running over 500 and 1000 pages? These paged books again running into ten and twenty volumes. How many people possess the brains to read and understand these books? How many people have money to buy these big books? The

---

165 NAI, Home Pol. File No.30/50/1931. Report of the Chief Commissioner, Delhi dated December 14 1931.

166 NAI, Home Pol. File No.130 & KW/1930, p.40. These workers unions were Punjab Mechanical Engineers Union, a Press Union and the Railway Porters' Union.

167 Ibid., p.41.

> Government can be overthrown only by small cheap pamphlets, which can reach the petty huts of poor peasants and workers.

One of the prime objectives of the Sabha was propagating the ideology it stood for and initiating a campaign among the people on those lines. Hence it decided to launch a Tract Society devoted to the publication and distribution of revolutionary socialist literature, impregnated with nationalism and secularism. Principal Chhabil Das[168], one of the well known scholars of Punjab and a founder member of the Sabha, was elected its first secretary. He wrote a number of sixteen-page tracts in Urdu, which were priced at two pice so that they may reach almost everyone, howsoever poor he or she may be. These tracts were extremely popular in the Punjab, U.P., Delhi and J&K, i.e. in all areas where Urdu was then predominant, and were printed and sold in thousands.

Principal Chhabil Das tried to expose the British imperialists in the very first tract by quoting Sir William Higgs, Home Secretary, Government of India. Higgs had said:

> We did not conquer India for the benefit of Indians. It is often said in missionary meetings that we are ruling India for the welfare of Indians. This is a cant. We are governing India for the export of British goods to India in general and for the sale of the Lancashire cotton goods in particular, and by the sword we will retain it.

Responding to such a brutal and blunt expression, the title page of the first tract written by Chhabil Das prominentaly displayed the following couplet as representing the message of the revolution :

> *Duniya se ghulami ka main nam mita dungi*
> *Ik bar zamane ko azad kara dungi*
> *Jo log gharibon par karte hain sitam nahaq*
> *Gar dam hai mira qayam gin gin kar saza dungi*

Translated into English it said :

---

168 Prof. Chhabil Das was the Principal of National College, Lahore. He took
   keen interest in the activities of the Sabha.

> I shall for all time put an end to slavery,
> And for once liberate the whole world;
> Those who perpetrate atrocities on the exploited people,
> Shall each and all be visited by deserved retribution.

The Tract Society published three pamphlets in the beginning, which were declared by the colonial administration as highly objectionable and "strongly impregnated with Bolshevik and Communist doctrines."[169] These pamphlets were 1. *The Wealth of Nations* by Hardayal, 2. *India and the Next Year* by Agnes Smedley and 3. *Bharat Mata Ka Darshan* by Chhabil Das. There are not enough details available to tell us about the content of these pamphlets. However, there were many more and fortunately we have some detailed information about them. It will be useful to relate the content of some of those tracts here.

Tract One

Ham Swaraj Kyon Chahte Hain (Why do we want Swaraj). This tract was a comparative compilation of statistical information regarding area, extent, population, education, health, wealth and daily income of Indians and the citizens of other civilised and developed countries. These statistics in some places startled the Indians. For example, whereas the average annual income of a man in USA was about Rupees 4000 in those days, the average annual income of an Indian was between Rupees 20 or 30 and the daily average income of an Indian was five paisa only. Due to this extreme poverty millions died of hunger and disease, crores were uneducated and illiterate, and the number of unemployed and beggars was staggering. Millions of tender age widows suffered untold miseries.

Tract Two

Naujawanon Se Do Baten[170] (A few words with the Young). This tract depicted the grim picture of poverty, illiteracy and superstitions,

---

169 NAI, Home Pol. F. No.130 & KW/1930.

170 Ibid.

and the question was raised as to who would rid India of these evils. It reminded the people that no God will descend from heaven to intervene and provide relief. The people themselves will have to tackle these evils. Again a question was raised as to who among the people will take on this task, when the crores in the villages were illiterate and did not know how and what to do; the traders and businessmen were busy accumulating money; pandits, maulvis and granthis were engaged in fasts, prayers and other such rituals; the Government employees spent their time in attending their office to receive monthly packets of pay and then spend the amount. The answer they proposed was that history was witness to all the adversities faced by mankind and it was only the educated courageous young men who took up the challenge. The young educated men and women had come forward valiantly and waged a hard struggle to overthrow kings and emperors to change the faces of their countries. This pamphlet thus urged the youth of the country to follow the example set by the young men of Ireland, Turkey, Japan and China in their respective struggles for independence; accused the English government of exploiting India and keeping its inhabitants impoverished and illiterate.[171] It clearly showed that the Sabha regarded Indian subjection baneful for the neighbouring countries when it said that "the state of slavery in which India was held had calamitous results on neighbouring countries".[172] It directly urged the students "to study such movements as communism and Bolshevism, the doctrines of freedom and equality, democracy and self-determination, which alone could bring self-government and economic freedom."[173]

Tract Three

This tract raised the question: *what is the greatest sin?* The answer again was: *poverty*. It emphasised that financial and educational

---

171 Ibid.

172 Ibid.

173 Ibid.

deprivation is the cause of most sins. There are millions of people who commit theft, dacoities and murders because of this. A large number of womenfolk are driven to sell themselves and their honour because of hunger. Then the question was raised as to how this problem could ultimately be solved. The answer, according to the revolutionaries, lay in the economic restructuring of society. Private property should be abolished. The means of production should be socially owned and all people should share work and benefits alike.

Tract Four

This tract also began with a question: *Who are the greatest men in the world*? The author described the following five categories :

> Conquerers and Generals – Alexander, Napoleon, Hitler.
> Wealthy men – Ford, Carnegie, Tata.
> Poets and writers – Kalidas, Shakespeare, Milton.
> Kindly people – Buddha, Christ, Confucius, Gandhi.
> Revolutionaries – Rousseau, Voltaire, Marx, Engels, Lenin.

The author then brought all these great men before the bar of the 20th century and administered the following judgements:

> If to kill a man is sin, generals and conquerers are the worst sinners for having killed thousands and lakhs of people.

> It is but fit that a man should earn, enjoy and save. But to exploit thousands of workers and then donate part of the earnings as charity to temples, mosques and churches is nothing but fraud.

> It is shameful to sing praises of kings and tyrants. One must sing to arouse the sleeping man to break his fetters.

> These in the 'Kindly people' category were respectfully welcomed as good men but their message of peace, it was said, was ill-suited because it blunted the edge of anger of the awakened, the down-trodden and the exploited poor.

> Then the final judgement was passed, and Voltaire, Rousseau, Marx, Engels and Lenin were showered with praises for having awakened and aroused the exploited people, and having shown them the new path of struggle for freedom and prosperity.

Tract Five

This particular tract was printed under the title, *Indian Peasant and Worker*. It went on to emphasise the role and contribution of peasants and workers to national life. It stated that if on any day the capitalists, money-lenders, princes, and landlords disappeared from the earth, it would hardly make any difference to the remaining humanity. But if on the other hand the peasants and workers disappeared or stopped all production, the world would face a catastrophe as there would be nothing to consume, and hunger and squalor would cover the world and death would reign supreme.

Tract Six

This tract was a Urdu translation of an article by Har Dayal. The author argued here that mountains, rivers, forests, gold mines, etc., do not constitute the entire index of the wealth of a nation. The wealth of a nation is created when the hearts, minds and the hands of its people are put to work. Men are the real creators of wealth. Tell the people to stop pilgrimages to forests, mountains and rivers, and by constructive thinking and labor build a new world and a new heaven on this earth, which no God has done for them till now.

Tract Seven

Here again the author of the tract attempted to arouse some sort of a class consciousness among the people. He reminded them that the world is witness to wars between kings and their subjects; between the black and the white; between labour and capital, between the feudal and the fascist rulers and the uprisings of the awakened men. The tract then went on to say that the people themselves should think, arise and decide whom to support.

Tract Eight

This particular tract was published with the title *Goron ki Kartut* and was reproduced in Gurmukhi as *Kachre Firangi* (Crafty Whites).

The earlier seven tracts were circulated among the people without much problem but this one infuriated the white bureaucracy, which went on to proscribe it.

The tract stated that the West has witnessed Industrial Revolution. There is steam power and big machines in the field. The whites require raw material for manufactures and markets for the sale of manufactured goods. To meet their need the white people colonised many backward countries of Asia, Africa and South America. To achieve this they created divisions among the backward nations and kept them illiterate. Well did Tolstoy say "the strength of a Government is in the ignorance of the people." So the masses were kept illiterate and ignorant and theories like the superiority of white nations were preached and spread, so that the subject nations will be convinced that the white rulers could alone govern and administer. There was unequal application of laws for the blacks, and the whites in a way became licensed murderers.

The Naujawan Bharat Sabha also published an 'Independent India Tract Series'. One of them was titled *Indian Peasants*, being a translation from Lala Har Dayal. Highlighting the importance of peasants and workers, it stated:

> If suddenly one night die all the rich people of the world like Tatas, Batas and Birlas, the people awaking in the morning, will not feel much about it. If on the contrary, all the peasants and workers meet the same fate, one would feel that the world is not worth living. It is worse than hell.[174]

In still another leaflet titled, *Worst Sin in the World is Poverty*, young men were exhorted to eradicate poverty root and branch, to make an equitable distribution of wealth and to have an equal opportunity to advance and share power.[175] It directly urged the students to study such movements as communism and Bolshevism, the doctrines of

---

174 Sukhdeoraj, op.cit., pp.26-27.

175 Ibid, p.27.

freedom and equality, democracy and self-determination, which alone could bring self-government and economic freedom.[176]

On the Students Front

These pamphlets of the Sabha, although aimed at the organisation of workers and peasants, evoked greatest response from youth and students. The revolutionary ideas of freedom, equality and economic emancipation stirred the youth to an unprecedented degree. The Sabha activities led to the founding of youth leagues and student unions in several towns and various centres of learning throughout north India.[177] The Lahore Students Union became an auxillary of the Naujawan Bharat Sabha. According to the reports of the Government "the Lahore Students Union was organised only as an appanage (appendage) to the Naujawan Bharat Sabha or as a recruiting ground for revolutionary work and from the very beginning the secret section of the Union kept working to achieve that object."[178] It attempted to channelise the students' activities along a revolutionary path. The students' enthusiasm so unnerved the authorities that they thought it fit to take stringent measures against the Sabha to check its rising influence. The British officials reported that the students had become obstinate and freely participated in all anti-Government activities of the Sabha. The Secretary of State in his letter to the Viceroy dated 29 September 1931, went to the extent of suggesting that the doors of the Government employment be shut against those youth who participated in 'terrorist' activities.[179] The Governor of Punjab went to the length of warning the management

---

176 NAI, Home Pol. F.No.130 & KW/1930.

177 SK Mittal, 'The Role of Meerut College in the Freedom Struggle of India', *Social Scientist*, No.76, pp.43–45.

178 NAI, Home Pol. File No.130 & KW/1930, p.6.

179 NAI, Home Pol. F.No.4/35/1931. After receiving this letter from the Secretary of State, the Viceroy wrote similar letters to the various Governors of states to gain information on the activities of the students and youth, and the measures taken by various governments to curb the tendency of revolt amongst them.

of the schools with stoppage of grants and recognition if they failed to curb the revolutionary tendencies of the students.[180] The teachers who preached revolutionary or anarchical ideas were threatened with removal from their services.[181] The Government adopted the dual policy of repression and reform in order to check the mounting revolutionary and anti-British feelings among the students. On the one hand the management and principals of the colleges were forced to weed out revolutionary elements from their colleges by means of repression such as suspension of teachers and grants. On the other hand, a Parents Society was formed to bring the parents in closer touch with the principals of the colleges with a view to exercise joint influence over the activities of their wards.[182] The repression only helped in rekindling the revolutionary spirit of the youth. As students activities in the Punjab increased, they, alongwith Naujawan Bharat Sabha, openly defied the authorities. The loyalists now formed the Punjab University Students Union to counteract the influence of the Sabha over the students.[183] It commanded enough financial resources and organised programmes of entertainment to depoliticise and derevolutionise the students. The sole purpose of this Union was to suppress the Naujawan Bharat Sabha or any other organisation of similar nature.[184] Even

---

180 Ibid.

181 Ibid. "In some cases, we stipulate for the removal of masters, who, we have proof, are giving a call for revolutionary or anarchical ideas. In one case, we suspended all grants to a private High School until three masters had been removed. This has had a good effect not only on the particular institution, but also on other institutions, as few schools can get on without the Government grant."

182 Ibid. "We got some leading non-officials to form a Parents Society in Lahore and the mofussil with the main object of keeping parents in closer touch with the principals of colleges and forcing the latter to take a deeper and more constant interest in the activites of their sons and the influences to which they may be exposed."

183 Ibid.

184 Ibid. "This has had a good and loyal influence and has really begun to make headway against the seditious Punjab Students Union, the Naujawan Bharat Sabha and other undesirable associations, because it has

the DAV College, Lahore became infested with the revolutionary spirit to an extent that Government was "chary of recruiting youths educated at the DAVCollege, Lahore, on account of the large number of seditious and revolutionary youth who have hailed from that College". Undaunted by the repression, which ruined many careers, the students participated enthusiastically in the activities of the Naujawan Bharat Sabha.[185]

Sabha and the Simon Commission

No event after the Jalianwala Bagh massacre stirred the Indian people so deeply as the imposition of the all white Simon Commission on India. It united all the active forces, parties, organisations of nationalists and revolutionaries cutting across the ideological lines. The Naujawan Bharat Sabha held a meeting on August 18, 1928 and carried out a vigorous propaganda for the boycott of the Commission.[186] But, it is significant that the basis for the boycott was different in Sabha's case. The Congress opposed the Commission only because no Congressmen could be its member, despite repeated requests. The Sabha, on the other hand, believed that "the English government had no right to decide our fate. Who are they to send a Commission?"[187] Only four days before the arrival of the Commission, the Sabha held another meeting, calling for a demonstration against the Commission in Lahore on October 30. As a matter of fact, it was the Sabha which led the demonstration against the Commission in Lahore and the Congress leaders had no option but to come forward and join the procession.[188] A day before, the Lahore SSP Scott had issued orders, directing the public to abstain from organising and joining the procession, which had

---

    really more to offer them owing to being in possession of more funds than the above organisations."

185 Ibid.

186 NAI, Home Pol. File No.130 & KW/1930, p.41.

187 Yashpal, op.cit., p.137.

188 Ibid.

not been permitted by him.[189] The same day a public meeting was called in the evening denouncing the order and urging the people to defy it. The order of the SSP was obeyed only in its breach and a veritable sea of humanity surged on to the streets of Lahore with anti-Simon slogans. The functionaries of a 'pride-hurt' Government resorted to deliberate and unprovoked lathi charge, injuring Lajpat Rai seriously, which led to his death after a fortnight. It was undoubtedly an affront to the whole nation. The youth were desperate and eager to vindicate the honour of Lalaji. During this period the Sabha held several public meetings and openly alleged that the British government was responsible for the murder of Lalaji. On December 17, meetings were held to celebrate 'Kakori Day' in Lahore and Amritsar, where the speakers glorified and praised the patriotic spirit of the revolutionaries.[190] On December 17, Saunders and his reader were killed and "the cirmustances of the murder suggested the knowledge, if not complicity, of several members of the Sabha and seven members were arrested."[191] In fact it was Bhagat Singh, the founder of the Sabha who killed Saunders on December 17. "Bhagat Singh did not become popular because of his act of terrorism, but because he seemed to vindicate, for the moment the honour of Lala Lajpat Rai and through him of the nation. He became a symbol, the act was forgotten, the symbol remained and within a few months each town and village of the Punjab and to a lesser extent in the rest of India resounded with his name and innumerable legends grew up about him. The popularity that the man achieved was something amazing."[192]

Naujawan – the Sabha's Press Organ

The Naujawan Bharat Sabha started a newspaper called *Naujawan* in October 1928. This paper was started with the declared policy of

---

189 NAI, Home Pol. File No.1–28/1928, Monthly Report.

190 Sohan Singh Josh, op.cit., pp.21-22.

191 NAI, Home Pol. File No.130 & KW/1930.

192 Jawaharlal Nehru, op.cit., pp.175-176.

"developing a spirit of patriotism in the hearts of young men, helping in the cause of the workers, peasants and the poor, evoking the memory of the martyrs who have sacrificed their lives for the sake of the country and providing young men with literature to induce them to make sacrifices for the liberty of the motherland."[193] The first issue of the paper published a detailed life-sketch of Madan Lal Dhingra[194] and also a message from Sohan Singh Josh. The paper, in its issue of November 13, 1928 published an article entitled 'The Time has Come', which made a revolutionary appeal to the youth and urged them to wake up and free the motherland. The paper exhorted the youth to cast off cowardice, timidity and shamelessness. It reminded them that "the sword of the alien was hanging at our mother's helpless breast to suck her blood" and called upon the youth to "rise, quench the blood-thirsty sword of the tyrants and cause blood to run in streams."[195] The paper continued to publish such articles exhorting young men to follow the path of revolutionaries like Kartar Singh Sarabha and others. It succeeded in developing hatred and contempt for the British government in the hearts of the young generation.

Second Provincial Naujawan Bharat Sabha Conference, 1929

The Provincial Naujawan Bharat Sabha held its second session in Lahore from February 22 to February 24, 1929, electing Sohan Singh Josh as its President. In this conference, imperialism was strongly condemned, complete independence was declared to be the creed of the youth of India and a mass revolution by workers and peasants was advocated. The Conference strongly criticised the Congress

---

193 NAI, Home Pol. File No.130 & KW/1930, p.44.

194 Madan Lal Dhingra was a young revolutionary who killed Sir Curzon Wylie in 1907 in London.

195 NAI, Home Pol. File No.130 & KW/1930, p.44.

demand for Dominion Status and "reflected the revolutionary, communist and anti-British spirit of the Naujawan Bharat Sabha".[196]

By the end of 1929, branches of the Sabha were established in many districts of western Uttar Pradesh.[197] In the city of Meerut, a branch of Naujawan Bharat Sabha was founded on October 22, 1929, in a meeting held at the residence of Radha Mohan Garg.[198] Similarly, in the province of Sindh, the Sabha was formed at Karachi,[199] which became quite active in the years to come, besides spreading its influence in the far off cities of Western India like Bombay and Surat.[200]

Bhagat Singh, who was a founder member of the Sabha and its first Secretary, was now an active member of the HSRA. On April 8, 1929, he alongwith BK Dutt threw bombs in the Assembly while the members were discussing the Public Safety Bill. They shouted the slogans, "Inquilab Zindabad", and ''Down with British Imperialism''. Both were arrested on the spot. The Sabha's activities gained momentum after the imprisonment of Bhagat Singh and his comrades. The subsequent hunger strike by Jatindra Nath Das,

---

196 Ibid.

197 *The Tribune,* 21 January, 1930. The U.P. General Secretary of the Sabha, comrade Ram Saran Das Johry, toured the state and established branches in Khurja, Bulandshahar, Sikanderabad, Saharanpur and Dehra Dun.

198 U.P. Police Secret Abstract, 2 November, 1929, para 686 cited by SK Mittal, 'The Role of Meerut College in the Freedom Struggle of India' in *Social Scientist*, November, 1978, No.76. The objectives of the Sabha were (1) to establish a free republic of workers and peasants in India; (2) to inspire youth with the spirit of patriotism and sacrifice to the end that India might become a full fledged national entity; (3) to cut off every connection with those bodies which propagate communalism or favour communal representations; (4) to organise workers and peasants; (5) to take interest in every anti-communal, economic, social or political movement leading to the ultimate goal of a free republic of workers and peasants in India.

199 NAI, Home Pol. File No.498/1930.

200 Home Deptt. (Special Branch) File No.141 (673–D) of 1931 (Naujawan Bharat Sabha), Maharashtra State Archives, Bombay.

Bhagat Singh, BK Dutt and others in the jail further added fuel to the fire.

Several public meetings were held throughout the province under the auspices of the Sabha to express sympathy with the hungerstrikers and to press the imperialist Government to accept their demands.[201] To congratulate Bhagat Singh, BK Dutt and KN Sehgal, the Sabha held meetings in Lahore and Amritsar on June 19, 1929. Sardar Kishan Singh, father of Bhagat Singh, was one of the speakers at the Lahore meeting. He said that "he was not sorry his son had been convicted and asked his audience to see that the object for which his son and BK Dutt had been punished was eventually achieved."[202] Milkhi Ram, one of the Sabha activists, ridiculed the idea that the adoption of Khaddar and the boycott of foreign cloth would lead to the emancipation of the country and advised those present to "wear hats and keep pistols".[203] A similar meeting was held in Amritsar where Ajit Singh, General Secretary of the Sabha, expressed the hope that India would produce many more young men like Bhagat Singh and BK Dutt who would destroy the British government.[204] The leaders of the Sabha observed June 30 as "Bhagat Singh Day" and all major cities and towns participated enthusiastically. At a meeting in Lahore, where about 6000 people gathered under Sardul Singh Cavisher's leadership, the former cry of "Bande Mataram" was replaced by shouts of "Long Live Revolution" and "Down with Imperialism". Much greater enthusiasm was generated at Amritsar, where Bhagat Singh Day was celebrated in the Jalianwala Bagh under the joint auspices of the City Congress Committee and the Sabha, where an address was also presented to

---

201 NAI, Home Pol. File No.244 & KW/1930, p.6.

202 NAI, Home Pol. File No.130 & KW/1930, p.47.

203 Ibid.

204 Ibid.

Master Mota Singh[205] on June 30, 1929.[206] Hakim Sikandar Khizr read the address of the Naujawan Bharat Sabha which welcomed Master Mota Singh and appreciated the sacrifice made by him in bearing unlimited troubles in jail for seven years, for the honour and dignity of the motherland. The address of the Sabha said that the country which was once a paradise had become desolate due to the exploitation of capitalists and imperialists. Still, the capitalist leaders of the poor people were rendering cooperation to the alien government "by framing Nehru Constitution, negotiating for compromise with imperialism, which was busy in crushing the political and economic struggle of the labourers and peasants by legitimate and illegitimate methods."[207] The Sabha cried halt to all compromises with imperialists, proclaimed the ideal of complete independence and declared the determination of its members to sacrifice their comforts and blooming youths at the altar of freedom. Unlike the elder leadership, the young men and their hearts were free from the encumbrances of what was regarded as tradition. In the end, it was said that the young men only needed a good leader and requested the Master to guide them like Lenin so that they might be able to rouse the peasants and workers from their abysmal state to a life of dignity.[208]

The Sabha celebrated July 21, 1929, as the All India Bhagat Singh–BK Dutt Day. An Appeal was made to the Congress youth

---

205 Master Mota Singh was a revolutionary, who was imprisoned for seven years and who worked with the Babbar Akalis. He was also a prominent communist leader of the province.

206 NAI, Home Pol. F.No.130 & KW/1930. In this meeting Dr Kichlew presided and the audience consisted of all communities, traders, businessmen, shookeepers, students etc. It was attended by prominent leaders like Ajit Singh of Naujawan Bharat Sabha, Gurbaksh Singh, Sohan Singh Sevak, Sikandar Khizr, Feroze din Mansoor, Dr Sant Ram Seth, Dr Sant Ram Arora, Daud Ghaznavi, Hasanuddin, Ratan Singh Azad, Mool Singh Chaurinda, Bhagwan Singh Langowal, Amokh Singh, Nudharak and Master Mota Singh.

207 Ibid.

208 Ibid.

and to all labour organisations in the country to observe the day by (1) Fasting; (2) Taking out processions and collecting funds for the defence of the accused in the Lahore Conspiracy Case; (3) Organising meetings in the evening to explain the significance and importance of the struggle in the cause of country's freedom, to record the country's protest against the treatment meted out to these prisoners. Wherever possible their photos and copies of their statements should be distributed.[209] In the meanwhile, the revolutionaries continued their struggle against the imperialist power even from the jail. They demanded an improvement in the condition of prisoners and the treatment meted out to them in the jail. When there was no response from the British bureaucracy, Bhagat Singh, Jatindra Das, BK Dutt and others went on a hunger-strike in protest. This hunger-strike continued for more than two months but the Government kept watching callously. At last on the 63rd day of his hunger-strike Jatin Das achieved martyrdom. This news spread like wild fire. It roused country-wide protests and public meetings were held to condemn the inhuman attitude of the Government. The two month long hunger-strike in the jail and the martyrdom of Das show that the soldiers of the Sabha did not represent merely physical-force, as many Gandhians would have us believe. On the contrary, their fast demonstrated the power of soul-force, and succeeded in bending the imperial government to grant concessions for political prisoners. In fact these revolutionaries believed in combining soul-force with physical-force.

A Naujawan Bharat Sabha Conference was held at Lahore on December 23, 1929, under the presidentship of Comrade Suhasini Nambiar, where a resolution was passed on the 'Martyrdom of Das'. It said: "This Conference pays its homage to the martyr JN Das on his exemplary self sacrifice and lays the responsibility for his death on the shoulders of the Government."[210] Comrade Suhasini in her address condemned the Dominion Status theory of the Congress

---

209 *The Tribune*, July 19 1929.

210 *The Tribune*, December 28 1929.

leaders and warned that those leaders who are making petty bargains with the Government would soon lose their hold on the masses.

To infuse patriotism and the spirit of sacrifice among the people of the country, the Sabha usually celebrated the memories of the old revolutionaries: Kakori Day was celebrated on December 19, 1929, at Bradlaugh Hall, Lahore.[211] The Sabha commemorated October 6, 1929, as "The Political Sufferers Day" and public meetings were held in all important cities of the province under its auspices.[212] The Sabha, in its Working Committee meeting in Delhi on February 3, 1930, decided that the Sabha will mark May 10 as the 'Revolution Day' and a programme was chalked out, which was to be followed everywhere on the proposed date.[213] The Committee resolved that the following programme be observed: (1) A procession with red flags be organised and workers and peasants be specially asked to join it; (2) The procession to terminate at a public place where the red flag be hoisted and saluted; (3) After the flag hoisting ceremony a public meeting be held where the statement, to be issued by the Working Committee, be read. It was also decided to arrange places, wherever the branches of the Sabha are located, to impart physical training to volunteers, including training in the use of rifles, swords, lathis, etc. The Working Committee of the Sabha also instructed the local Sabhas to carry on a campaign of boycott of British goods throughout the country.[214]

Naujawan Bharat Sabha and Civil Disobedience

Gandhi had begun preaching the ideas of Civil Disobedience in 1929 and 1930. These ideas were welcomed and hailed by the Naujawan Bharat Sabha. From the platform of the Sabha, Dr Kitchlew said in Amritsar on October 6, 1929, that the country was ready for the Civil Disobedience or any other programme proposed by the

---

211 *The Tribune*, December 20 1929.

212 *The Tribune*, October 8 1929.

213 *The Tribune*, February 9 1930.

214 Ibid.

Congress for the freedom of the country. Mahatma Gandhi launched his nation-wide Civil Disobedience campaign in the beginning of March 1930. This programme of the Congress was enthusiastically supported by the Naujawan Bharat Sabha and its members plunged themselves into the struggle. Several members of the Sabha were arrested while recruiting volunteers for the Civil Disobedience in Biharsharif.[215] Similarly, the Sabha alongwith the Congress held public meetings in the urban and rural areas of Saharanpur, which perturbed the district officials.[216] The Naujawan Bharat Sabha's platform was openly used for the propagation of the Congress creed of Civil Disobedience. The Congress had to enlist the support of the Naujawan Bharat Sabha because there was a noticeable decline in the popularity of the Congress while the youth movement had received impetus from the Lahore Students Conference held on October 19 and 20.[217] During the year 1929, the youth movement continued to be regarded as a source of danger to the Government, and another organisation on lines similar to the Naujawan Bharat Sabha sprang into existence at Jullunder under the name *Doaba Balik Sabha*.[218] Though the Sabha assisted the Congress in its recruiting campaign, there was an obvious distinction between them, and the leaders of the Sabha warned the Congress leaders to stand clear of the way of the young men.[219] But the co-operation between the two organisations continued throughout the Civil Disobedience movement. The Punjab Congress called for a Hunger Strike Week in February, 1930 and was zealously supported by the

---

215 *The Tribune*, March 23 1930.

216 *The Tribune*, April 4 1930.

217 NAI, Home Pol. File No.17/1929. This Conference was presided over by Subhash Chandra Bose and was attended by a large number of students from the local colleges.

218 Ibid.

219 Ibid. Pandit Shiv Dutt Ranga, while speaking at the Naujawan Sabha meeting in Multan on October 1 1929, warned the Congress leaders to stand clear of the way of the young men.

Sabha.[220] Simultaneously, the Sabha worked hard to collect funds for the defence of the Lahore Case. The Naujawan Bharat Sabha became so popular among the masses of the Punjab that the Government had to take strong measures to curb its activities. But no step of the Government could stem the tide of the rising enthusiasm and the Sabha continued to gain ground. It celebrated March 20, 1930, as the 'Meerut Day', processions were taken out and funds were collected for the Meerut Communist Conspiracy Case.[221] Ultimately, the wrath of the white bureaucracy fell on the Sabha. The Punjab Government notified that the Naujawan Bharat Sabha constituted a danger to the public peace, interfered with the maintenance of law and order, and declared it an unlawful organisation on June 23, 1930.[222] The offices of the Sabha were vigorously searched and its leaders were rounded up throughout the state. The imperialist government had to take similar steps in Sind where the Naujawan Bharat Sabha had overshadowed all other political organisations including the Congress. Here the initiative passed from the hands of the Congress – an ostensibly non-violent body, which failed to make any real progress – into those of a more violent set of organisations of which the Naujawan Bharat Sabha was the chief.[223] The Sabha exhorted the youth to go and work in the villages, like the Russian youth. They needed to explain there the real meaning of the forthcoming revolution in India. Villagers were to be made to understand and feel that the new revolution would not be confined to merely changing the rulers; it would mean the establishment of a completely new socio-political order. It would therefore, be a

---

220 *The Tribune*, February 16 1930.

221 *The Tribune*, March 19 1930. It was on this day when the Meerut prisoners were put on a trial.

222 NAI, Home Pol. File No.498/1930, p.17.

223 Ibid.

revolution of the people and by the people. In other words, it would be a *swaraj* for 98% of people.[224]

The Special Tribunal to try Bhagat Singh and his comrades on its part shamelessly staged a drama of hearings that continued for 6 months, and finally, on the October 7, 1930, Bhagat Singh, Sukhdev and Rajguru were sentenced to death. Once more, the nation's soul was stirred, this day was seen as a black day and Bhagat Singh became almost an object of worship by crores of Indians. He was now a symbol of unprecedented courage in the struggle against imperialist power. The Civil Disobedience movement of Gandhi also gained momentum and was spreading rapidly but was suddenly withdrawn, and the Mahatma agreed for a dialogue with the Viceroy. On the other hand, Bhagat Singh Appeal Committees were formed throughout the state in various districts.[225] The Naujawan Bharat Sabha, which had been declared illegal in June 1930, was revived, though in a camouflaged form, through these committees. In this connection, the Government fortnightly report says that there started "an energetic campaign to secure signatures to a memorandum praying for the reprieve of those sentenced to death." The Committee, which conducted this campaign was, reported the Government avowedly, a camouflaged revival of the Naujawan Bharat Sabha.[226] In Lahore and Amritsar almost all members of the committees were the old Sabha activists.[227] The object of these committees was to stir the people to such a pitch of excitement that

224 Manifesto issued by the Sabha in 1929 and published in *Yuvakranti*, July 1972, New Delhi, p.10.

225 NAI, Home Pol. F.No.130 & KW/1931. The Bhagat Singh Appeal Committees were reported from (1) Kasur, Distt. Lahore, (2) Moga, Distt. Ferozepore, (3) Ferozepore, (4) Sialkot, (5) Ludhiana, (6) Lyallpur, (7) Phagwara, (8) Poilga, Distt. Jullunder, (9) Banga, Distt. Jullundur, (10) Batala, Distt. Gurdaspur (11) Okara, Distt. Montgomery, (12) Gujaranwala, (13) Amritsar, (14) Jaranwala, Distt. Loyallpur, (15) Sheikhupura.

226 NAI, Home Pol. File No.18/1/1931. Fortnightly Report on the internal political situation for February,1931.

227 For example, in Lahore, Sodhi Pindi Das was a leading worker while Gurdit Singh and Ahmad Din were its active members in Amirtsar.

on the day of the execution they would take part in offensive and possibly violent demonstrations. Bhagat Singh Day was observed throughout the province on February 17, 1931. Almost all colleges were affected; particularly in the DAV and Sanatan Dharma colleges all students absented themselves from their classes. A procession was taken out and in the evening a meeting of about 15,000 persons was held. It was addressed by S Sardul Singh, Dr Satyapal, Baba Sohan Singh and others.[228] Dr Satyapal, while speaking at the meeting said that the execution of Bhagat Singh would be a certain challenge to all the lovers of motherland, and all chances of peace would be jeopardised in future.[229]

The Bhagat Singh Appeal Committee collected signatures of as many people as possible on a printed appeal to be sent to the Viceroy for clemency. The enthusiasm of the extremists was so great that even the mildest supporters of the Congress were carried away.[230] It was clear that if the Congress did not demand the commutation of these sentences as one of the terms for opening negotiations with the Government, it would be most unpopular.[231] On February 16, 1931 the appeal of Sardar Bhagat Singh and his companions was rejected by the Privy Council. A week later, the famous leader of the HSRA, Chandrashekhar Azad, was killed during a police action in Allahabad. The Naujawan Bharat Sabha held a public meeting to commemorate the martyrdom of Azad on March 13, 1931, in Delhi.[232]

Gandhi-Irwin Pact

---

228 NAI, Home Pol. File No.18/1/1931.

229 Ibid.

230 Ibid.

231 Ibid. Ahmad Din, a leader of the Sabha, had warned the leaders at Amritsar that if they do not strive for the release of the revolutionaries then all the released political workers will be greeted with black flags and with cries of "Gandhi go back" and "Go back Jawaharlal".

232 NAI, Home Pol. File No.KW 159/1931.

A little before the death of Azad, parleys between Mahatma Gandhi and Lord Irwin succeeded leading to the suspension of the Civil Disobedience movement and an assurance by the Government to release all political prisoners. But it was made clear that only the political prisoners connected with the non-violent movement would be set free. The Sabha proclaimed that the young men were not satisfied with the peace terms and as a mark of protest spread a black cloth over its camp in the Jalianwala Bagh.[233] The Naujawan Bharat Sabha workers dubbed the peace terms as abject surrender of the Congress to the British government and even raised slogans like 'Down, Down with Mahatma Gandhi'.[234] Thus, the Gandhi–Irwin Pact indirectly helped the Government to isolate the revolutionaries and to hang Bhagat Singh and his companions.[235] Inspite of an uproar throughout the country, the Government persisted with its scheme and the three revolutionary freedom fighters were hanged on March 23, 1931. The Naujawan Bharat Sabha openly held Mahatma Gandhi responsible for the death of Bhagat Singh and his comrades. It said:

> If Mahatma Gandhi had made it a condition of peace, the execution might not have taken place.[236]

P Sitaramayya, the Congress leader and Gandhi's disciple wrote:

> But I think the revolutionaries were not aware of the fact that Mahatma Gandhi had himself appealed to the Viceroy that if the boys should be hanged, they had better be hanged before the Congress (Karachi) Session, than after it."[237]

The hanging of these patriots cast a gloom over the Karachi Session of the Congress which was held only three days later.

---

233 *The Tribune*, March 11 1931.

234 Ibid.

235 Chaman Lal Azad, *Revolutionary Movement in India*, Delhi, pp.40-41.

236 *The Tribune*, April 9 1931.

237 Pattabhi Sitaramayya, *History of the Indian National Congress*, Vol.1, Bombay, 1946, p.442.

According to Sitaramayya:

> It is no exaggeration to say that at the moment Bhagat Singh's name was as widely known all over India and was as popular as Gandhi's.[238]

On March 25, when the Mahatma arrived to attend the Karachi Session, he was welcomed with black flags and had to face a hostile reception at the hands of the infuriated young men and the members of the Naujawan Bharat Sabha. Slogans like "Down with Gandhi" were raised.[239] The Naujawan Bharat Sabha held its Conference at the same time in Karachi and Subhas Chandra Bose was invited to preside. While speaking at the Conference, Bose declared that the Delhi Truce revealed the defeatist mentality of the Congress.[240] In his Presidential address, Bose also said:

> I want a Socialist republic in India. The message I have to give is of complete freedom and until these radical or revolutionary elements are stirred up, we cannot get freedon, and we cannot stir up revolutionary elements among us, except by inspiring them with a new image which comes from the heart and goes straight to the heart.[241]

He further said:

> I want a socialist Republic of India. I want political freedom and complete economic emancipation. Every human being must have the right to work and right of living wage. There shall be no drones in our society and no unearned incomes. There must be equal opportunities for all. Above all, there should be a fair, just and equitable distribution of wealth. For this purpose it may be necessary for the state to take over the control of the means of production and distribution of wealth. And thirdly I want social equality for all. There should be no caste, no depressed classes. Every man will have the same rights and the same status in society. Further, there shall be no inequality

---

238 Ibid.

239 NAI, Home Pol. File No.136/1931.

240 Ibid.

241 *Selected Speeches of Subhas Chandra Bose*, Publications Division, Government of India, New Delhi, 1974, pp.58-59.

between the sexes, either in social status or in the law, and women shall be, in every way equal partner of men.[242]

Swami Govindanand, Chairman of the Reception Committee welcoming the delegates called upon the audience to realise the ideal of "the establishment of a Socialist Government for the masses."[243] He wanted India to give an Indian garb to Russian Socialism and said:

> Complete socialistic independence could alone be the goal of the youth for which they must always be prepared to lay down their lives.[244]

During its five year long eventful existence, the Sabha's slogans 'Long Live Revolution' (*Inquilab Zindabad*) and 'Down with Imperialism' reverberated from the North-West Frontier to Gujarat.

---

242 Samar Guha, 'Socialist Image of Netaji Subhas Chandra Bose', *National Herald*, New Delhi, August 15 1971.

243 *The Amrita Bazaar Patrika*, March 28 1931.

244 Ibid.

Chapter Three

Trials, Congress and Revolutionaries

The second Lahore Conspiracy Case of 1929-30 occupied a place of pride in the liberation movement, which is characterised by a number of conspiracies and trials.[245] It assumed an unusual importance because the principal accused or revolutionary enthusiasts chose death in order to propagate their ideology and programme. They also displayed great courage, heroisn, determination and a breadth of vision unparalleled in the history of revolution.

It all began with the arrest of Bhagat Singh and Batukeshwar Dutt on April 8, 1929, after the Bomb explosion in the Assembly. A case was instituted against them for depriving His Majesty of the sovereignty of India. It began on May 7th, 1929 and continued for about a month in the Delhi Jail. Both the comrades in arms or accused utilised this opportunity for the propagation of the ideology

---

245 Before the celebrated second Lahore Conspiracy Case there were numerous such cases and trials resulting in death penalties and imprisonments of patriots: First Lahore Conspiracy Case, Alipore Conspiracy Case, Kakori Case, Delhi Conspiracy Case, etc.

of the HSRA. Bhagat Singh, in fact, after throwing the bomb got himself arrested for this purpose alone. They utilised every little occasion to issue a statement. Their statement of June 6, 1929, assumed historical importance for it unravelled their unequivocal commitment to socialism. It also made clear that the revolutionaries were not "perpetrators of dastardly outrages and therefore a disgrace to our country"; instead they made a "practical protest against the institution, which since its birth has eminently displayed, not only its worthlessness, but also its far-reaching power for mischief."[246] It was also stated by them that "revolution does not necessarily mean sanguinary strifes nor is there any place in it for individual vendetta. It is not the cult of the bomb and pistol."[247] To them revolution meant that "the present order of things, which was based on manifest injustice must change."[248] Their statement ended with the capsuled expression *Inquilab Zindabad* which was to echo and re-echo as the war cry of the youth. On June 13, 1929, Bhagat Singh and BK Dutt received the court judgement in the Assembly Bomb Case, with the twin cries of "Long Live Revolution" and "Long Live the Proletariat".[249] Both of them were sentenced to transportation for life and immediately Bhagat Singh was transferred to Lahore Jail and Dutt was sent to the jail at Mianwali.

Bhagat Singh beautifully utilised the trial of Assembly Bomb Case for the propagation of the objectives of the party. It was he and BK Dutt, who for the first time, raised the slogans of 'Long Live Revolution' and 'Long Live the Labour' in the open court of Delhi.[250] They were courageous enough to admit that they were members of a revolutionary party. Moreover, in their statement they exhorted people to organise labour and peasant parties for the attainment of a veritable prosperity bringing *swarajya*. The joint statement of

---

246 Bhagat Singh and Dutt's Statement of June 6 1929.

247 Ibid.

248 Ibid.

249 *The Tribune*, June 14 1929.

250 JN Sanyal, op.cit., p.74.

Bhagat Singh and Dutt was secretly sent out and was published in several Indian and foreign newspapers like *La Humanite* of France and *Pravda* of Russia.[251] It had a lightening influence on the people of the country, particularly the youth. Several important leaders had to amend their previous statements of outright condemnation of the bomb throwing in the Assembly. Nehru and other notable leaders had to appreciate the objectives of the revolutionaries.[252] The Naujawan Bharat Sabha played a useful role in propagating the views of Bhagat Singh expressed in the statement.

Thus, Bhagat Singh and Dutt proved the futility of the notion that they were rash, mindless and trigger happy youth. They even convinced the judiciary that they cherished certain ideas and programme for the liberation of their country. Medilton, the presiding officer of the session's court in Delhi, had admitted that the undertrials had a well defined political creed. He was apprehensive of the 'malinfluence' the ideas of these revolutionaries were bound to exercise on the minds of the youth. He stated in his judgement:

> These persons (Dutt and Bhagat Singh) used to enter the court with the cries of 'Long Live Revolution', 'Long Live Proletariat' etc. which shows clearly what sort of political idea they cherish. In order to put a check in propagating these ideas I transport them for life.[253]

As a matter of fact, the Assembly Bomb Case proved a useful medium for the real objectives of HSRA. It enhanced the prestige of the party and its two representatives and fired the imagination of the youth of the country. While the nation was lamenting over the severity of punishment given to Bhagat Singh and Dutt, the discovery of a large bomb factory at Lahore and later on at Saharanpur led to the arrest of several important members of the HSRA. Some of them like Jai Gopal, Phanindra Ghosh and Hansraj proved traitors and became approvers. Their information led to the arrest of several party members and thus they caused maximum damage to the

251 Ibid.

252 Ibid.

253 NAI, Home Pol. File No.244 and KW 1930.

revolutionary party. After their arrest, the imperialist government lost no time in instituting the Lahore Conspiracy Case against them. Dutt and Bhagat Singh who had already been sentenced to transportation for life, were brought to Lahore as accused in the Lahore Case. Dutt's name was later dropped as he could not be implicated in the Saunders murder.

The Hunger Strike Against Imperialist Discrimination

As referred to earlier, the prisoners in Indian prisons were given a treatment which no civilized government would meet out to its worst criminals, much less to its political prisoners. Efforts were made by the Kakori prisoners earlier but they could achieve only temporary concessions from the colonial government. Before the formal beginning of the proceedings of the Lahore Case, Bhagat Singh and Dutt picked up the fight from where it had been left by their predecessors of the Kakori Case. The Bhagat Singh–Dutt hunger strike emphasised that there was a specific class of political prisoners struggling against the foreign rule whose existence and rights should be recognised.[254] The revolutionaries had two objectives in resorting to hunger-strike: first, to secure better facilities as political prisoners and second, to propagate their revolutionary ideals by getting publicity for their hunger-strike.[255]

Bhagat Singh and BK Dutt began their hunger-strike in mid-June 1929. These two young men declared their resolve that they will lay down their lives for their cause but will not accept the humiliation of being treated as felons.[256] To express sympathy with their cause and their *tapasya*, June 30 was observed as the Hunger-strike day.[257] The other comrades of Lahore Conspiracy Case also observed a one day token hunger strike on June 30, 1929 to express sympathy with Bhagat Singh and Dutt. Large public meetings were held throughout

254 JN Sanyal, op.cit., p.78.

255 Shiv Verma, op.cit., p.42.

256 *The People*, June 27 1929.

257 Ibid.

the country at various places.[258] The proceedings of the Lahore Conspiracy Case formally commenced on July 11, 1929.[259] The other prisoners of the Lahore Conspiracy case joined in the hunger strike on July 13, 1929. Bhagat Singh wrote a letter to the Home member of the Government of India on July 14, requesting him to accept the demands of the revolutionaries.[260] But the Government remained adamant and refused to extend the same facilities to Indian prisoners as were extended to European prisoners.[261] Several noted leaders like Jawaharlal Nehru, Madan Mohan Malaviya and others appealed to the Government to accept the just demand of the revolutionaries and relieve them of the suffering they were undergoing. Nehru said that the Government ought to have behaved with them just as a brave enemy behaves with his brave counterpart in times of war.[262] MM Malaviya warned the Government that the treatment of the Lahore prisoners was attracting the attention of the whole country, and that the whole country wanted the matter to be settled early in a fair and humane way.[263]

The condition of the hunger strikers went on deteriorating day by day. The Government decided to force-feed them and thus prolong the agony. The strikers decided against taking any medicine and resisted forced feeding. The Government adopted several measures to tempt the revolutionaries and thus to make them break their fast. For instance, well cooked food was kept in the cells so that the aroma might weaken the resolve of some. But the revolutionaries threw the food out of the grating in the presence of jail officials.[264] Among all the hunger strikers, the condition of

---

258 *The People*, June 27 1929.

259 NAI, Home Pol. File No.172/1930.

260 JN Sanyal, op.cit., pp.81-82.

261 NAI, Home Pol. File No.21/57/29.

262 *The Tribune*, July 7 1929.

263 NAI, Home Pol. File No.21/57/29.

264 Jai Dev Kapoor, 'Amar Shaheed Jatindranath Das', in the *Souvenir,* on the occasion of Jatin Das's 50th *Balidan Diwas,* Sept. 13, 1979, issued by All

Jatin Das deteriorated most. Nehru came to see the hunger strikers and issued a statement saying, "The condition of Jatin Das is very bad. He has become so weak that he cannot turn in his bed. He can speak only slowly. Indeed he is inching towards his death."[265] When this went on about two months, the Government gave an assurance for the redressal of their grievances. On September 2, 1929, all undertrials except Jatin Das broke their fasts. His condition soon became critical and he developed pneumonia. He even refused to come out on bail and uttered only one sentence, "I will stick to the last". On September 12, 1929, Jinnah said in the Assembly:

> The hunger strike is the declaration of war. You know that these people are determined to sacrifice their lives. Everyone cannot begin a fast unto death. Such an individual can neither be an ordinary human being nor an accused of a cruel murder. The people oppose this abhorent governing system and remind that there are thousands of youth outside.[266]

The very next day, on September 13, 1929, Jatin Das achieved martyrdom, on the 63rd day of his hunger strike. The whole country was stunned and the anger of the youth reached a high pitch.[267] Condolence messages were received from various parts of the world. Among those, one came from the family of Terence McSwiney, who sacrificed his life in similar conditions in Ireland. The message said: "Family of Terence McSwiney have heard with grief and pride of the death of Jatin Das. Freedom will come."[268] To die on the battlefield or on the scaffold is child's play compared to the grim suffering that Jatindra underwent; so said a news report.[269] When McSwiney died under similar circumstances Lloyd George is said to have exlaimed

---

India Freedom Fighters Organisation, Delhi Pradesh. Also MN Gupta, *Bhagat Singh and His Times*, Delhi, 1977, p.174.

265 Ibid, p.175.

266 JN Sanyal, op.cit., p.91.

267 SK Mittal op.cit., p.43.

268 SC Bose, *The Indian Struggle 1920–34*, Calcutta, 1948, p.227.

269 *The People*, September 19 1929.

that he was a great patriot and a martyr. Here some friends of the Government called Jatindra's death a suicide. But, continued the news report, "his is an example that will shine brilliantly in the annals of the great and glorious deeds of the country and will cast a unique lustre on the great acts of heroism that follow."[270]

Bhagat Singh and his comrades now thought that the recommendations put forward by the Jail Enquiry Committee would be enough reward for the first phase of their struggle, and they unanimously gave up their hunger strike. The soul force was used to such an extent that the revolutionaries staked their precious lives and one of them achieved martyrdom in the course of unusual display of soul-force.[271] Soon after, Bhagat Singh formed a Committee of three persons, comprising Sukhdev, Vijay Kumar Sinha and himself. The aim was to chalk out a plan to fulfil the objectives of the party during the trial. First, they wanted that the restrictions imposed by the Government on people's entry in the court during the trial should be lifted. They fought for this and succeeded. Now a large number of people, particularly young men and women, started visiting the courts. The proceedings used to begin with the cries of "Long Live Revolution", "Down with Imperialism" and "Long Live the Working Classes". These slogans certainly impressed a large number of people collected to witness the proceedings.[272]

Secondly, the accused themselves cross questioned the approvers during the proceedings and in this way forced them to speak everything before the collected people about the objectives of the party and also about the reality behind any revolutionary activity. In this way, Bhagat Singh and his comrades wanted to dispel the misunderstandings being spread about their activities among the

---

270 *The People*, September 26 1929.

271 Interview with Rajendra Pal Singh 'Warrior', who was a member of the HSRA and had an opportunity to work with Bhagat Singh and Chandrashekhar Azad.

272 JN Sanyal, op.cit., p.94.

people and also to infuse a new inspiration and awakening among the youth through the trial proceedings in the conspiracy case.

Thirdly, they utilised the opportunity for demonstration in the court. They celebrated Kakori Day, Lenin Day, May Day and Lajpat Day in the open court.[273] By all these activities, the undertrial revolutionaries wanted to excite the political feelings of the people. They, no doubt, succeeded in propagating the socialistic principles of their revolutionary party and identified themselves with the toiling masses of the country. It was made clear that they wanted a *swarajya* in which socio-economic inequality and communalism will have no place.

The trial of the accused and the manner in which they behaved in the court room generated profound enthusiasm and sympathy among the masses, particularly among the younger sections. Innumerable public meetings and demonstrations were held in various parts of the country, particularly in the Punjab. The All India Bhagat Singh–Dutt Day was celebrated on July 21, 1929.[274] Motilal Nehru also appeared to help Lahore Conspiracy Case accused with funds and said that donors will be serving the cause of justice and humanity.[275]

The Congress observed 'Hunger Strike Week' in the Punjab in February 1930 and also collected funds for the defence of the Lahore prisoners. The revolutionaries became so popular among the youth that a thirteen year old boy of class IX was arrested in Amritsar for possesion of letters bearing the slogans "Long Live Revolution" and "Long Live Bhagat Singh".[276]

The Imperialist government was worried by the awakening caused by the undertrials during the case. It wanted to end the court proceedings and to pronounce its pre-meditated judgement. This judgment came on October 7, 1930. Bhagat Singh, Rajguru

---

273 Ibid, p.95.

274 *The Tribune*, July 19 1929.

275 *The Tribune*, December 22 1929.

276 *The Tribune* March 8 1930.

and Sukhdev were sentenced to death. Others were awarded varying terms of imprisonment, ranging from three years to life imprisonment. The day of judgment was kept secret by the Government but the secrecy could not be maintained. Wherever the news reached, it led to spontaneous *hartal* and a wave of indignation gripped the country. The news spread like jungle fire in Lahore. Despite imposition of Section 144 in the city, a mammoth public meeting was held outside the municipal grounds in Lahore.[277] The leaders condemned the one sided hearing of the case and severe punishments. The next day Naujawan Bharat Sabha convened a meeting of students and youths at Bradlaugh Hall and here the revolutionary leaders were extolled and inspiring speeches were delivered. The public agitation gained momentum day by day, many people were arrested and others were *lathi*-charged.

On the other hand, to continue the legal battle, an appeal was made to the Privy Council, which was undoubtedly an exercise in futility. The condemned revolutionaries had no courtroom now to propagate their ideas. They thought it wise to appeal to the Privy Council to highlight the high-handedness of the tribunal and to let the world know about the cherished principles of the revolutionary party in India. This appeal was made by the Defence Committee, which was functioning since the case began in 1929. Among the prominent national leaders, Dr Saifuddin Kitchlew, S Sardul Singh Caveeshar, Purushottam Das Tandon, Dr Gopi Chand and Lala Duni Chand were its members. The aim of this Committee was to collect funds to support the families of the accused and for the defence of the revolutionaries in the Lahore Case.[278]

As referred to earlier, Bhagat Singh and his comrades, through this appeal, wanted to tell the civilized world about how inhumanly political prisoners were treated in India. Secondly, through this appeal they wanted to inform the enemies of England about the existence of a revolutionary socialist party in India. Thirdly, they

277 JN Sanyal, op.cit., pp.102-103.
278 Ibid, p.105.

wanted to delay the executions till the moment the execution may have the maximum impact on the people. Bhagat Singh and his comrades had an idea that the Congress would soon enter into an 'ignominous' pact with the Government and then the executions will expose the hollowness of the Congress on the one hand and the party of the youth will be strengthened on the other.[279] When the executions came they were in consonance with the strategy of Bhagat Singh and proved his farsightedness. A public memorandum was presented to the Viceroy for the commutation of death sentences. It contained about 20,000 signatures including some of the members of the Legislative Assembly, Municipal commissioners, etc.[280]

The citizens of Bombay organised a meeting in March 1931, which was marked by the slogans of 'Bhagat Singh and Comrades *Zindabad*'. A well-known Congress leader KF Nariman presided over the meeting and said in his address that if the execution of Bhagat Singh is carried out, it will arouse the bitterest of feelings and influence the proceedings of the forthcoming Karachi Congress.[281] He further warned the Government:

> If Bhagat Singh is hanged India will never forget the wrong.

Mr Abid Ali, Secretary of the BPCC also declared:

> it would be impossible for the Congress to sit silent if the Government disregarded the voice of the whole country....Congress had suspended its fight, the people had not given up the war mentality and they would resume it if their voice was not heard.[282]

The Muslims of Lahore also decided to ask Maulana Abul Kalam Azad to prevail upon Mahatma Gandhi to get the sentence commuted by the Viceroy.[283] A wave of resentment was witnessed even in London where a meeting was organised to protest against

---

279 Ibid, pp.105-106.

280 NAI, Home Pol. File No.4/20/1931.

281 *The Bombay Chronicle*, March 24 1931.

282 Ibid.

283 *The Tribune*, March 3 1931.

the sentences, which was addressed by several British members of Parliament.[284]

Martyrdom of the Trinity

The Gandhi–Irwin Pact was signed on March 5, 1931. As a result of this pact all political prisoners, except those accused of violent crimes, were released. But Gandhi had now realised that the executions will have an adverse affect on the Karachi session, due to begin in the end of March 1931. He, therefore, suggested to the Viceroy to postpone the executions till the session was over. But Irwin opposed the idea saying that postponement is beyond his power. He further said that postponment may lead to false hopes and he did not wish to be called dishonest by the falsification of hopes.[285] In this way Irwin defeated Mahatma Gandhi by his own weapon of honesty. Bhagat Singh, Sukhdev and Rajguru, were executed on March 23, 1931, at 7:33 pm in the Lahore Central Jail.

As it happened, the execution of Bhagat Singh made Indian people seethe with resentment against the British as well as against the Gandhian ambivalence, and created popular sympathy for the cause of the revolutionaries. Bhagat Singh and his comrades had firm faith in the ultimate victory of their ideals – the doom of imperialism and capitalism – and throughout their life, they felt proud that they had relentlessly waged war against these systems.[286]

'Ihe Mahatma had a tough time at the hands of the Naujawan Bharat Sabha members who demonstrated against him at the Karachi session. MN Roy, who also attended the Session in the guise of Dr Mahmud,[287] and, in his own words, "a semi-official guest of the Congress bosses",[288] described the Delhi Pact as "a

---

284 *The Leader*, Allahabad, March 4 1931.

285 *Mukti*, July 1972, New Delhi, p.16.

286 Shiv Verma, op.cit., pp.46-47; also JN Sanyal, op.cit., p.118.

287 JP Haithcox, *Communism and Nationalism in India*, Bombay, p.187.

288 Letter from MN Roy to Louise Geissler, Karachi, March 30 1931, cited in Ibid, p.187.

betrayal of India by the bourgeoisie"[289] and as inconsistent with the Lahore Independence resolution. Jamnadas Mehta, a labour leader, said that if anyone other than Gandhi had been responsible for the agreement he would have been thrown into the sea.[290] But soon Gandhi prevailed over all opposition. He adopted tactics not unknown among democratic party leaders framing slogans for an electioneering campaign.[291] To the businessmen he held out visions of great wealth and at the request of Jawaharlal, he advertised a 'Utopia for the teeming millions'.[292] In this manner, the Mahatma deliberately tried to placate the people of different classes while at heart he was aware that most of his promises were in conflict with each other.

The young Congressmen of Delhi were also up in arms against Gandhi for his condemnation of the revolutionaries, and said that the Mahatma was doing all this 'to please the Government and the British people.'[293] They further accused the Mahatma of attempting to crush the enthusiasm of the youth of the country because he was incapable of understanding the "urge of the revolutionary which moves him to face untold sufferings and dangers."

There was, justifiably, a lot of hue and cry at the executions. The youth of the country called Mahatma the murderer of the revolutionaries and many other such accusations were levelled against him for his failure to save their lives. But what the three comrades felt about their life and death was clear from the letter of Bhagat Singh, which he wrote during those last days:

> It is but natural that I should desire to live. I do not want to conceal this, but it is conditional in the sense that I do not live with my freedom curbed...My weaknesses are not known to the public. If I am saved from the gallows, they would become known to everybody.

---

289 *The Times* (London) March 30 1931, p.12.

290 *The Tribune*, March 30 1931.

291 NAI, Home Pol. File No.136/1931.

292 Ibid.

293 *The Tribune*, August 8 1931.

Thus, the symbol of revolution would fade and even dissolve, but if I die wreathed with smiles, Indian mothers would wish their children to emulate Bhagat Singh, and thus the number of formidable freedom fighters would increase so much that it would be impossible for the satanic forces of imperialism to stop and stem the march of revolution....[294]

The Congress and the Revolutionaries

The Indian National Congress, the biggest political organisation of the country, was transformed under Mahatma Gandhi's leadership into a fighting machine wedded to *swaraj*. It remained in the vanguard of the freedom struggle working overtly to achieve freedom from the British. The revolutionaries, although working covertly, fought with courage and determination to wrest freedom from the British hands. The twin movements of the revolutionaries and the Congress, with all their differences of ideology, philosophy, means and methods, were aimed at a common goal, i.e., the achievement of freedom.

These two diverse currents in the national struggle for freedom ironically strengthened each other, and undoubtedly, both played a significant role in the mass awakening and national upsurge in India. "If Gandhi–Nehru (Congress) and the Socialist and Communist parties gave a decisive shape to the Indian freedom struggle, Lala Hardayal's *Ghadr* Party and later Bhagat Singh's Hindustan Socialist Republican Army and the countless sacrifices of brave revolutionaries had an equally decisive role to play."[295]

Before the emergence of Gandhi at the epicentre of Indian politics, and as the *el supremo* of the Congress, the revolutionaries discovered their fount of inspiration in the extremist 'trio' of the Congress – BG Tilak, BC Pal and Lajpat Rai.[296] A large number of revolutionaries were also active in the Congress.[297] Their influence

---

294 MN Gupta, *Bhagat Singh and His Times,* p.194.

295 Shivdan Singh Chauhan (ed.), *Prithvi Singh Azad in Lenin's Land,* Delhi, 1980, p.15.

296 Ram Gopal, *How India Struggled for Freedom,* Bombay, 1967, pp.181–197.

297 David M Laushey, op.cit., pp.25-26.

in the national organisation was so great that CR Das had to act as a mediator to bring about a meeting between Gandhi and the revolutionaries. This meeting took place in September 1920. The revolutionaries were persuaded to halt their activities and support the Gandhi led movement of non-co-operation.[298] CR Das had realised that unless the youth force is harnessed to the Congress movement, it had no prospects in Bengal. Thus, he urged the revolutionaries to "sheath your swords and join us in our path".[299]

Dr Jadugopal Mukherjie has also described in detail the private conversation he had with Gandhi. At the end of the conversation Gandhi appealed to the revolutionies to at least not obstruct him in Bengal even if they could not persuade themselves to accept his path. Mukherjee assured Gandhi that instead of obstructing him they would continue to help him so long as he himself did not call a halt to the struggle.[300] Gandhi had also realised after his tour of Bengal that it would not be possible for him to build any organisation and movement there by ignoring the revolutionaries. That is why he acquiesced in the revolutionaries joining the Congress.[301] Almost all the revolutionary groups joined the Congress while maintaining and endeavouring to strengthen their secret organisation. An official report describes the situation thus:

> Many of their leaders obtained responsible positions in district Congress committees and used their positions to consolidate their followers. This penetration of the Congress had very important consequences, for it helped the terrorist party internally in the matter of recruitment and organisation, and externally in the matter of public sympathy.[302]

This part of the report concluded by expressing the apprehension:

---

298 SC Bose, op.cit., p.60.

299 Bhupendra Kishore Rakshit Roy, *Bharater Sahastra Biplab*, Calcutta, p.230.

300 *Biplabi Jiboner Smriti*, Calcutta, p.461.

301 SN Mazumdar, op.cit., p.118.

302 *Terrorism in India*, p.15.

> ...the time was to come when there would be few districts in the
> province where terrorists were not represented on local Congress
> Committees.[303]

During 1920–22 no major terrorist activities were planned. Early in 1922 the failure of the Non-cooperaton Movement led to the controversy over means – non-violent or violent – to be employed for wresting independence from British hands. Barring Gandhi and his ilk, the Congress leaders were not so besotted with the concept of non-violence. Mahatma Gandhi was, of course, most uncompromising in his stance against violent methods. As he was the virtual 'dictator' of the party, his opinion counted most within the Congress. Yet there were other leaders of national stature in the Congrees who certainly had a soft corner for the young revolutionaries. Prominent among them were Jawaharlal Nehru and Subhas Chandra Bose. Any reference to the activities of the revolutionaries on the Congrees forums revealed the schism, and an open demonstration of sympathy for the revolutionaries was visible in Congress conferences. A survey of the period clearly shows that except for the national leadership, the Congress cadre was always sympathetically inclined towards the revolutionaries and their daring exploits. Many of the Congress leaders even made common cause with the Naujawan Bharat Sabha.

Mahatma Gandhi and the revolutionaries both shared the resentment against the British rule. *Satyagraha* and non-violence were Gandhi's tools of struggle, while the revolutionaries discarded his "philosophy of non violence as a philosophy arising out of despair".[304] While launching his first mass movement in 1920-21, Gandhi appealed to the revolutionaries to halt their activities for one year and to co-operate with him.[305] The revolutionaries, who had been waging a relentless struggle against British imperialism, halted their movement to give a fair chance to the Gandhian

303 Ibid.

304 SN Sanyal to Gandhi published in *Young India*, February 12 1925.

305 *Collected Works of Mahatma Gandhi (CWMG)*, Vol.XXI, p.557.

experiment. But seeing the embarassing end of the movement, they were "thoroughly disgusted with Gandhi who had made a fetish of non-violence."[306] Sachindranath Sanyal informed Gandhi that "now the experiment is over and therefore the revolutionaries are free from their promise, or, as a matter of fact, they promised to remain silent only for a year and no more".[307]

Despite the co-operation extended by the revolutionaries, the Mahatma remained hostile to their programme. He even said that a "revolutionary's sacrifice, nobility and love are not only waste of effort, but being ignorant and misguided, do and have done more harm to the country than any other activity. For, the revolutionaries have retarded the progress of the country".[308] Gandhi was infuriated when CR Das praised the courage and sacrificing spirit of Gopinath Saha. A resolution was moved in the AICC at Gandhi's instance in June 1924, and Saha's action was characterised as misguided love of country, and it disapproved emphatically of all political murders as inconsistent with the Congress creed. This resolution could be passed by 78 in favour and 70 against.[309] Though Gandhi won, he considered the passing of the resolution by a thin margin as his defeat. He declared himself as 'Defeated and Humbled'.[310] The voting pattern exhibited the extent of sympathy the revolutionaries enjoyed within the Congress despite an open and virulent opposition by Gandhi.

During 1924 and 1925 the revolutionaries and Mahatma Gandhi entered into a series of polemical arguments. In his presidential address at the Belgaum session of the Congress, Gandhi characterised revolutionary actions as the 'insane pressure of anger

---

306 MN Gupta, 'Gandhi and the Revolutionaries', in M B Rao (ed.), *The Mahatma: A Marxist Symposium*, p.92.

307 *Young India*, February 12 1925.

308 *Young India*, April 9 1925, Mahatma Gandhi's reply to the letter of a revolutionary.

309 MR Jayakar, *The Story of my Life, 1922–25*, Bombay, 1959, Vol.II, p.320.

310 *CWMG*, XXIV, p.334.

and ill will', far less effective than the pressure of non-violent acts born of goodwill and gentleness.[311] On behalf of the revolutionaries, Sachindranath Sanyal addressed to him an 'open letter' in defence of the revolutionary creed. He held Gandhi guilty for persuading "the whole nation to accept the spirit of *Ahimsa* irrespective of *desh* (place, environment), *kal* (time) and *patra* (suitability/suitable object)…which was a matter of individual *sadhana* (spiritual practice) with the Indians". Sanyal hit hard at Gandhi's vagueness about India's ultimate political goal, i.e., the self-government. He quipped, "A sovereign, independent Indian republic in alliance or in federation with the other independent nations of the earth is one thing, and self-governing India within this imperialistic British empire is perfectly another thing." He asserted: "The non-violence that India preaches is not non-violence for the sake of non-violence but non-violence for the good of humanity and when this good for humanity will demand violence and bloodshed, India will not hesitate to shed blood just in the same way as a surgical operation necessitates the shedding of blood."[312]

The polemics continued, even after the arrest of Sanyal. The revolutionaries disagreed with Gandhi's interpretation of India's history as being one of peace, non-violence and love. They would not accept Gandhi's dictum : "India's path is not Europe's." They pointed to the fact of huge standing armies in ancient India and recalled the Gita's refrain of *Vinashaya cha dushkritam* (Destruction of the wicked). They accused the Mahatma of spreading 'philosophical cowardice' by preaching non-violence throughout the length and breadth of the country, and asked if he did not believe, like Mazzini, that 'ideas ripen quickly when nourished by the blood of martyrs?' To Gandhi's charge that their (revolutionaries') movement is not a mass movement, the revolutionaries replied that "the masses are not for the revolution but the revolution is for the masses". Gandhi's responses were inconsistent and often contradictory

311 Ibid, p.473; *Young India*, December 26 1924.

312 *Young India*, February 22 1925.

but he continued to cling to the opinion that the 'modern Indian revolutionary' does not know his work and that "revolutionary activity is suicidal at this stage of the country's life at any rate, if not for all time in a country so vast, so hopelessly divided and with the masses so deeply sunk in pauperism and so fearfully terror-struck".[313] The last remark of Gandhi implied that in a changed milieu he might not oppose the revolutionary method.

Gandhi ignored the socio-economic, political and psychological conditions that gave rise to revolutionary conditions. There is a need to therefore break out of the confines of merely the criticism of the 'mistaken methods' of the early revolutionaries to assess this social phenomenon as an integral part of the national libration movements of the twentieth century.

The Mahatma had accepted the policy of non-violence as a religion – to be followed everywhere, in politics or out of it. But the others in the Congress had no such sentimental attachment to the creed of Gandhi.[314] Jawaharlal Nehru, like many others, had "accepted non-violence only as a policy, not as a creed".[315] He could not stomach the Chauri Chaura retreat and expressed doubts about the efficacy of the non-violent creed.[316]

Similarly, Subhas Chandra Bose too, was not obsessed by ahimsa and for him an act of violence was not an obstacle in the struggle for freedom. He was called by the British "a would be

---

313 Ibid, April 9 1925.

314 For Gandhi ji it was a creed, for the majority of Congressmen it was a policy. For him means and ends were inter convertible terms. One could always have control over the means and never on the end. To many Congressmen the end justified the means." (Tendulkar, *Mahatma*, Vol.III, Ahmedabad, 1952, p.366). When Gandhiji tried to introduce the words, "truthful and non-violent means" in place of the words, "legitimate and peaceful means" in the Article 1 of the Congress constitution, he failed to carry the amendment. (Proceedings of the Working Committee, 20th to 29th October, 1934, Bombay, KK Mitra, op.cit., October 1934, p.207).

315 Dhananjay Keer, *Mahatma Gandhi, Political Saints and Unarmed Prophet*, Bombay, 1973, p.624.

316 Manmathnath Gupta, *They Lived Dangerously*, p.56.

Mussolini in Bengal" who "holds the Bengal extremists on his side".[317] That Subhas was in league with the revolutionaries is proved by the Bengal Intelligence Report which says that when Bose assumed power in the Calcutta corporation, many terrorists were given jobs in the city administration.[318]

Besides Nehru and Bose, there were other prominent Congressmen who unhesitatingly sympathised with the revolutionaries and provided them with monetary support whenever required. Chandrashekhar Azad received financial assistance from Motilal Nehru. Similarly, Purshottamdas Tandon of Allahabad and Shiv Prasad Gupta of Varanasi secretly supplied money for the revolutionary activities.[319] Ganesh Shankar Vidyarthi, a prominent Kanpur Congressman and the President of the UPCC, was virtually a godfather to the revolutionaries. For some time Bhagat Singh also worked in his paper *Pratap* and wrote under the pseudonym 'Balwant'. Leaders like Maulana Shaukat Ali and Krishna Kant Malaviya supplied revolvers to Sachindranath Sanyal.[320] The Mahatma's message of non-violence was overlooked by the Congressmen who gladly helped the revolutionaries morally, financially and in any other way in which their support was required. The Mahatma, despite having his way in the Congress by condemning the revolutionaries, could not deter the people within the Congress who had a soft corner for the revolutionaries, from giving material help to them.

The various revolutionary acts and the reactions of the Congress leaders and workers towards these acts would be helpful in understanding the attitude of the Congress towards them in more concrete terms.

---

317 J Coatman, *Years of Destiny*, London, 1932, p.96.

318 Ray, 'Brief Note on the Alliance of Congress with Terrorism in Bengal', NAI, Home Pol. F. No.4/21, 1932.

319 JN Sanyal, op.cit., p.45.

320 Ibid. p.26.

The murder of Saunders in December 1928 in Lahore brought to light the existence of an active group of young revolutionaries who were prepared to sacrifice their lives for regaining the dignity of the country. Mahatma Gandhi called the murder a "dastardly act which will decidedly retard the progress of this quiet building".[321] Jawaharlal Nehru did not appreciate this denunciation and said that it was unjustified to condemn these persons or acts "without seeking to understand the springs of action, the causes that underlie them".[322] Trying to assess the reasons for Bhagat Singh's popularity, he wrote:

> Bhagat Singh did not become popular because of his act of terrorism, but because he seemed to vindicate, for the moment, the honour of Lala Lajpat Rai, and through him of the nation. He became a symbol, the act was forgotten, the symbol remained, and within a few months each town and village of the Punjab, and to a lesser extent in the rest of northern India, resounded with his name. Innumerable songs grew about him and the popularity that the man achieved was something amazing.[323]

Immediately after the Saunders murder, Jawaharlal sent a message to Naujawan Bharat Sabha, assuring that many in "India are full of sympathy for them and are prepared to help them as much as they can". He further affirmed that the Sabha will "grow in strength to take a leading part in forming a national India".[324]

The next revolutionary activity was the Assembly bomb explosion of April 1929 which rocked the foundations of the imperialist government. Gandhi's reaction was a bitter denunciation:"The bomb-throwers have discredited the cause of freedom in whose name they threw the bombs". "Congressmen", he wrote, "should not give, even in secret, any approval to the deed". He further observed: "The Government could prevent its use by conceding the national demand gracefully in time." Gandhi thus condemned the action of Bhagat Singh as madness, but used it for

---

321 *CWMG*, Vol.38, pp.274–276.

322 Jawaharlal Nehru, *An Autobiography*, New Delhi, 1956, pp.174-75.

323 Ibid, pp.175-76.

324 *Searchlight*, January 11 1929.

promoting the cause of the nation.[325] On the other hand, Jawaharlal informed the Viceroy that "it is absurd to talk of unqualified condemnation of the young men who did it." He ridiculed the rulers' attempt to connect the bombs with Moscow, saying that "for them everything they (rulers) do not like comes from Moscow."[326] Nehru was courageous enough to publish the statements of Bhagat Singh and Dutt in the *Congress Bulletin* for which he was duly reprimanded by the Mahatma. Apologising, Nehru wrote to Gandhi, "I am sorry you disapproved of my giving Bhagat Singh and Dutt's statement in the *Congress Bulletin*"; and expressing his helplessness, he wrote that he was "compelled to publish the statement because there was very general appreciation of it among Congress circles".[327] For Subhas, the Assembly Bomb explosion was "a visible expression of the revolutionary movement," which "excited not only public interest but public sympathy as well".[328]

The explosion led to the arrest of Bhagat Singh and BK Dutt and a vigorous hunt for the arrest of other comrades. All arrested revolutionaries stood trial in the Lahore Conspiracy Case. But, this was not an end of their struggle. They began a hunger-strike against maltreatment of political prisoners in jails. This struggle won the sympathies of the nation, irrespective of party affiliations. But, the Mahatma maintained a sphinx-like silence throughout the struggle. In one of his letters to Nehru, he even dubbed it as an "irrelevant performance".[329] The martyrdom of Jatin Das stirred the heart of the nation. But Gandhi did not come out with a word of appreciation for this heroic self-sacrifice. Later, he wrote that he had purposely

---

325 *CWMG*, Vol.40, pp.259-60. Gandhi knew that Congressmen secretly approved of the various revolutionary acts.

326 *The Tribune* April 17 1929.

327 *Selected Works of Jawaharlal Nehru, (SWJN)*, Vol.4, p.157.

328 SC Bose, *op.cit.*, p.160.

329 *CWMG*, Vol.41, p.153.

refrained from commenting because if he had done so, he would have been forced to write something unfavourable.[330]

Jawaharlal Nehru differed from Gandhi. Moved by their sacrificial ordeal, he said:

> No Indian can refrain from admiring their great courage and our hearts must go out to them now in their great and voluntary suffering. They are fasting not for any selfish ends but to improve the lot of all political prisoners. As days go by, we shall watch with deep anxiety this hard trial and shall earnestly hope that the two gallant brothers of ours may triumph in the ordeal.[331]

Jawaharlal Nehru went to meet the hunger strikers and saw their agony inside the jail. He personally met all of them and described their pathetic conditions movingly. He was convinced of their selfless sacrificing spirit and said: "I gathered from them that they would adhere to their resolve, whatever the consequences to their individual selves might be. Indeed, they did not care very much for their own selves."[332] In a speech at Lahore on August 9, 1929, Jawaharlal compared the careerist and selfish Congressmen with the selfless hunger-striking prisoners:

> We should realise the great value of the struggle that these brave young men are carrying on inside the jail. They are not struggling to get honours from the people or laurels from the crowd for their sacrifice. What a contrast this is, compared with the unfortunate wrangles among Congressmen and the fighting for securing positions in the Congress and the reception committee. I am ashamed to hear of these internecine differences amongst the Congressmen. But my heart is equally delighted by witnessing the sacrifices of the young men who are determined to die for the sake of the country.[333]

He even exhorted the people to follow in their footsteps and "free the country from foreign bondage by similar sacrifices".[334] Jatin

---

330 Ibid, p.528.

331 *The Tribune*, July 7 1929.

332 Ibid, August 10 1929.

333 Ibid, August 11 1929.

334 Ibid.

Das died on the 63rd day of his ordeal and Nehru later wrote in his *Autobiography* that his "death created a sensation all over the country. It brought the question of the treatment of political prisoners to the front".[335]

Going a step further than Jawaharlal's moral support and verbal sympathy, Subhas actively came out in support of the hunger-strikers and was even tried for sedition by the imperialist government. He believed that after Jatin's death "the whole country gave him an ovation which few men in recent history of India have received".[336] Bose sent Rupees 600 so that Jatin's body could be brought in a special compartment to Calcutta.[337] Subhas Bose frankly admitted that "his martyrdom acted as a profound inspiration to the youth of India and everywhere youth and student organisations began to grow".[338]

In the autumn of 1929, with the prospect of a nationwide mass movement in the offing, the Chittagong Congress Party was divided between those who would follow Gandhi's lead and those who had no confidence in non-violent methods. In a rather stormy meeting on September 21, 1929, the Gandhians were defeated and the executive committee of the Chittagong Congress came under the control of persons sympathetic to terrorist methods.[339]

The Punjab Congress observed a "Hunger Strike Week" in February 1930 with the zealous support of the Naujawan Bharat Sabha. The Congressmen in Punjab did not hesitate in using the Sabha platform for preaching their creed of Civil Disobedience during 1930. The Congress popularity suffered a decline as most of its young cadre was active in the Sabha which was in command

---

335 J Nehru, op.cit., p.194.

336 Bose, op.cit., pp.161-62.

337 MN Gupta, *History of the Indian Revolutionary Movement*, p.123.

338 SC Bose, op.cit., p.162. See also S K Mittal, op.cit., p.43.

339 Kali Charan Ghosh, *The Roll of Honour*, Calcutta, 1965, p.462.

in the Punjab and Sindh.[340] The hunger strike in jails and the civil disobedience movement outside received full support and sympathy of the Congress and the Sabha simultaneously.

The attempt in Delhi to blow up the Viceregal Special on December 23, 1929, caused a commotion throughout the British Empire. The Lahore Congress Session, a few days later, revealed clear division among the Congress rank and file on the issue of the bomb explosion. Mahatma Gandhi himself moved a resolution congratulating the Viceroy on his escape and condemning the attempt of the revolutionaries. It read:

> This Congress deplores the bomb outrage perpetrated on the Viceroy's train and reiterates its conviction that such action is not only contrary to the creed of the Congress but results in harm being done to the national cause. It congratulates the Viceroy and Lady Irwin and their party including the poor servants on their fortunate and narrow escape.[341]

Gandhi congratulated Lord Irwin for his narrow escape like a friend. But the revolutionaries believed that as "the author of the Meerut prosecutions and Lahore and Bhusawal persecutions" Irwin could "appear a friend of India only to the enemies of her freedom".[342]

The resolution of the Mahatma did not have a smooth-sailing within the Congress. Many Congressmen stood up to challenge it as an exercise in futility – an exercise that was both undesirable and unnecessary. These Congressmen included Swami Govindanand from Sindh, HD Rajah from Tamil Nadu, Dr Mohammad Alam and Baba Gurdit Singh. Swami Govindanand asserted that the non-violent creed of the Congress "is not binding upon the people who choose to stand outside the Congress, and it is the duty of the Congress to persuade the parties that stand outside the Congress not by condemnation but by sweet reasoning, sweet arguments to

---

340 SK Mittal and S Irfan Habib, 'Towards Independence and Socialist Republic – The Naujawan Bharat Sabha', *Social Scientist*, No.87, p.35.

341 *CWMG*, Vol.42, p.341.

342 *The Philosophy of the Bomb*.

come round to our view of things...." Dr Alam contended that the resolution was "unimportant, improper and harmful, and hence needed rejection". Pleading for the rejection of the resolution, he appealed to the delegates not to vote out of regard for any personality. As a new era was dawning, it was their duty to vote according to the dictates of their conscience.[343] Rajah declared that the resolution was contrary to the anti-imperialist outlook of the Congress. What mattered it to them whether the bomb hit the Viceroy or a donkey?[344] The enthusiasm in the Congress *pandal* was such that the supporters of the Mahatma's resolution like Dr Ansari were hooted down when they rose to speak and red flags were repeatedly waved amidst the cries of 'Up, Up, with Revolution' and 'Down, Down with Imperialism'.[345] When put to vote, the resolution could be carried by a trifling majority of 81, with 904 in favour and 823 against. This again proved that the Congress was as much with revolutionaries as it was with the Mahatma.

Jawaharlal, being mindful of his position as the President of the Congress, could not, this time, afford to annoy the Mahatma and maintained studied silence on this popular issue. His Presidential address left this episode untouched. The nation celebrated the 'Independence Day' on 26th January 1930 with great fanfare. Popular enthusiasm crossed all limits and surprised even Nehru.[346] The demonstators made an effort in Bombay to hoist the red flag alongside the tricolour during the 'independence day' celebrations. The left Congressmen rejoiced over the incident while the rightist elements were horrified. However, Jawaharlal adopted a balanced attitude and issued a statement to the press:

---

343 Report of the Lahore Congress Session, 1929.

344 Ibid. Later the word donkey was replaced by 'any other'.

345 Ibid.

346 Letter to Secretaries, League Against Imperialism, AICC File No.FDI/1929-30, pp.47–61. NMML.

> There is, and should be, no rivalry between our national tricolour flag and the workers' red flag. I honour and respect the red flag, because it represents the blood and suffering of the workers.[347]

Subhas was in complete agreement with the revolutionaries as far as the objective of the bomb explosion was concerned. The HSRA declared that it aimed at preventing a meeting between the Viceroy and the Congress leaders, "whose attitude was described as one of begging".[348] Subhas thus wrote about the Mahatma's resolution:

> ....the feeling in the Congress was that that clause was uncalled for in a political resolution but the Mahatma insisted on retaining it probably because he wanted to placate Lord Irwin and prepare the ground for a rapproachment in future.[349]

Not satisfied with the passage of the resolution at Lahore, Gandhi again entered into polemical arguments with the revolutionaries. He denounced the latter and their creed in an article 'The Cult of the Bomb'.[350] However in the next breath he expressed his indebtedness to the revolutionaries "for the Morley Minto Reform, Montague Reforms and the like".[351] But Bhagwati Charan hit back saying:

> these the British Government threw before the constitutionalised agitators to lure them away from the right path. This was a bribe paid to them for their support to the Government in its policy of crushing and uprooting the revolutionaries. These toys – as Gandhi calls them – were sent to India for the benefit of those, who, from time to time, raised the cry of 'Home Rule', 'Self Government', 'Responsible Government', 'Full Responsible Government', 'Dominion Status' and such other names for slavery....They (the revolutionaries) raised the standard of independence long ago.[352]

Bhagwati Charan was not wrong. It had been the policy of the imperialist government to keep busy the leaders of the country

---

347 *The Hindoo*, January 29 1930.

348 *The Tribune* March 2 1930.

349 SC Bose, op.cit., p.174.

350 *Young India* January 2 1930.

351 Ibid.

352 *The Philosophy of the Bomb.*

in various constitutional problems and thereby avoid any serious revolutionary outbreak. As Wavell argued in 1944,

> unless we have previously diverted their energies into some more profitable channel, i.e., into dealing with the administrative problems of India and into trying to solve the constitutional problem, it would be difficult to stem the tide of agitation and revolution.[353]

Gandhi further declared that his faith in the efficacy of non-violence had increased and he hoped to convert the enemy through the gospel of love.[354] The revolutionaries countered by asking Gandhi:

> Will he let the world know how many enemies of India he had been able to turn into friends? How many O'Dwyers, Dyers, Readings and Irwins has he been able to convert into friends of India? If none, how can India be expected to share his growing faith, that he will be able to persuade or compel England to agree to Indian independence through the practice of non-violence.[355]

The Mahatma ascribed the awakening of the 1920's to his 'preaching of non-violence'. The revolutionaries dismissed the assertion as absurd and stressed:

> It is wrong to assign to non-violence the widespread awakening of the masses which, in fact, is manifested wherever a programme of direct action is adopted. In Russia, for instance, there came about widespread awakening among the peasants and workers, when the

---

353 Wavell to Churchill, October 24, 1944, *Transer of Power 1942–7*, Vol.V, pp.131 and 132. It is interesting to note that the mass revolutionary upsurge was sought to be diverted by the rulers through the revival of constitutional activity. The unity of the revolutionary forces which was emerging due to the activities of the HSRA and the Congress-led Civil Disobedience movement was broken by the Delhi Pact and the Round Table Conferences. Again the phenomenon of mass unity and the tidal waves of revolution (INA demonstration, RIN upsurge, labour militancy, etc., in 1945-1946) were disrupted by the constitutional proposals of the Cabinet Mission plan. See also Sumit Sarkar, 'Popular movements, National Leadership and the coming of Freedom with Partition, 1945–47', in DN Panigrahi (ed.), *Economy, Society and Politics in Modern India*, New Delhi, 1985.

354 *Young India*, January 2 1930.

355 *The Philosophy of the Bomb.*

> Communists launched forth their great programme of Militant Mass Action, though nobody preached non-violence to them.[356]

Holding Gandhi and his creed responsible for the failure of the movement, the revolutionaries believed that "it was mainly the mania for non-violence and Gandhi's compromise mentality that brought about the disruption of the forces that had come together at the call of Mass Action".[357] It is a paradox that Gandhi believed in winning foes through the gospel of love while he indulged in bitter denunciation of those who disagreed with him in his own country, and disagreed for the common cause of the country's liberation.

There were local outbursts of popular militancy, crossing the bounds of Gandhian orthodoxy, for which many Congressmen expressed their sympathy. Most notable among these was an incident at Peshawar in April-May, 1930 where Garhwali Hindu soldiers refused to open fire on Muslim crowds, sending the Chief Commissioner into "a state of mental prostration".[358] Unrest and militancy were also visible in the *ghat* areas of Nasik, Ahmadnagar and Poona districts where *Kolis* "armed with spears, swords and other weapons" joined in large numbers the anti-grazing fee movement with Congress slogans on their lips.[359] The official *Fortnightly Reports* revealed the mood of popular militancy in parts of Bengal, Bihar, Bombay and the United Provinces. The Bombay City Congress, echoing the sentiments of the revolutionaries, issued a cyclostyled bulletin on November 4, 1930 entitled *Freedom Be Thou My Soul, Sedition Be My Song*.[360] Popular militancy manifested itself in a well planned revolutionary capture of the Chittagong Armoury in 1931.

---

356 Ibid.

357 Ibid.

358 Irwin to Wedgewood Benn, May 1 1930, Halifax Papers, NMML.

359 NAI, Home Pol. File No 18/XII/1930.

360 This cyclostyled bulletin is preserved in Thakurdas Papers, File No.101/1930, NMML.

The Congress attitude towards the revolutionaries took a new turn after the Gandhi–Irwin Pact of March 1931 and the subsequent execution of the Bhagat–Sukhdev–Rajguru trinity on March 23, 1931. All hopes were pinned on Gandhi but he could not save the three revolutionaries. As in 1920-21, the Mahatma had appealed again to the revolutionaries to desist from violence and give him a chance to save the condemned young men from the gallows.[361] But the outcome was similarly embarassing for them. The city of Delhi resounded with the slogans 'Down with Gandhi' and even the humbler Congress camp followers believed that Gandhi had nice-places being made for himself and his immediate entourage.[362]

A little before his execution, Sukhdev wrote an open letter to Gandhi. He accused Gandhi, arguing that his Pact had ignored the revolutionary prisoners languishing in prisons since 1915, and scores of others belonging to different Conspiracy cases. As for their own fate, he wrote: "As a matter of fact the executions are expected to do greater good than the commutation of the sentences." He further said that Mahatma Gandhi's public appeals asking them to call off their movement had harmed them because "appeals mean you are joining hands with the bureaucracy to crush that movement, and your appeals amount to preaching treachery, desertion and betrayal amongst them".[363] To this Gandhi retorted: "...authors of political murder count the cost before they enter upon their awful career. No action of mine can possibly worsen their fate." Gandhi went to the extent of alleging that the delay in freedom was due only to the revolutionary activities and if he "had a completely peaceful atmosphere we would have gained our end already".[364]

Jawaharlal Nehru kept quiet before the executions lest a word of his may annoy the Mahatma. But soon after the executions, he came out with a statement in defence of his silence. He said, "I have

361 *The Tribune*, March 8 1931.

362 *The Pioneer*, March 27 1931.

363 *Young India*, April 23 1931.

364 Ibid.

remained silent though I felt like bursting, and now all is over."[365] He might have been speaking the truth because in another context he had accepted, "I was being compelled by force of circumstances to do things I was in thorough disagreement with."[366] He further said, "Not all of us could save him who was so dear to us and whose magnificent courage and sacrifice have been an inspiration to the youth of India. India today cannot save her dearly loved children from the gallows."[367]

Subhas accused Gandhi of blundering in making peace and not securing the release of all the prisoners and said that *Naujawans* would carry on the fight in any case.[368] After the executions, he wrote:

> Bhagat Singh had become the symbol of the new awakening among the youths... The feeling among a considerable section of the youth was that the Mahatma had betrayed the cause of Bhagat Singh and his comrades.[369]

The Karachi session of the Congress in March 1931, repeated the history of Lahore. A resolution of executions was hotly discussed before it was declared carried with a sizable number of Congressmen voting against it. The main opposition was directed against the words "whilst dissociating itself from and disapproving of political violence in any form or shape".[370] The resolution was moved by Nehru on behalf of Gandhi who had drafted it. While speaking before the resolution, Nehru praised Bhagat Singh and felt indebted to him for the great awakening. He said:

> He was a clean fighter who faced his enemy in the open field. He was a young boy full of burning zeal for the country. He was like a

---

365 *The Bombay Chronicle*, March 25 1931.

366 Jawaharlal Nehru, op.cit., p.156.

367 *The Bombay Chronicle*, March 25 1931.

368 NAI, Home Pol. File No.136/1931.

369 Bose, op.cit., p.205.

370 *AICC Report, Karachi Session*, March 1931, NMML; also Mitra, *The Indian Annual Register*, 1931, Vol.I, pp.266-67.

spark which became a flame in a short time and spread from one end of the country to the other dispelling the prevailing darkness everywhere.[371]

The atmosphere at the session revealed the Congress attitude towards the revolutionaries and the extent to which the Congressmen could go to oppose the Mahatma's unqualified hostility towards the revolutionaries. MM Malaviya, who seconded the resolution, accepted that Bhagat Singh was not only a lover of the motherland; he was a representative of our youth. Voicing the views of the left wing within the Congress, Swami Govindanand said that the Gandhi–Irwin Pact had set back the clock of India's progress to independence. Yusuf Meherali felt that the truce was a betrayal of the national movement. He declared:

> We do not believe in the change of heart theory, to which Mahatmaji attaches so much importance. To our mind, imperialism has no heart to change, it has only pockets to fill.[372]

Meherali denounced the Pact as a "great triumph for British diplomacy", and "a great national mistake". Attacking "the politics of compromise" and of "change of heart", he made sharp references to the string pullers of the Congress – "the Birlas, the Purushottamdas Thakurdass, Walchand Hirachands, Husseinbhai Laljis" – who were then "out and busy in making efforts to obtain the fruits of the suffering and sacrifices of others". He predicted the failure of the Round Table negotiations and hoped to hear the call for militant action. "We patiently await the call to fight. *Inquilab Zindabad*."[373]

---

371 *Report of the Karachi Session, March 1931*; SWJN, Vol.4, pp.505-506.

372 *Report of the Congress Session*, Karachi, March 1931.

373 *Report of the Congress Session*, Karachi, 1931, NMML. Sumit Sarkar has revealed the crucial role played by business pressures in bringing about a change in Gandhi's political stance in February-March, 1931. 'The Logic of Gandhian Nationalism: Civil Disobedience and the Gandhi–Irwin Pact 1930-31', in *The Indian Historical Review*, July 1976, Vol.III, No.1, pp.114–146. Bipan Chandra has also pointed towards the capitalist pressures on the national movement in RS Sharma and V Jha (ed.), *Indian Society: Historical Probings*, New Delhi, 1974, pp.390–413; also 'Jawaharlal Nehru and the

The resolution was declared carried but a number of Congressmen condemned it as a half-hearted and stunted appreciation of the daring revolutionaries.

The revolutionaries and their activities were appreciated by their countrymen, irrespective of party affiliations. Congressmen like the two Nehrus, Bose, GS Vidyarthi and a host of others did not bring in the creed of non-violence and openly exhorted them to work for the country's freedom. It was Gandhi alone who remained adamant and obsessed with his non-violence and the gospel of love. On the one hand he was winning co-operation of the revolutionaries through CR Das and on the other hand he was appealing against the 'mad worship' of Bhagat Singh which, he believed, had "led to goondaism and degradation."[374] Even after the executions, when the All India Bhagat Singh–Rajguru–Sukhdev Memorial Committee approached Gandhi for his support, he bluntly dissociated himself from it as it aimed at immortalizing men who had followed the path of violence.[375] The majority of the Congressmen did not believe in the indispensability of the non-violent creed and so, exhorted the revolutionaries to follow their own path to accelerate the pace of freedom struggle. But this was of hardly any practical value as Gandhian ideology was supreme in the Congress once it came to policy decisions and action. And we have seen what Gandhi's attitude was.

Capitalist Class, 1936', in Debiprasad Chattopadhyaya (ed.), *History and Society*, Calcutta, 1978, pp.513–534.

374 *The Tribune*, August 1 1931.

375 SK Mittal and S Irfan Habib, op.cit., No.87, p.38.

Chapter Four

The Ideology of the National Revolutionaries, 1926–32

The revolutionaries have been constantly depicted as irresponsible and unscrupulous elements with a criminal bent of mind, saturated with emotions of abstract nationalism and an ever burning desire to lay down their lives for the motherland. They were called 'deluded patriots' and men 'past reason'.[376] Their heroism and sacrifice was dubbed as 'waste of energy' and they were branded as the 'enemies of the country'.[377] The result was that even their admirers lauded their heroic actions but considered them mindless patriots having no ideas and no programme for the reconstruction of society. The public mind was fed with only a romantic image of the revolutionaries. The revolutionaries were aware of this misconception being sedulously spread about them by the alien government. Unfortunately, many people were taken in by the ceaseless propaganda of the Government. The common masses were told about revolutionary activities as dastardly crimes, committed for the gratification of money and blood lust. The revolutionaries courted death to remove untruth and misconceptions. One of their declarations said:

---

376 Mahatma Gandhi in *Young India*, January 2 1930; also *CWMG*, Vol.42, pp.361–64.

377 Ibid, February 12 1925.

> There are few to question the magnanimity of the noble ideals they cherish and the grand sacrifices they have offered, but their normal activities being mostly secret, the country is in the dark as to their present policy and intentions.[378]

The revolutionaries of the Hindustan Socialist Republican Association were cast in heroic mould as far as their capacity for physical endurance and mental development were concerned. Although Bhagat Singh was hanged barely at the age of twenty three, he impressed Jawaharlal Nehru with his intellectual looks. Nehru's first impression of Bhagat Singh as having an "attractive, intellectual face, remarkably calm and peaceful," is revealing.[379] MM Malaviya, also attested to the intellectual prowess of the revolutionaries.[380] GS Vidyarthi, the doyen of Hindi journalism, was greatly impressed by the qualities of head and heart of the revolutionaries.[381] The imperial bureaucracy dreaded their ideas most for being the best dissolvent of imperialism.[382] The judge who tried the revolutionaries was aghast at their irrefutable logic and arguments.[383] The revolutionaries of the period under study were neither 'blood-thirsty tyrants' who 'enjoyed shedding human blood' nor 'misguided patriots', but were men committed to higher values of life. They had developed an understanding of revolution, had made a class-analysis of society and stood for the 'Dictatorship of the Proletariat'.[384]

---

378 The HSRA Manifesto distributed at the Lahore session of the Congress in December 1929, Appendix.

379 Jawaharlal Nehru, op.cit., p.193.

380 Report of the Karachi Session of the Congress, March 1931, NMML.

381 A Tribute by Balkrishna Sharma 'Navin', in *Ganesh Shankar Vidyarthi ke Shreshtha Nibandh*, Delhi, 1964 (being the collection of his articles contributed to *Pratap*), p.1.

382 NAI, Home Pol. File No.130 & KW 1930.

383 Mr Medilton, the presiding officer of the session's court at Delhi in the Assembly Bomb Case had admitted to the intellectual acumen of the undertrials.

384 *The Philosophy of the Bomb.*

The revolutionary party cherished certain ideals and goals. The HSRA men were very clear about their objectives. They were unequivocal in their commitment to (1) Freedom from the yoke of British imperialism, (ii) Revolution or overthrow of the present system of relationship based on manifest inequality and exploitation, (iii) Socialism which will sound the death-knell of capitalism, (iv) Establishment of the Dictatorship of the Proletariat. They envisaged the realisation of their objectives in a broader perspective, and their commitment to freedom was not limited to India; they desired the end of all imperialisms and from all corners of the world. They had many ideas regarding the solution of the religious and social problems peculiar to Indian situation and ethos.

The revolutionaries were wedded to the ideal of complete independence.[385] They had identified themselves with freedom to the extent that they proclaimed it by their deeds, 'Give us Liberty or Death'.[386] Quoting Thomas Jefferson, Bhagat Singh wrote in his diary:

> The tree of liberty must be refreshed from time to time with the blood of patriots and tyrants. It is its natural manure.[387]

In their joint statement, Bhagat Singh and BK Dutt had proclaimed:

> Freedom is the imprescriptable birth right of all.[388]

They had analysed that all ills and evils in Indian society and polity accrue from the existence of this fact, i.e. the loss of liberty.

---

385 The Congress adopted the goal of complete independence in 1929 but its commitment to that goal was ambivalent as its representatives participated in constitution making processes on the basis of dominion status even after 1929 and upto as late as 1946. The voluminous correspondence among Indian and British leaders reveals that the former were prepared to negotiate with the British on the basis of self-government. See N Mansergh (ed.), *Transfer of Power* in several volumes (so far 8 vols. published).

386 Unpublished Diary of Bhagat Singh. He quotes Patrick Henry and cries with him 'Give me Liberty or Death'.

387 Ibid.

388 Bhagat Singh and Dutt's joint statement of June 6 1929.

Therefore freedom was a preliminary or necessary prerequiste for the establishment of socialism or fair or just order, and India must sever all connections with the imperialists, throw them out of the country and establish complete political freedom.[389] The Naujawan Bharat Sabha also declared that it will be contented only when the English leave the country and Indians rule instead.[390] It had reiterated complete independence to be the creed of the youth of India. The Sabha believed that the Congress was not fighting for complete independence, and since it was incapable of doing so, the youth should struggle for complete independence of the country.[391] When the Congress adopted complete independence as its goal in 1929, the revolutionaries commented :

> This year it has accepted the ideal which the revolutionaries have preached and lived upto for more than a quarter of a century.[392]

The 'freedom' of the conception of the revolutionaries had a wider meaning and a greater scope. Their struggle against the imperialist masters was not going to end with the attainment of freedom for India. In the freedom of India they visualised the end of all imperialisms and the breaking down of all chains that fetter mankind.

> India's freedom shall ultimately be the freedom of all slave nations and peoples.

Bhupendranath Sanyal echoed the sentiments of all revolutionaries at a meeting of the Sabha held in Mathura on May 22, 1931:

> Our ideal is freedom...I invite the youth to organise and come under the flag of Naujawan Bharat Sabha with a view to fight the battle for freedom. We, keeping the freedom of our own country and that of

---

389 NAI, Home Pol. File No.27/VII of 1932.

390 NAI, Home Pol. File No.27/5/1931.

391 Ibid.

392 *The Philosophy of the Bomb.*

other countries in view, are required to start our work. Today it is very necessary to put an end to British and other imperialisms.[393]

The sentiment of freedom and its expression was not just a vague ideal with the revolutionaries. The revolutionary leaders exhorted their followers to prepare themselves to stand against the imperialist forces of the world. They declared their resolve to cut the sinews of war, through which moral, material help flowed from India only to bring more blood and bounty to imperialist tigers. The frontiers of the revolutionary movement were boundless and embraced the submerged nationalities of the world. They called for the unity of the 'enslaved' against the slavery merchants. BN Sanyal appealed:

> It is also necessary that China and Kabul be with us. If any atrocities are perpetrated on them (enslaved nations)...we shall have to check it and ask the people of our country...not to fire at, kill them and enslave the innocent people...If those countries are in bondage it is our first and foremost duty to free them...[394]

They visualised the freedom of mankind long before the Indian National Congress, the biggest political party in India. Such a clean and wide enunciation of the concept of freedom was seen in the Congress documents only in the 'Quit India' resolution of 1942 which says that the freedom of India shall be a prelude to the freedom of Afro-Asian nations:

> The possession of empire, instead of adding to the strength of the ruling Power, has become a burden and curse. India, the classic land of modern imperialism has become the crux of the question, for by the freedom of India will Britain and the United Nations be judged, and the people of Asia and Africa be filled with hope and enthusiasm...A free India...will bring all subject and oppressed humanity on the side of the United Nations, and give these Nations... the moral and spiritual leadership of the world...The freedom of India must be the symbol of and prelude to this freedom of all Asiatic nations....[395]

---

393 NAI, Home Pol. File No 27/5/1931.

394 Ibid.

395 *Transfer of Power*, Vol.II, 'Quit India', pp.621–23; also Pattabhi Sitaramayya, op.cit., Vol.II, New Delhi, 1969, pp.343-44.

The revolutionaries of the HSRA proved to be the forerunners of the spirit manifested in the 'Quit India' resolution of the AICC. They called for a halt to all exploitations in the form of imperialism. They also envisaged the creation of a World Order which will free humanity from the scourge of capitalism and imperial wars. They proclaimed:

> Unless...Imperialism is brought to an end, the suffering and carnage with which humanity is threatened today cannot be prevented and all talk of ending wars and ushering in an era of universal peace is undisguised hypocrisy...a World Federation should redeem humanity from the bondage of capitalism and the misery of imperial wars.[396]

For the revolutionaries, independence was thus a stepping stone to achieve real freedom – social, economic and religious freedom.[397] Will the real freedom dawn like manna from heaven at the outstretched hands? If it were so India would have been free long ago at the request of moderate leaders of the pre- and post-Gandhi Congress. A relentless war had to be waged to achieve independence. They propounded the theory of revolution to wrest freedom from British hands and then use it as an instrument for the achievement of economic emancipation. Thus their second commitment was revolution which meant forcible overthrow of the existing system and social relations and their replacement by another system, more humane, responsive and responsible. The members of the HSRA gave expression to their faith in revolution in a catchy slogan, *Inquilab Zindabad* (Long Live Revolution) which became as popular with the masses as the *Bande Matram* in an earlier period or the *Jai Hind* afterwards. *Inquilab Zindabad*, coined and introduced by Bhagat Singh, became the mode of salutation and homage among patriots and it formed the war cry of the militant masses.

---

396 Bhagat Singh and Dutt's statement of June 6 1929.

397 Many leaders of the HSRA, quite a large number of whom had joined the CPI, dubbed the transfer of power from the British to Indian hands as false freedom. (*yeh azadi jhooti hai*).

This *Inquilab Zindabad* was not merely an emotional war cry for the revolutionaries but had a lofty ideal which was explained by the HSRA thus:

> The Revolution will ring the death knell of capitalism and class distinction and privileges...It will give birth to a new state – a new social order.[398]

Another manifesto of the HSRA declared that "Revolution is not a philosophy of despair or a creed of desperadoes." It ended with the words:

> Individual liberty shall be safe. The sovereignty of the proletariat shall be recognised. We court the advent of such a Revolution.[399]

Bhagat Singh was even more definitive in his statement in the court on June 6, 1929. He said :

> Revolution is not a culture of bomb and pistol. Our meaning of revolution is to change the present conditions, which are based on manifest injustice.[400]

Bhagat Singh agreed with Karl Marx that a radical revolution is not utopian. "What is utopian is the idea of a partial, an exclusively political revolution, which would leave the pillars of the house standing."[401] The HSRA aimed at such a revolution which would usher in a new era, demolishing the existing socio-economic and political structure of the Indian society. Their revolution was not for anarchy or lawlessness but for social justice.

The spirit of revoluton must be kept alive until and unless the third objective of the revolutionaries was not realised, i.e. socialism. This goal was not based on hazy and wooly notions or youthful impetuosity. A great deal of intensive study and discussion had gone into the making of their ideology. Bhagat Singh had helped

---

398 *The Philosophy of the Bomb.*

399 The manifesto of the HSRA circulated at Lahore Congress in December 1929.

400 Suresh, *Krantikari Bhagat Singh*, Delhi, 1971, pp.91-92.

401 Quoted in the Unpublished Diary of Bhagat Singh.

the Dwarkadas Library to acquire a rare collection of literature on the revolutions of Russia, Ireland and Italy. He had organised a number of study circles with the help of Sukhdev and others and carried on intensive political discussions. These study circles were on the patterns of Russian social revolutionary Kropotkin. Young revolutionaries, both in the Punjab and U.P., were taking keen interest in socialism.[402] As early as 1929, Lala Lajpat Rai publicly described Bhagat Singh as a Russian agent and complained that Bhagat Singh wanted to "make me into a Lenin".[403] JN Sanyal, his co-prisoner in the Lahore Conspiracy Case, made in 1931 the following evaluation of Bhagat Singh as an intellectual:

> Bhagat Singh was an extremely well-read man and his special sphere of study was socialism...Though socialism was his special subject, he had deeply studied the history of the Russian revolutionary movement from its beginning in the early 19th century to the October Revolution of 1917. It is generally believed that very few in India could be compared to him in the knowledge of this special subject. The economic experiments in Russia under the Bolshevik regime also greatly interested him.[404]

His intellect developed in leaps and bounds in prison and he wrote several books of which four were prominent: *Autobiography, The Door to Death, The Ideal of Socialism* and *The Revolutionary Movement of India.* Unfortunately, all the manuscripts have been lost.[405] His unpublished diary brings to light his reading habits and the wide range of authors he keenly read, including Marx, Engels, Russell, Tom Paine, Upton Sinclair, Lenin, Wordsworth, Tennyson, Tagore, Bukharin, Trotsky, and several others.[406] Similarly Bhagwati Charan and Sukhdev also made wide study of socialist literature. Sukhdev was a man of great intellectual ability and his brother has

---

402 Yashpal, op.cit., Vol.1, p.96.

403 V Sandhu, *Yugdrashta Bhagat Singh*, Delhi, 1968, p.316.

404 JN Sanyal, op.cit., p.113.

405 V Sandhu, op.cit., pp.237 and 306; also Balbir Singh, 'Krantikari Pathyakram' in *Mukti*, July 1972, p.38.

406 Unpublished Diary of Bhagat Singh.

called him the Chanakya of the HSRA.[407] Yashpal writes that in 1924-25, Bhagwati Charan, inspired by revolutionary feelings, had come close to the communist groups and all papers from Europe were received on his address.[408] He regarded Karl Marx and Lenin as his 'political gurus and guides'. He had unshakable faith in socialism.[409] Later, Yashpal took the lead and he not only read Rajni Palme Dutt's *Modern India* but also translated it into Hindi.[410]

The equally important point is that Bhagat Singh and fellow comrades worked hard to see that other party members grasp the ideals and principles of socialism. The *Naujawan Bharat Sabha* came to be formed mainly to preach the ideals of socialism, organise the workers and peasants and thus accelerate the pace of revolutionary outbreak. Bhagat Singh emphasized the importance of ideas in his statement before the Lahore High Court that "the sword of revolution is sharpened at the whetstone of thought."[411] Bhagwandas Mahour has also narrated how Bhagat Singh urged him to read Marx's *Capital* and other books.[412]

It can be safely said that the members of the HSRA had developed a fairly good understanding of socialism and Marxism. They may not have become great scholars in the short time they had at their disposal but they were no mere novices either. They had traversed some distance and were gradually feeling, studying and thinking their way towards a scientific socialist understanding of the problems of the Indian Revolution. Bhagat Singh, in his last message appears to have grasped that socialism as a system is not the product of a mere subjective longing for a desirable system but far more the

---

407 Mathura Das Thapar, *Amar Shaheed Sukhdev*, Delhi, 1980, p.170.

408 *Souvenir*, Amar Shaheed Chandrashekhar Azad Balidan Ardhshatabdi, February, 1981, Allahabad, p.35.

409 Jaidev Kapoor, 'Amar Balidani Bhagwati Bhai', in Himanshu Joshi (ed.), *Utsarg*, Lucknow, 1980, p.65.

410 Yashpal, op.cit., Vol.II, p.11.

411 V Sandhu, op.cit., p.196.

412 Bhagwandas Mahour in Banarsidas Chaturvedi (ed.), *Yash ka Dharohar*, in Hindi, Delhi, 1968, pp.27-28.

objective product of the necessity of the social circumstances.[413] He defined the aim of socialism in the words of Trotsky that "it is absolutely unchallenged that the aim of socialism is to eliminate force, first of all in its most crude and bloody forms, and afterwards in other more concealed forms."[414] Bhagat Singh wrote to Sukhdev, whose mind was tormented with doubts and who was awaiting the execution of the death sentence with him:

> If we had not entered the field, would it have meant that no revolutionary action would have occurred? You are wrong if you think so. It is true that we helped to a large extent change the (political) atmosphere. At the same time, we are mere products of the necessity of our times. I would even say that the creator of Communism, Marx, was in fact not the creator of this ideology. It was the industrial Revolution in Europe, which produced many persons of a particular way of thinking. Marx was just one of these men. In this situation Marx undoubtedly helped impart a particular motion to the movement of his times. I and you have not created the socialist or communist ideas in this country. On the other hand, they are the result of the impact on us of our time and circumstances. Undoubtedly, we have contributed in a simple and humble manner to the propagation of these ideas.[415]

Chandrashekhar Azad met Nehru in 1930 and during their conversations the latter asked the former as to what type of a socialist was he? Azad replied that he believed in the precepts of Scientific Socialism and those who believed in the precepts of Karl Marx could remain in their movement.[416] The HSRA leadership clearly grasped that socialism was a product of the historical process and therefore, as a system it was the antithesis of capitalism. Hence, the prerequisite for ushering in socialism is the elimination of capitalism.

---

413 Bhagat Singh's last message, see Appendix three to JN Sanyal, op.cit., pp.138-139.

414 Trotsky, *Where is Britain Going*, quoted in Bhagat Singh's Unpublished Diary.

415 Cited in V Sandhu, op.cit., p.241.

416 Sushila Azad, 'Heroic Martyrdom of Chandrashekhar Azad', in *Blitz*, Bombay, July 16 1960, p.14.

In their joint statement of June 6, 1929, Bhagat Singh and Dutt further elaborated on this point:

> Producers or labourers, inspite of being the most necessary element of society, are robbed by their exploiters of the fruits of their labour and deprived of their elementary rights. On the one hand, the peasant who grows corn for all starves with his family. The weaver who supplied the world market with his textile fabrics cannot find enough to cover his own and his children's bodies. Masons, smiths and carpenters, who rear magnificent palaces, live and perish in slums, and on the other hand, capitalist exploiters, parasites of society, squander millions on their whims.... Radical change, therefore, is necessary, and it is the duty of those who realize this to reorganize society on a socialistic basis.[417]

Delivering the Presidential Address at the Naujawan Sabha Conference in Lahore, Comrade Suhasini Nambiar said that "every industrial strike, every economic dispute between the tenants and the landlords, the *sahukar* and the peasant, is definitely a part of the struggle against imperialism, and is a preparation of the final overthrow of all exploiters."[418] The HSRA did not make any difference between the British rule and capitalism and believed that one cannot be banished without expelling the other. In one of its pamphlets, the HSRA stated:

> If we drive out this rapacious English government from the country, we can easily put an end to the tyranny of capitalism, and if we can efface capitalism, the English government cannot hold its sway over this land.... It is the belief of the HSRA that the easiest and best method of driving out the British government is to establish socialism, for which a revolution is indispensable."[419]

It continued:

> We are opposed to injustice and tyranny perpetrated by man on man or by one race on another. In order to eradicate violence and

---

417 Gopal Thakur, *Bhagat Singh – The Man and his Ideas*, New Delhi, 1976, p.36; also Mitra, *Indian Annual Register, 1929*, Vol.I, pp.78-80.

418 *The Tribune*, Jamuary 1 1930.

419 NAI, Home Pol. File No.27/VII of 1932. A red pamphlet in Hindi entitled Hindustan Socialist Prajatantra Sangh issued by Prakasho Devi, Secretary, Publicity Department of the HSRA.

injustice, we socialist revolutionaries are doing our level best to counter capitalism and imperialism.[420]

The HSRA challenged the native capitalists in these words:

> The time is not far off when our party will decide as to who should be made the mark of pistol and when the capitalism of these capitalists... which has stupified them... should be mixed with dust under their eyes...unless they change their attitude our party will wipe out their whole family and their capitalism from the face of the earth.[421]

They knew that socialism will remain a remote dream till the state apparatus remains in the hands of the exploiting classes. In a message from prison in October, 1930 Bhagat Singh said:

> We mean by revolution the uprooting of the present social order. For this, capture of state power is necessary. The state apparatus is now in the hands of the privileged class. The protection of the interests of the masses, the translation of our ideal into reality, that is the laying of the foundation of society in accordance with the principles of Karl Marx, demand our seizure of this apparatus.[422]

Bhagat Singh expressed himself categorically on the issue of revolution and socialism in his message to political workers, among the last before he was hanged a month later. He told the young political workers:

> We want a socialist revolution, the indispensable preliminary to which is the political revolution. That is what we want. The political revolution does not mean the transfer of state (or more crudely, the power) from the hands of the British to the Indian, but to those Indians who are at one with us as to the final goal, or to be more precise, the power to be transferred to the revolutionary party through popular support. After that, to proceed in right earnest is to organise the reconstruction of the whole society on the socialist basis.[423]

---

420 Ibid.

421 NAI, Home Pol. File No.4/36/31 (KW) 1931. "Bande Matram" (Lahore), December 13 1930. Posters of the HSRA found pasted in Amritsar.

422 Gopal Thakur, op.cit., p.38.

423 Bhagat Singh's *Message to Young Political Workers*, February 2, 1931.

The HSRA had no doubt that after the effacement of the British rule, "the structure of the Indian society can be metamorphosed on the lines of Soviet Russia".[424] The salvation of the country is possible "only when the power passes from the handful of persons to the masses at large."[425] Hence, the Naujawan Sabha emphasised on the organisation of the oppressed workers, or peasants or the petty shopkeepers who cannot find food to fill their stomachs. They wanted the 98% to rule in place of the 2% capitalists, who hold the state apparatus for the exploitation of the majority.

The HSRA had no illusions about the nature of the native bourgeois leadership and so, its manifesto had declared:

> The hope of the proletariat is, therefore, now centred in socialism which alone can lead to the establishment of complete independence and the removal of all social distinctions and privileges.[426]

It repeatedly affirmed its faith in socialism and the necessity of organizing the proletariat for the achievement of social justice. Here, Bhagat Singh's views were in perfect consonance with Marx, who had said:

> Great are great because
> We are on knees
> Let us Rise![427]

This growing socialist consciousness of the HSRA revolutionaries enabled them to understand the linkages between the foreign and native capitalisms. They clearly perceived the collaborationist, comprador relationship of the Indian capitalist class and the native bourgeoisie with the foreign capitalists, both of whom joined hands to deprive the masses of what was theirs. They believed that India is enslaved by a class – constituting of Indian as well as foreign

---

424 NAI, Home Pol. File No.27/VII of 1932.

425 NAI, Home Pol. File No.27/6/1931.

426 The HSRA manifesto circulated at the Lahore Congress in December 1929.

427 Unpublished Diary of Bhagat Singh.

elements. This understanding is reflected in various slogans and leaflets where freedom was linked with the ending of exploitation of man by man. They came face to face with the domestic exploiters and declared that they were as dangerous to the interests of the masses as the foreign capitalist rulers. The manifesto of the HSRA also clearly said:

> The position of the Indian proletariat is, today, extremely critical. It has a double danger to face. It has to beat the onslaught of Foreign Capitalism on the one hand and the treacherous attack of Indian capital on the other; the latter is showing a progressive tendency to join forces with the former...Indian capital is preparing to betray the masses into the hands of Foreign Capitalism and receive as a price of this betrayal, a little share in the Government of the country.[428]

Bhagat Singh, in a message from the prison, wrote that 'the peasants have to liberate themselves not only from the foreign yoke but also from the yoke of landlords and capitalists.'[429] He was even more explicit in his message of March 3, 1931 saying:

> ...the struggle in India would continue so long as a handful of exploiters go on exploiting the labour of the common people for their own ends. It matters little whether these exploiters are purely British capitalists, or British and Indians in alliance, or even purely Indians.[430]

The end of exploitation and the realization of the socialist state of workers and peasants were possible only through the organization of the above classes. The HSRA dealt with the question: Who would fight for the revolution or what would be the social base of the movement? They were aware of the fact that their movement was to be based on the organisation of masses, the labourers and peasants, and the radical intelligentsia. They believed that "the labourer is the real sustainer of society. The sovereignty of the people is the ultimate destiny of the workers".[431] Bhagat Singh, particularly, had visualized

428 The HSRA manifesto circulated at the Lahore Congress in December 1929.

429 Gopal Thakur, op.cit., p.39.

430 Ibid.

431 Bhagat Singh and Dutt's joint statement of June 6 1929.

the future when the struggle of national freedom would be brought to a successful culmination by the active participation of the working class and peasantry. The Kanpur meeting of the HSRA's Central Council in January 1930, in which, among others, Chandrashekhar Azad, Bhagwati Charan Vohra, Yashpal and Kailashpati participated, decided to intensify the work among the students, peasants and workers, and to form for the purpose, a separate section of the party to by headed by Seth Damodar Swarup as President and Bhagwati Charan as Secretary.[432]

There was one more important reason for their emphasis on the organisation of workers and peasants. The HSRA leaders were convinced that the capitalists and the upper classes were showing a tendency of joining hands with the foreign power and abandoning the freedom struggle midway.[433] The Naujawan Sabha manifesto, while attacking such classes and leaders, said:

> There are also people among us who try to hide their inactivity behind the cover of internationalism. They say that they believe in *Atmvatasrvabhuteshu* and on account of it even the English are our brothers; we need not fight them. Perhaps, they do not understand the meaning of *Atmvatsarvabhuteshu*. It means that the exploitation of man by man and nation by nation should be made impossible for ever and the British rule in India pointblank negates this principle...[434]

In this situation, only the masses could be relied upon and the freedom struggle could be carried to its logical end only on their shoulders. The revolutionaries believed that "neither the working class nor the oppressed peasantry can any day think of making a compromise with British Imperialism if they are to remain true to their economic interests."[435] While on the other hand they knew that the Indian capitalists can never come into the struggle against imperialism because they need imperial support to maintain

---

432 Kailashpati's evidence, *Proceedings of the Delhi Conspiracy Case*, Vol.I, p.229;also Yashpal, op.cit., Vol.II, pp.153-54.

433 Bhagat Singh quoted in Gopal Thakur, op.cit., pp.38-39.

434 Shiv Verma, 'Bhagwati Charan Vohra', in Himanshu Joshi, op.cit., p.53.

435 *The Tribune*, January 1 1930.

themselves.[436] Thus, the work of the HSRA and the Naujawan Sabha reflected an emphasis on the potentialities of these oppressed sections of the society and an eagerness to enlarge their social base among them. The Sabha did some work in this direction and made attempts to mobilise the workers and the peasants. These two sections were specially exhorted to join the Sabha activities.[437] The Sabha openly declared that it believes more in the organisation of workers and peasants than in holding public meetings.[438] The Naujawan Bharat Sabha condemned the Delhi Pact of 1931 because it did not give anything to the workers and peasants. It took part in some agrarian agitations in 1929, exhorted the millions of youth to spend their valuable lives in villages like the Russian youth. They had to explain there the real meaning of the forthcoming revolution in India. Villagers were to be made to understand and feel that the new revolution would not be confined to merely changing the rulers. It would work for the establishment of a completely new socio-political order. It would, therefore, be a revolution of the people and by the people. In other words, it would be a *swaraj* for 98% of people.However, despite the Sabha's commitment to the cause of the workers and peasants, it could not mobilize them effectively. It could not identify itself with them though it was known to be the organisation for workers and peasants. Its appeal could not go beyond the urban youth and student community. It was confined to the middle and lower middle class sectors of the cities.

The HSRA leaders worked for a militant mass revolution and had no illusions about violence or terrorism. Any terroristic activity was described as an 'Action for propaganda'[439] and was not merely a desire for shedding human blood. The revolutionaries were not

---

436 Ibid.

437 *The Tribune*, February 9 1930.

438 Ibid, October 8 1929. Several workers of the Sabha toured villages and preached their message.

439 *The Pioneer*, March 30 1931. Sukhdev's unfinished letter to his brother; also NAI, Home Pol. File No.139/1931.

trigger-happy but believed only in surgical bloodshed.[440] Through these actions, they wanted to awaken the masses from their slumber so that they may rise and shake off the yoke of slavery. The HSRA leaders repeatedly denied the allegations that they were bloodthirsty tyrants and aimlessly fired at and threw bombs to kill innocent human beings. In the course of their statement, Bhagat Singh and Dutt dealt with their aim in throwing the bombs without hurting anybody. They explained what violence was and what it was not:

> Force, when aggressively applied is violence and therefore morally unjustifiable. But when it is used in furtherance of a legitimate cause it has its moral justification. Elimination of force at all costs is utopian and the new movement which has arisen in the country and of which we have given a warning is inspired by the ideals which guided Guru Gobind Singh, Shivaji, Kamal Pasha, and Reza Khan, Washington and Garibaldi, Lafayette and Lenin.[441]

Dealing with the question of violence and non-violence, *The Philosophy of the Bomb* further clarified the stand of HSRA:

> ...Violence is physical force applied for committing injustice, and that is certainly not what the revolutionaries stand for. On the other hand, what generally goes by the name of non-violence is in reality the theory of soul-force, as applied to the attainment of personal and national rights, through courting suffering and hoping thus to finally convert your opponent to your point of view. When a revolutionary believes certain things to be his right, he asks for them, pleads for them, argues for them, wills to attain them with all the soul force at his command, stands the greatest amount of suffering for them, is always prepared to make the highest sacrifice for their attainment, and also backs his efforts with all the physical force he is capable of. You may coin what other word you like to describe his methods but you cannot call it violence, because that would constitute an outrage on the dictionary meaning of that word. Satyagraha is insistence upon Truth. Why press for the acceptance of Truth by soul force alone? Why not add physical force also to it? While the revolutionaries stand for winning independence by all the forces, physical as well moral at their command, the advocates of soul-force would like to ban the use of physical force. The question really, therefore, is not whether

---

440 Author's interview with Manmathnath Gupta.

441 KK Mitra, *The Indian Annual Register*, Vol.I, 1929, p.79.

you will have violence or non-violence, but whether you will have soul force plus physical force or soul force alone.[442]

Bhagat Singh dealt with the question of violence while writing an introduction to *The Dreamland*, a political work of an old revolutionary Lala Ram Saran Das.[443] He wrote:

> Lala Ram Saran Das was the member of the revolutionary party which was held responsible for many a violent deed. But this by no means proves that the revolutionaries are blood thirsty monsters, seeking pleasure in destruction.

In support of his argument, he quotes a few lines from the book:

> If need be, outwardly be wild,
> But in thy heart be always mild
> Hiss if need be, but do not bite,
> Love in thy heart and outside fight.[444]

He was convinced that violence is crucial for a revolutionary change and felt that "destruction is not only essential but indispensable for construction...resort to violent means is a terrible necessity".[445] Another manifesto of the HSRA also dealt with the twin question of violence and terrorism saying:

> Non-violence may be noble ideal, but it is a thing of the morrow.... The world is armed to the very teeth. And the world is too much with us. All talk of peace may be sincere, but we, of the slave nation, cannot, and must not, be led away by such false ideology.[446]

The manifesto clarified the HSRA's attitude towards terrorism saying that "terrorism is never the object of revolutionaries, nor do they believe that terrorism alone can bring independence," but terrorism, according to them, was an "effective means of retaliation. The British

---

442 *The Philosophy of the Bomb.*

443 *Gopi Chand Bhargava Papers*, NMML, New Delhi. The introduction was written by Bhagat Singh in jail on January 15, 1931.

444 Ibid.

445 Ibid.

446 The HSRA manifesto circulated at the Lahore Congress Session in December, 1929.

government exists, because the Britishers have been successful in terrorizing the whole of India....Only counter terrorism on the part of the revolutionaries can checkmate effectively this bureaucratic bullying."[447]

The faith in violence and terrorism waned in the later phase of the HSRA. Its leaders realized the futility of their faith in individual acts of violence and came over to militant mass revolution. In theory, they stood for it from the very beginning but practically they remained away from this ideal owing to the limitations imposed by the then political circumstances. Bhagat Singh even declared in one of his last messages "that I am not a terrorist and I never was, except perhaps in the beginning of my revolutionary career. And I am convinced that we cannot gain anything through these methods."[448]

The HSRA was opposed to all kinds of sectarianism, obscurantism and the religious fanaticism rampant in the Indian society. Unlike in the early revolutionary movements, religion was not allowed to have precedence over the secular and nationalistic outlook of its organisers who belonged to different religious groups in the country. To overcome the dogmatic and socially prejudicial caste outlook and to develop healthy secular nationalist feelings in the people, the Naujawan Sabha used to arrange social gatherings, and public lectures to discuss socio-political affairs.

The revolutionaries attached great importance to the inculcation of a spirit of scientific materialism over mystical metaphysics. Bhagat Singh expressed the feelings of the HSRA while discussing God and religion with one of his associates. He said:

> Yours is the way of passivity, of inactivating the youth of the country by administering them the drug of fatalism under the cover of selfless action. It can never be my way. The people who consider this world unreal and regard its inhabitants as shadows or illusions, they can

---

447 Ibid.

448 Bhagat Singh's *Message to Young Political Workers*, February 2, 1931.

never struggle for the good of the world or fight honestly for the freedom of this country.[449]

The manifesto of the Sabha condemned the forces which fomented communal strife and attacked the blind faith in religion:

> When the great Russia is playing the role of the world's benefactor; what are we Indians doing? The mere cutting of a branch of the *Pipal* tree hurts the religious feelings of the Hindus. They get excited. God (*Allah*) gets infuriated at the mere tearing of the paper *Tazia* of the Iconoclasts and they do not rest content till they shed the blood of the unholy Hindus. Man is more valuable than animals. But, here in India, we are breaking one another's head in the name of holy animals. The morbidity of communalism has blurred our sight while the youth of the world are thinking in terms of internationalism.[450]

Bhagat Singh dealt with religion and atheism in detail in one of his articles entitled 'Why I am an Atheist'. Before elaborating on his own views about religion, Bhagat Singh first deals with the religiosity of his predecessors. He points out that in the absence of a scientific understanding of their own political activity they needed irrational religious beliefs and mysticism to sustain them spiritually, to fight against personal temptation, to overcome depression, to be able to sacrifice their physical comforts, and even life. For all this a person requires deep sources of inspiration. This requirement was, in the case of early revolutionaries, met by mysticism and religion.[451]

He made it clear that the revolutionaries now needed no religious inspiration as they had an advanced revolutionary ideology, based on reason instead of blind faith. Regarding his opinion about God, Bhagat Singh writes:

> He (God) was to serve as a father, mother, sister and brother, friend and helper...so that when man be in great distress having been betrayed and deserted by all friends, he may find consolation in the idea that an ever true friend was still there to help him, to support him and that He was Almighty and could do anything. Really that

---

449 Shiv Verma, op.cit., pp.38-39.

450 Shiv Verma, 'Bhagwati Charan Vohra', in Himanshu Joshi, op.cit., p.52.

451 *The People*, Lahore, September 27, 1931.

was useful to a society in the primitive age. The idea of God is helpful to man in distress.[452]

How close Bhagat Singh was to the thinking of young Marx. This is what Marx wrote in 1844:

> Religion is the general theory of that world, its encyclopedic compendium, its logic in a popular form, its spiritualistic *point d'houneur*, its enthusiasm, its moral sanction, its solemn complement, its universal source of consolation and justification...Religious distress is at the same time the expression of real distress and also the protest against real distress. Religion is the sigh of the oppressed creature, the heart of the heartless world, just as it is the spirit of spiritless conditions. It is the opium of the people. To abolish religion as the illusory happiness of the people is to demand their real happiness.

Even though Bhagat Singh could not have read this passage, he understood better than most others what Marx meant when he described religion as "the opium of the people".[453]

At another place, while discussing the position of God, Bhagat Singh said to his associate:

> You talk of the omnipotent God. I ask you that inspite of being omnipotent, why does your God not eliminate injustice, oppression, starvation, poverty, exploitation, inequality, slavery, epidemics, violence and war? Despite possessing the power to eliminate all these, if He does not emancipate mankind from these curses, definitely, he cannot be called a benevolent God...and its immediate extinction is in the public interest.[454]

"The Philosophy of the Bomb" of the HSRA also declared that the revolutionaries see the "advent of the revolution in the restlessness of youth, in its desire to break free from the mental bondage and religious superstitions that hold them." In another pamphlet, the HSRA reiterated its stand on God and faith in man

---

452 Ibid..

453 Bipan Chandra in an introduction to *Why I am an Atheist* by Bhagat Singh, Delhi, 1979, p.6.

454 Shiv Verma, op.cit., p.39.

when it said: "Revolution may be anti-God but is certainly not anti-Man."[455]

Bhagat Singh was convinced that religion is a tool in the hands of exploiters who keep the masses in constant fear of God for their own interests.[456] All religions and creeds are the props of tyrannical and exploiting institutions, men and classes. He wrote: "Rebellion against King is always a sin according to every religion."[457] He agreed with Bertrand Russell who said that religion is "a disease born of fear, and a source of untold misery to the human race."[458] The revolutionaries of the HSRA realized that all moral ideals and religions were useless for an empty stomach and for him only food was God. "Morality and religion are but words to him who fishes in gutters for the means of sustaining life, and crouches behind barrels in the street for shelter from the cutting blasts of a winter night."[459]

This scientific approach of the HSRA leaders matured with the passage of time. The majority of them came close to the ideals of communism, which believed in mass action instead of individual terroristic actions.[460] Chandrashekhar Azad also felt that "clearly

---

455 The HSRA manifesto circulated at the Lahore Congress in December, 1929.

456 Interview with Manmathnath Gupta.

457 *Why I am an Atheist.*

458 Cited in the Unpublished Diary of Bhagat Singh.

459 Horace Greeley cited in Ibid.

460 The leaders of the HSRA had close affinity with the communist ideology. Why did they not join the Communitst Party of India? The CPI did not function as an open political party in the pre-independence era. It was founded in Tashkent and its adherents faced persecution at the hands of the British from the very beginning. The Peshawar Conspiracy Case (1921), the Kanpur Conspiracy Case (1923), the Meerut Conspiracy Case (1929–32) and numerous other oppressive measures of the Government made it impossible for the party to function openly. The instinct of survival led it to adopt tactics of organising workers, peasants and students organisations. Most of the survivors of the HSRA later became active in the Communist parties. Some of the prominent survivors were Shiv Verma and Jaidev Kapoor, who became state committee members of

something was wrong with the notion that a band of heroic and self sacrificing youth could, by their action, influence the national movement as a whole in a revolutionary direction."[461] He was convinced of the necessity of a widespread mass movement and the uselessness of the secret terroristic activities.[462] Azad came to believe "that as many comrades as possible should now go in for mass work and organise the workers and peasants to develop a mass socialist movement leaving him and a few others to resort to armed actions only when the needs of that movement demanded it".[463] Sukhdev wrote similarly to his friend and made clear that secret activities should now cease, and open work should begin because masses now understand their ideals. Bomb explosions were now not required.[464] Bhagat Singh had read Karl Marx and Lenin in jail and had gone into the details of the success of the Bolshevik Revolution in Russia. He had come face to face with these basic questions regarding India's true struggle. What should be the character and shape of the future political, economic and social set up? Would the levers of power be manipulated by the princes, *nawabs*, feudal lords, priests, capitalists and money lenders after the white overlords were overthrown? Bhagat Singh thought that these elements were the biggest stooges and props of British power in India and collaborated with them in exploitation, violence and suppression of the people.[465] Bhagat Singh had come to understand clearly that without doing away with these lackeys of imperialism, the Indian freedom would be only for the rich, the communalists, the toadies and the affluent sections of the upper castes, and not for the 95% of the poor and helpless people. The HSRA leadership wanted that some of their

---

the CPI (M) in Uttar Pradesh and Kundanlal, who was associated with the Punjab CPI (M).

461 Ajoy Ghosh, op.cit., p.31.

462 Mahour, op.cit., p.133.

463 Ajoy Ghosh, op.cit., p.31.

464 Mathra Das Thapar, op.cit., pp.220-221.

465 Prithvi Singh Azad, op.cit., p.21.

comrades should go to the Soviet Union to learn the tactics of anti-imperialist fight. Merely studying Marx, Lenin and others was not enough. Sukhdevraj felt it when he said: "Books enable us only to surmise. They give us no practical solutions."[466] For this practical understanding of the Bolshevik methods of revolution, Bhagat Singh directed Prithvi Singh Azad to go to Russia.[467]

The HSRA's veering round to communism was noted by the Government and it is clear from the official report, which said:

> In the United Provinces it was recognised that the terrorists had decided to call a halt in the face of strong Government action directed against them. Here, there was exhibited a tendency to accept communist doctrines and the communist argument that individual terrorism merely leads to the strengthening of Government measures for resisting political change.[468]

A document was seized in connection with the Inter-Provincial Case bearing the title 'The Constitution of the Hindustan Socialist Revolutionary Party' with headquarters at Bhagwati Charan Nagar, Bengal. Bhagwati Charan was a noted leader of the HSRA who died in a bomb explosion in May 1930. This document was far more advanced in its thinking and the adoption of the proletarian outlook.[469] Its identification with the oppressed classes was complete when it declared that our aims are nothing but the interests of our class, the exploited class which constitutes 98% of the population and whom we represent.[470] It reiterated that "we the socialist revolutionaries as against the other types of revolutionaries are to work with the workers and peasants of India."[471]

---

466 Ibid. p.22. This Sukhdeoraj is different from the martyr Sukhdev.

467 Ibid. p.23.

468 *Terrorism in India.*

469 SN Mazumdar, op.cit., pp.244–46.

470 Printed judgement of the Inter Provincial Case, pp.413-414, cited in ibid, p.244.

471 Ibid, p.245.

It is unfortunate that despite its vocal commitment to the cause of the workers and peasants, the appeal of the HSRA could not go beyond the lower middle class youth. It stood for the organisation of the downtrodden and accepted the proletariat as its social base but it could do little to organise it. Its class struggle remained confined to its various manifestos, pamphlets and the statements of its leaders. The Naujawan Bharat Sabha made some attempts in this direction and it did convey the message of the socialist revolutionaries into the remote villages, but its activities were limited to the state of Punjab. The Sabha also organised several workers unions in the Punjab.

But the fact was that the main concentration of the HSRA was upon the power of the radical nationalist youth of the country, who were considered useful in two ways. They were to act as the conveyers of the revolutionary socialist message to workers and peasants,[472] and they were also to be the soldiers in the struggle against imperialism. The Naujawan Bharat Sabha was founded by Bhagat Singh to enlist young cadre for revolutionary work and the Lahore Students Union was also organised as an appendage to the Naujawan Bharat Sabha or as a recruiting ground for revolutionary work.[473] The entire emphasis of the HSRA was, thus, on the youth which was to be the vanguard of the revolutionary struggle. This faith in the youth was further reiterated in a HSRA poster, which said:

> Youths ye are the source of liberty, the hope of the country, nay the saviour of the motherland....Make India another Ireland and the reins of the Government are in your hands.[474]

Moreover, in practice also the 'propaganda by death' was directed towards the youth. The young cadre from the lower middle class formed the veritable social base of the revolutionary movement.

---

472 *The Tribune*, October 22 1929. Bhagat Singh and Dutt's message to the Students' Conference in Lahore.

473 NAI, Home Pol. File No.130 & KW 1930.

474 The poster of the revolutionary party was found pasted at St. John's College, Agra in January, 1930.

Almost the entire membership of the HSRA was drawn from this section of the society.[475] Bhagat Singh believed that such selfless youth were required who might do organisational and other essential work for the socialist revolution. The youth must, therefore, be the vanguard of the revolution, they must act to stir the people and arouse them through their work and sacrifices.[476]

Despite HSRA's commitment to socialism, its leaders could not shed their petty-bourgeois revolutionism which still persisted to a considerable extent. Their faith in heroic terrorism or 'propaganda by action' led them to sacrifice their most useful comrades and in the process, decimated their ranks. They could not withstand bureaucratic suppression and the hostility of the bourgeois nationalist leadership. Their belief that propaganda by deed or by death could help in creating a revolutionary socialist consciousness proved unfounded. Where were the political forces – parties, groups, individuals – in the country which could take advantage of the sentiments released and aroused by their immense sacrifices?[477] Their actions aroused nationalist consciousness but could not convey their message of socialism to the masses. This nationalist enthusiasm generated by revolutionary actions was made use of by the bourgeois leadership of the Congress. Gandhi's Dandi March' in March 1930 was preceded by such 'action deeds' like the Assembly Bomb explosion and the Viceregal train explosion in 1929. The HSRA could not preach its own programme through its own leaders' sacrifices while the same was done by the parties which it decried. The very bourgeois nationalist leadership which they had desired to replace through exposure of its pro-capitalist character harnessed their names and sacrifices to make popular

---

475 Yashpal, op.cit., Vol.I, p.232.

476 Bhagat Singh quoted in V Sandhu, op.cit., p.323.

477 Bipan Chandra, 'The Ideological Development of the Revolutionary Terrorists in Northern India in the 1920s' in BR Nanda (ed.), *Socialism in India*, p.187.

their own brand of nationalism.[478] If any success can be ascribed to the Gandhi led Civil Disobedience Movement, 1930–32, in terms of mass court arrest the credit must be given to the heroic sacrifices made by the members of the HSRA in 1928, 1929 and 1930. By their dare-devil acts they aroused great political consciousness in the people who, not sharing their level of sacrifices were prepared to take to the path of lesser sacrifices charted out by the Congress in the beginning of 1930.

The HSRA, with all its weaknesses, was the first mass organization which attempted to preach the gospel of socialism in India. Its leaders devoured literature on communism and socialism, read Marx, Lenin, Trotsky and others. Whatever socialist understanding they developed was enough because the country was hermetically sealed against the entry of such literature. The existence of communist literature in India baffled the British government so much that by a notification dated September, 10, 1932, issued under the Sea Customs Act, all documents issued by or emanating from the Communist International or publications which contained substantial extracts from communist documents were ordered to be confiscated.[479] It is noteworthy that the notification was preceded by the Lahore and the Meerut Conspiracy cases. The revolutionaries of the HSRA "decided to advance towards socialism which they did not differentiate from communism at that time".[480] Their contribution both to the national movement as a whole and to the cause of attracting the younger generation of revolutionaries towards socialism was foundational and vital.

---

478 Ibid, p.187.

479 SN Mazumdar, op.cit., Preface p.xviii.

480 *The Hindustan Times*, March 23 1981. An article by Ram Chandra, the associate of Bhagat Singh, entitled 'We, The Accused'.

CHAPTER V

CONCLUSION

The rise of national revolutionary ideology is not a twentieth century phenomenon in Indian politics. Neither is it the result of British imperialism alone, although it proved to be the greatest single factor for the outbreak of armed revolutionary activities in India. The roots of revolutionary sentiment lie much deeper in history, and many factors, events, ideas and personalities provided the backdrop for the origin, growth and flowering of revolutionary ideology, programme and the eventual deeds.

The love of freedom is inherent in human breast. The outbreak of numerous revolts, uprisings and mini rebellions in the late 18th century and their continuance in the nineteenth and twentieth centuries emanated from this basic instinct.[481] These rebellions could not succeed because of India's social system and backwardness or, contrarily, because of the advanced, scientific and modern system of the enemy who had profited immensely from the gifts of the industrial revolution. Among these outbursts of revolutionary sentiments, the uprising of 1857 proved to be the most formidable challenge to the British imperialism in India.

---

481 SB Chaudhuri has dealt with some of these revolts and rebellions in *Civil Disturbances during the British Rule in India, 1765–1857*, 1955.

The armed revolutionary movement was an outcome of socio-economic and political exploitation of the Indian massses by their imperialist masters. The revolutionaries clearly perceived the socio-economic basis of Indian servitude. They were aghast to see that the Indians were held in economic bondage and were merely hewers of wood and drawers of water in their own country. Their heart bled at the sight of colossal poverty and its expanding grip over the people because of the determined thrust of Pax Britannica in the sub-continent and around.

Peasantry – the most numerous section in the countries of Asia and Africa – was worst hit on account of imperialist greed. The alien Government devised measures which impoverished the peasantry. The land revenue systems and the periodic increase in revenue demand constituted the one great source of peasant exploitation. The village economy was completely destroyed. Ground down by the worsening economic conditions, the peasantry fell into the clutches of moneylenders. The rural masses eked out an existence which was no better than that of cattle. The lot of the urban labour was as unenviable as that of the rural proletariat. Denied the bare necessities of life they moved to death's door as skeletons.

The revolutionaries were shocked to read the accounts of poverty and wretchedness of the Indian masses rendered by the liberal Indian politicians and economists like Dadabhai Naoroji, RC Dutt, DE Wacha, and S Iyer. The Indian nationalist press also came out against the imperialist policy of exploitation.

The early revolutionaries, who were imbued in oriental traditions, resented the cultural onslaught, let loose by the imperial masters. The imperialists had a very low opinion of Indian cultural values. They practised racial discrimination against the Indians. The experience of 1857 added impetus to this policy of the Britishers and the various Governor-Generals like Lytton and Curzon added fuel to the fire by their various acts. When the cup of indignation overflowed, the Indians took to revolutionary terrorism to shake off the yoke of slavery and subjugation.

Many other influences, native as well as foreign, went into the shaping of the revolutionary creed. The Congress had bowed and prayed before the haughty imperialist bureaucracy but without any tangible result. The aspirations of the people went far ahead of the Congress ideals. The renaissance had awakened the Indians to the values of ancient Indian traditions and the hatred for everything alien increased day by day. The revolutionary leaders of this era were deeply religious in outlook and drew inspiration from India's ancient past. The Gita became the fountain head of inspiration for the leaders of both Maharashtra and Bengal. Tilak in Maharashtra, and Bankim Chandra, Aurobindo Ghosh and Vivekanand in Bengal provided the leadership and ideas in their respective provinces.

Tilak's revolutionary interpretation of the *Gita* and his speeches and writings led to the formation of *Hindu Dharam Sanrakshini Sabha* by Chapekar brothers. Savarkar, inspired by Chapekars, formed *Mitra Mela* at Nasik, the early version of *Abhinav Bharat Society* of Poona. Similarly, under the impetus of Bankim, Aurobindo and Vivekanand, P Mitra founded *Anushilan Samiti* in 1901, which was later joined by various celebrities. The Goddess *Durga* was sought to be made a symbol of *Shakti* to kill all the oppressors of the motherland.

The ideas of foreign revolutionary personages like Mazzini and Garibaldi were very popular among the Indian revolutionaries of the pre-1924 period. The victory of Japan over Russia in 1905 imparted a spirit of self-confidence among the Indians. In this atmosphere, the partition of Bengal and the accompanying acts of Governmental repression proved to be the catalytic agent for the appearance of bomb and pistol in Indian politics with greater vigour. Several hated imperialist officers were killed by the revolutionary young men.

The period, 1908–1915, can be characterised as the spring time of revolutionary nationalism in the Indian liberation movement. On the one hand the revolutionary groups of *Yugantar–Sandhya* vintage were active in Bengal and on the other the *Abhinava Bharat* and *Anushilan Samiti* were gaining influence in the Bombay

Presidency and the United Provinces. Led by Hardayal, the Delhi group of revolutionaries was also forging its way. Rash Behari Bose's arrival in northern India accelerated the pace of revolutionary activities and an abortive attempt was made on the life of Viceroy Lord Hardinge in December 1912. He also made an unsuccessful bid for an armed uprising throughout India, and escaped to Japan to continue his struggle against imperialism. The revolutionary enthusiasm remained undiminished, notwithstanding the imperial oppression. Many of the revolutionaries used foreign lands for the accomplishment of their mission, i.e. the end of British hegemony in India. The Ghadarites led by Hardayal in the USA; Shyamji Krishna Verma in London; Madam Bhikaiji Cama, Rana and VN Chattopadhaya in Germany; Raja Mahendra Pratap and Maulana Barkatullah in South-East Asia kept the torch of revolution burning.

The revolutionaries of this era, however, had no concrete and clear-cut conception about the future state of India. They were emotionally committed to their motherland and yearned for the elimination of British imperialists from the land of their birth. Yet, they were not devoid of the clamour for new ideas. They were religious men and for them religion was the main source of inspiration. But they considered religion only an instrument to arouse political nationalism. For them, religion was not a disintegrating force but a tool for strengthening their organisation.

The revolutionaries of the pre-war period knew nothing about the concept of Marxian class consciousness yet they talked of the downtrodden and the welfare of the peasantry. There are instances where political demands of *swarajya* and *swadeshi* were accompanied by vague demands of economic justice. To them Indian degradation and misfortune were the results of the alien rule. They attributed all evils in India to British imperialism. The native exploiters, the foreign capitalists and the lackeys of British imperialism seemed to have escaped their attention altogether. Despite their weaknesses, the revolutionaries generated a dare-devil spirit among the countrymen and awakened the nation by their courageous deeds. They tried to break the traditional bonds of custom and untouchability. The romanticism and emotionalism gradually gave way to a well defined revolutionary creed with the inflow of socialist ideas, particularly after 1920.

The Great War proved disastrous for the belligerent nations and their economy was in shambles. Capitalism showed signs of decay everywhere and the Bolshevik revolution succeeded in Russia. The World War and the Russian socialist revolution made a tremendous impact on the revolutionary forces.

The expectations of the people aroused by the war promises came to nothing with the imposition of the Rowlatt Act. It spurred a mass movement in the country joined by students, teachers, advocates and others. But Gandhi, the aspostle of non-violence, withdrew the mass movement at the first glow of revolutionary tendencies. The non-cooperating soldiers of the Mahatma, particularly the youth, felt tricked and frustrated at the withdrawal of the movement. They had left their studies and promising careers for the freedom of the country, which Gandhi had promised to be theirs in one year. They had not intended their sacrifice at the altar of non-violence. Dismayed with Gandhism, they went back to their old faith in armed revolution. They also devoted their energies to evolve an alternative to Gandhism and the bourgeois Congress. This led them to form the Hindustan Republican Association (HRA) with the objective of establishing a "Federal Republic of the United States of India where there will not be any exploitation of man by man." The Constitution, objectives and the literature of the HRA clearly revealed the disenchantment with bourgeois leadership and the growing influence of the Bolshevik Revolution in Russia. Cutting themselves loose from the bonds of romanticism, the revolutionaries in India showed a clear proclivity towards democracy and socialism. Their ideological commitments to socialism became more pronounced with the passage of time. This ideological shift was clearly expressed in its manifesto *The*

Revolutionary in 1925. Despite their growing faith in socialism, they could not shed their religious commitments. They welcomed the new ideas from Russia but also appealed to follow in the footsteps of ancient Indian *rishis*. The HRA could not accept a materialistic world-view and the influence of traditionalism persisted. Yet, for the first time the revolutionary stream of the national movement moved towards socialism and felt the need for transforming the prevalent order of things along socialist lines.

The year 1928 constituted a landmark in the annals of the national revolutionary movemnt when the HRA adopted an advanced socialist and internationalist outlook owing to the efforts of Bhagat Singh and his comrades. Its name was also changed to Hindustan Socialist Republican Association (HSRA). Its existence came into light when its members avenged the death of Lajpat Rai by killing the police officer Saunders in Lahore in December 1928. Next, the party reacted against the repressive measures being enacted by the imperialist government to check the growth of communism and suppress the workers movement. Two bombs were thrown by Bhagat Singh and BK Dutt in the Assembly in April 1929 to broadcast the new gospel of socialist revolution and to express their determined opposition to the twin anti-people measures – the Public Safety Bill and the Trade Disputes Bill – which the Viceroy wanted passed through his special powers of certification. Several HSRA leaders were rounded up; yet, many of them remained active outside. An attempt was made to blow up the Viceregal Special in December 1929, which proved abortive. The act was condemned as 'dastardly' by Gandhi but, the resolution he moved to congratulate the Viceroy on his escape, could be passed only by a narrow margin. Gandhi, disparaging the revolutionary creed wrote 'The Cult of the Bomb' which prompted the revolutionary leaders to refute the allegations in their manifesto 'The Philosophy of the Bomb' in January 1930. This manifesto aimed at clearing innumerable misconceptions about the revolutionaries being spread among the people. These three daring acts of the HSRA brought imperialist wrath to an extreme and all prominent activists, except Azad, were put behind the bars.

The struggle did not cease even in jail and the revolutionaries took up the cause of political prisoners. A memorable hunger strike began against the imperialist policy of racial discrimination in prisons and in the process they sacrificed the life of Jatin Das. The believers in violence made a historic use of the weapon of soul-force. [482]

Chandrashekhar Azad was also killed in February 1931 in a police encounter in Allahabad. He had tried for the commutation of death sentences of the revolutionary trinity through various Congress leaders but failed. He even made attempts to send a few of his associates to Soviet Union to learn from their experience of revolutionary struggle. His death rendered the HSRA weak and ineffective.

The HSRA had as its public organisation the Naujawan Bharat Sabha, which openly propagated the ideals of revolution and socialism among people. It was founded in 1926 by Bhagat Singh and aimed at the organisation of workers and peasants. It inspired the youth to come forward and join in the revolutionary struggle against the imperialists. The Sabha had secular ideals. It was so popular that the Congress had to enlist its support for the success of the Civil Disobedience movement in the Punjab and Sindh in 1930-31. The Sabha was very active in mobilising public opinion against the Gandhi–Irwin Pact and in demanding the commutation of the death sentences of the trinity. During its short existence, till

---

482 In the polemics over violence and non-violence, physical force v/s soul force, the followers of the Mahatma waxed eloquent on Gandhi's use of soul-force expressed through fasts, satyagraha and self-suffering. Gandhi undoubtedly wielded enormous soul force and moral power but the revolutionaries possessed no less soul force and power of self suffering. Gandhi's fast never went beyond 21 days during which he took orange juice on 5th day on doctor's advice while the revolutionaries' spell of fasting was from 63 to 80 days without any intake.

1931, the Sabha infused a revolutionary socialist spirit among the people of the Western United Provinces and the Punjab.

In the popular imagination, the revolutionary fighters were men of unbounded courage, passionately committed to the freedom of the country but without any ideas of revolution and reconstruction. Contrary to this, HSRA members were men of high understanding and stood for the ideals of socialism. They had made a class analysis of the society and wished to change the prevalent socio-economic and political structure through armed revolution.[483] They wanted freedom for the 98% people instead of merely the 2% capitalists – native or foreign. The HSRA openly stood for the dictatorship of the proletariat. The belief in violence and terrorism did not emanate from their so-called love for shedding human blood. The HSRA stood for "surgical bloodshed" and "counter terrorism" to face the British terrorism. The party had no faith in traditional beliefs which, in its opinion, were bound to lead to religious fanaticism and obscurantism. Religion and God were the tools for exploiters to keep the masses in perpetual thraldom. The revolutionaries had clearly perceived the disintegrating forces inherent in the complex, polyglot socio-economic and religious structure of the Indian people.

Despite the progressive scientific approach of the HSRA, its appeal could not go beyond the lower middle class urban youth. Rural India remained unaware of the cries of 'Long Live Revolution' and 'Down with Imperialism' which reverberated only in the cities. The urge to die for the motherland decimated their ranks. Yet, the

---

483 The imperial Government dreaded the armed revolutionaries more than anything else in India. The closing years of the British rule revealed that it was the defection of the armed forces and its unreliability which became a major factor in the British decision to withdraw from India. The sequence of events from the Quit India movement to the INA demonstrations and Naval Ratings is unmistakable. The British helmsmen of the Indian administration had recognised that these revolutionary incidents had knocked the bottom of the British will to stay in India. The voluminous correspondence published in *Transfer of Power* is an eloquent testimony to this fact.

HSRA activists aroused the nation from its slumber and tried to give a socialist colour to the struggle for freedom.

The Congress and the revolutionaries had a strange love-hate relationship during this period of study. Gandhi, being obsessed with non-violence, remained adamant in his condemnation of the revolutionary acts. Others like Jawaharlal Nehru and Subhas Chandra Bose accepted non-violence merely as a policy and they often appreciated the spirit of sacrifice and suffering of the revolutionaries. The Congress cadre was always in sympathy with the revolutionary youth. In fact, there was an inner connection between the movements of the Congress and the revolutionaries. Not only did the rank and file of the Congress sympathise with the revolutionaries but many among the top brass of the Congress provided shelter and money to the revolutionaries. Many of the revolutionaries manned the Congress organisation at the district, tehsil and taluka levels. However, their allegience to Gandhi and their desire to be near the centre of power, which Gandhi undoubtedly was, locked their mouths and they could not come out openly in support of the revolutionary ideology.

APPENDIX A:

READING LIST OF BHAGAT SINGH

A.   The names of books and authors, read by Bhagat Singh, available from his unpublished diary, with his personal comments on the margins

1.   *Capital* by Karl Marx
2.   *The Origin of the Family, Private Property and the State* by Friedrich Engels
3.   *Where is Britain Going?* by Leon Trotsky
4.   *A World History for the Workers* by Alfred Barton
5.   *Rights of Man* by Tom Paine
6.   *The Cry for Justice* by Upton Sinclair
7.   *From Marx to Lenin* by Morris Hillquit
8.   *The Iron Heel* by Jack London
9.   *Wastes of Capitalism* by Theodor Hertzka
10.   *Children of the Dead End* by Patrick MacGill
11.   *Poverty and Riches* by Scott Nearing
12.   *The Lessons of October* by Leon Trotsky
13.   *Les Miserables* by Victor Hugo
14.   *Crime and Punishment* by Fyodor Dostoevsky
15.   *The House of the Dead* by Fyodor Dostoevsky
16.   *The New Spirit* by B C Pal
17.   *Indian Unrest* by Valentine Chirol
18.   *Tracticus Politicus* by Spinoza

19.　　*Citizen and Man* by Emile
20.　　*Essays in Application* by Henry Van Dyke

B.　　The list of books read, available from the letter of Bhagat Singh, written to his friend Jaidev from the prison on July 24, 1930:

1.　　*Militarism*
2.　　*Why Men Fight*
3.　　*Soviets at Work*
4.　　*Collapse of the Second International*
5.　　*Left Wing Communism*
6.　　*Mutual Aid*
7.　　*Fields, Factories and Workshops*
8.　　*Civil War in France*
9.　　*Land Revolution in Russia*
10.　　*Theory of Historical Materialism*

C.　　The names of authors and poets read by Bhagat Singh, available from his diary:

Bertrand Russell, JS Mill, Thomas Jefferson, Karl Kautsky, Nikolai Bukharin, Edmund Burke, VI Lenin, Thomas Aquinas, John Locke, Austin, Georges Danton, Charles Edward Russell, Omar Khayyam, James Russell Lowell, William Wordsworth, Lord Tennyson, VN Figner, Rabindranath Tagore, NA Morozov, Horace Greeley, Wendell Phillips, Frederic Harrison, J Campbell, George D Herrson, Herbert Spencer, Henry Maine, Jean-Jacques Rousseau.

To Make the Deaf Hear
Notice of Hindustan Socialist Republican Association

This is the text of the leaflet thrown by Bhagat Singh and Batukeshwar Dutt in the Central Legislative Assembly on April 8, 1929, after the bomb explosion. It briefly outlined the objectives of the revolutionary party and categorically declared that they wanted 'to make the deaf hear'.

"It takes a loud voice to make the deaf hear." With these immortal words uttered on a similar occasion by Valliant, a French anarchist martyr, do we strongly justify this action of ours.

Without repeating the humiliating history of the past ten years of the working of the reforms and without mentioning the insults hurled down on the head of the Indian nation through this House, the so-called Indian Parliament, we see that this time again, while the people expecting some more crumbs of reforms from the Simon Commission, are ever quarrelling over the distribution of the expected bones, the Govt. is thrusting upon us new repressive measures like those of the Public Safety and Trade Disputes Bill, while reserving the Press Sedition Bill for the next session. The indiscriminate arrests of labour leaders working in the open field clearly indicate whither the wind blows.

In these extremely provocative circumstances, the Hindustan Socialist Republican Association, in all seriousness, realising the full responsibility, had decided and ordered its army to do this particular action, so that a stop be put to this humiliating farce and to let the alien bureaucratic exploiters do what they wish, but to make them come before the public eye in their naked form.

Let the representatives of the people return to their constituencies and prepare the masses for the coming revolution. And let the Government know that, while protesting against the Public Safety and Trade Disputes Bills and the callous murder of Lala Lajpat Rai on behalf of the helpless Indian masses, we want to emphasise the lesson often repeated by history that it is easy to kill individuals but you cannot kill the ideas. Great empires crumbled but the ideas survived. Bourbons and Czars fell while the revolution marched ahead triumphantly.

We are sorry to admit that we who attach so great a sanctity to human life, who dream of a glorious future, when man will be enjoying perfect peace and full liberty, have been forced to shed human blood. But the sacrifice of individuals at the altar of the great revolution that will bring freedom to all, rendering the exploitation of man by man impossible, is inevitable.

Long Live The Revolution!

Sd/_
Balraj
Commander-in-Chief

Statement in the Sessions Court

This is the oft-cited statement of Bhagat Singh and BK Dutt, which was read out by Mr Asaf Ali in the Sessions Court on June 6 1929. It was drafted by Bhagat Singh and remains an important policy document on the aims and objectives of the revolutionary movement.

We stand charged with certain serious offences, and at this stage it is but right that we must explain our conduct.

In this connection, the following questions arise:

1. Were the bombs thrown into Chamber, and, if so, why?
2. Is the charge, as framed by the Lower Court, correct or otherwise?

To the first half of first question, our reply is in the affirmative, but since some of the so-called 'eye witnesses' have perjured themselves and since we are not denying our liability to that extent, let our statement about them be judged for what it is worth. By way of an illustration, we may point out that the evidence of Sergeant Terry regarding the seizure of the pistol from one of us is a deliberate falsehood, for neither of us had the pistol at the time we gave ourselves up. Other witnesses, too, who have deposed to having seen bombs being thrown by us have not scrupled to tell lies. This fact had its own moral for those who aim at judicial purity and fair play.

At the same time, we acknowledge the fairness of the Public Prosecutor and the judicial attitude of the Court so far.

Viceroy's Views Endorsed

In our reply to the next half of the first question, we are constrained to go into some detail to offer a full and frank explanation of our motive and the circumstances leading up to what has now become a historic event.

When we were told by some of the police officers, who visited us in jail, that Lord Irwin, in his address to the joint session of the two houses described the event as an attack directed against no individual but against an institution itself, we readily recognized that the true significance of the incident had been correctly appreciated.

We are next to none in our love for humanity. Far from having any malice against any individual, we hold human life sacred beyond words.

We are neither perpetrators of dastardly outrages, and, therefore, a disgrace to the country, as the pseudo-socialist Dewan Chaman Lal is reported to have described us, nor are we 'lunatics' as *The Tribune* of Lahore and some others would have it believed.

Practical Protest

We humbly claim to be no more than serious students of the history and conditions of our country and her aspirations. We despise hypocrisy. Our practical protest was against the institution, which since its birth, has eminently helped to display not only its worthlessness but its far-reaching power for mischief. The more we have pondered, the more deeply we have been convinced that it exists only to demonstrate to the world India's humiliation and helplessness, and it symbolises the overriding domination of an irresponsible and autocratic rule. Time and again the national demand has been pressed by the people's representatives only to find the waste paper basket as its final destination.

Attack on Institution

Solemn resolutions passed by the House have been contemptuously trampled underfoot on the floor of the so called Indian Parliament. Resolutions regarding the repeal of the repressive and arbitrary measures have been treated with sublime contempt, and the Government measures and proposals, rejected as unacceptable by the elected members of the legislatures, have been restored by mere stroke of the pen. In short, we have utterly failed to find any justification for the existence of an institution which, despite all its pomp and splendour, organised with the hard earned money of the sweating millions of India, is only a hollow show and a mischievous make-believe. Alike, have we failed to comprehend the mentality of the public leaders who help the Government to squander public time and money on such a manifestly stage-managed exhibition of India's helpless subjection.

No Hope for Labour

We have been ruminating upon all these matters, as also upon the wholesale arrests of the leaders of the labour movement when the introduction of the Trade Disputes Bill brought us into the Assembly to watch its progress. The course of the debate only served to confirm our conviction that the labouring millions of India had nothing to expect from an institution that stood as a menacing monument to the strangling of the exploited and the serfdom of the helpless labourers.

Finally, the insult of what we consider, an inhuman and barbarous measure was hurled on the devoted heads of the representatives of the entire country, and the starving and struggling millions were deprived of their primary right and the sole means of improving their economic welfare. None who has felt like us for the dumb-driven drudges of labourers could possibly witness this spectacle with equanimity. None whose heart bleeds for them, who have given their life-blood in silence to the building up of the economic structure, could repress the cry which this ruthless blow had wrung out of our hearts.

Bomb Needed

Consequently, bearing in mind the words of the late Mr SR Das, once Law Member of the Governor-General's Executive Council, which appeared in the famous letter he had addressed to his son, to the effect that the 'Bomb was necessary to awaken England from her dreams', we dropped the bomb on the floor of the Assembly Chamber to register our protest on behalf of those who had no other means left to give expression to their heart-rending agony. Our sole purpose was "to make the deaf hear" and to give the heedless a timely warning. Others have as keenly felt as we have done, and from under the seeming stillness of the sea of Indian humanity, a veritable storm is about to break out. We have only hoisted the "danger-signal" to warn those who are speeding along without heeding the grave dangers ahead. We have only marked the end of an era of 'Utopian non-violence,' of whose futility the rising generation has been convinced beyond the shadow of doubt.

Ideal Explained

We have used the expression Utopian non-violence, in the foregoing paragraph, which requires some explanation. Force when aggressively applied is "violence" and is, therefore, morally unjustifiable, but when it is used in the furtherance of a legitimate cause, it has its moral justification. The elimination of force at all costs is Utopian, and the new movement which has arisen in the country, and of that dawn we have given a warning, is inspired by the ideals which guided Guru Gobind Singh and Shivaji, Kamal Pasha and Riza Khan, Washington and Garibaldi, Lafayette and Lenin.

As both the alien government and the Indian public leaders appeared to have shut their eyes to the existence of this movement, we felt it is our duty to sound a warning where it could not go unheard.

We have so far dealt with the motive behind the incident in question, and now we must define the extent of our intention.

No Personal Grudge

We bore no personal grudge or malice against anyone of those who received slight injuries or against any other person in the Assembly. On the contrary, we repeat that we hold human life sacred beyond words, and would sooner lay down our own lives in the service of humanity than injure anyone else. Unlike the mercenary soldiers of the imperialist armies who are disciplined to kill without compunction, we respect, and, in so far as it lies in our power, we attempt to save human life. And still we admit to having deliberately thrown the bombs into the Assembly Chamber. Facts speak for themselves and our intention would be judged from the result of the action without bringing in Utopian hypothetical circumstances and presumptions.

No Miracle

Despite the evidence of the Government expert, the bombs that were thrown in the Assembly Chamber resulted in slight damage to an empty bench and some slight abrasions in less than half a dozen cases. While Government scientists and experts have ascribed this result to a miracle, we see nothing but a precisely scientific process in all this incident. Firstly, the two bombs exploded in vacant spaces within the wooden barriers of the desks and benches; secondly, even those who were within 2 feet of the explosion, for instance, Mr P Rau, Mr Shanker Rao and Sir George Schuster were either not hurt or only slightly scratched. Bombs of the capacity deposed to by the Government expert (though his estimate, being imaginary, is exaggerated), loaded with an effective charge of potassium chlorate and sensitive (explosive) picrate, would have smashed the barriers and laid many low within some yards of the explosion.

Again, had they been loaded with some other high explosive, with a charge of destructive pellets or darts, they would have sufficed to wipe out a majority of the Members of the Legislative Assembly. Still again we could have flung them into the official box which was occupied by some notable persons. And finally we could have ambushed Sir John Simon whose luckless Commission was loathed by all responsible people and who was sitting in the President's gallery at the time. All these things, however, were beyond our intention and bombs did no more than they were designed to do, and the miracle consisted in no more than the deliberate aim which landed them in safe places.

We then deliberately offered ourselves to bear the penalty for what we had done and to let the imperialist exploiters know that by crushing individuals, they cannot kill ideas. By crushing two insignificant units, a nation cannot be crushed. We wanted to emphasise the historical lesson that lettres de cachets and Bastilles could not crush the revolutionary movement in France. Gallows and the Siberian mines could not extinguish the Russian Revolution. Bloody Sunday, and Black and Tans failed to strangle the movement of Irish freedom.

Can ordinances and Safety Bills snuff out the flames of freedom in India? Conspiracy cases, trumped up or discovered, and the incarceration of all young men who cherish the vision of a great ideal, cannot check the march of revolution. But a timely warning, if not unheeded, can help to prevent loss of life and general sufferings.

We took it upon ourselves to provide this warning and our duty is done.

"Revolution" does not necessarily involve sanguinary strife nor is there any place in it for individual vendetta. It is not the cult of the bomb and the pistol. By "Revolution" we mean that the present order of things, which is based on manifest injustice, must change. Producers or labourers, in spite of being the most necessary element of society, are robbed by their exploiters of their labour and deprived of their elementary rights. The peasant who grows corn for all, starves with his family; the weaver who supplies the world market with textile fabrics, has not enough to cover his own and his children's bodies; masons, smiths and carpenters who raise magnificent palaces, live like pariahs in the slums. The capitalists and exploiters, the parasites of society, squander millions on their whims. These terrible inequalities and forced disparity of chances are bound to lead to chaos. This state of affairs cannot last long, and it is obvious, that the present order of society in merry-making is on the brink of a volcano.

The whole edifice of this civilisation, if not saved in time, shall crumble. A radical change, therefore, is necessary and it is the duty of those who realise it to reorganise society on the socialistic basis. Unless this thing is done and the exploitation of man by man and of nations by nations is brought to an end, sufferings and carnage with which humanity is threatened today cannot be prevented. All talk of ending war and ushering in an era of universal peace is undisguised hypocrisy.

By "Revolution", we mean the ultimate establishment of an order of society which may not be threatened by such breakdown, and in which the sovereignty of the proletariat should be recognised and a world federation should redeem humanity from the bondage of capitalism and misery of imperial wars.

This is our ideal, and with this ideology as our inspiration, we have given a fair and loud enough warning.

If, however, it goes unheeded and the present system of government continues to be an impediment in the way of the natural forces that are swelling up, a grim struggle will ensure involving the overthrow of all obstacles, and the establishment of the dictatorship of the proletariat to pave the way for the consummation of the ideal of revolution. Revolution is an inalienable right of mankind. Freedom is an imperishable birth right of all. Labour is the real sustainer of society. The sovereignty of the people is the ultimate destiny of the workers.

For these ideals, and for this faith, we shall welcome any suffering to which we may be condemned. At the altar of this revolution we have brought our youth as an incense, for no sacrifice is too great for so magnificent a cause. We are content, we await the advent of Revolution.

Long Live the Revolution!

Why I Am An Atheist

This is the most extensive and serious piece of writing left behind by Bhagat Singh. He wrote this in response to a prisoner's taunt in the jail that he will pray for his life once his end is near. Instead Bhagat Singh wrote this article a few days before he was hanged. He boldly put down his views on religion in this pamphlet, which was smuggled out and published in *The People* on September 27, 1931.

A new question has cropped up. Is it due to vanity that I do not believe in the existence of an omnipotent, omnipresent and omniscient God? I had never imagined that I would ever have to confront such a question. But conversation with some friends has given me, a hint that certain of my friends, if I am not claiming too much in thinking them to be so, are inclined to conclude from the brief contact they have had with me, that it was too much on my part to deny the existence of God and that there was a certain amount of vanity that actuated my disbelief. Well, the problem is a serious one. I do not boast to be quite above these human traits. I am a man and nothing more. None can claim to be more. I also have this weakness in me. Vanity does form a part of my nature. Amongst my comrades I was called an autocrat. Even my friend Mr BK Dutt sometimes called me so. On certain occasions I was decried as a despot. Some friends do complain and very seriously too that I involuntarily thrust my opinions upon others and get my proposals accepted. That this is true up to a certain extent, I do not deny. This may amount to egotism. There is vanity in me in as much as our cult as opposed to other popular creeds is concerned.

But that is not personal. It may be, it is only legitimate pride in our cult and does not amount to vanity. Vanity or to be more precise "Ahankar" is the excess of undue pride in one's self. Whether it is such an undue pride that has led me to atheism or whether it is after very careful study of the subject and after much consideration that I have come to disbelieve in God, is a question that I, intend to discuss here. Let me first make it clear that egotism and vanity are two different things.

In the first place, I have altogether failed to comprehend as to how undue pride or vaingloriousness could ever stand in the way of a man in believing in God. I can refuse to recognize the greatness of a really great man provided I have also achieved a certain amount of popularity without deserving it or without having possessed the qualities really essential or indispensible for the same purpose. That much is conceivable. But in what way can a man believing in God cease believing due to his personal vanity? There are only two Ways. The man should either begin to think himself a rival of God or he may begin to believe himself to be God. In neither case can he become a genuine atheist. In the first case he does not even deny the existence of his rival. In the second case as well he admits the existence of a conscious being behind the screen guiding all the movements of nature. It is of no importance to us whether he thinks himself to be that supreme being or whether he thinks the supreme conscious being to be somebody apart from himself. The fundamental is there. His belief is there. He is by no means an atheist. Well, here I am. I neither belong to the first category nor to the second. I deny the very existence of that Almighty Supreme Being. Why I deny it shall be dealt with later on. Here I want to clear one thing, that it is not vanity that has actuated me to adopt the doctrines of atheism. I am neither a rival nor an incarnation nor the Supreme Being Himself. One point is decided, that it is not vanity that has led me to this mode of thinking. Let me examine the facts to disprove this allegation. According to these friends of mine I have grown vainglorious perhaps due to the undue popularity gained during the trials – both Delhi Bomb and Lahore conspiracy cases. Well, let us see if their premises are correct. My atheism is not of so recent origin. I had stopped believing in God when I was an obscure young man, of whose existence my above-mentioned friends were not even aware. At least a college student cannot cherish any sort of undue pride which may lead him to atheism. Though a favourite with some professors and disliked by certain others, I was never an industrious or a studious boy. I could not get any chance of indulging in such feelings as vanity. I was rather a boy with a very shy nature, who had certain pessimistic dispositions about the future career. And in those days, I was not a perfect atheist. My grandfather under whose influence I was brought up is an orthodox Arya Samajist. An Arya Samajist is anything but an atheist. After finishing my primary education I joined the DAV School of Lahore and stayed in its Boarding House for full one year. There, apart from morning and evening prayers, I used to recite "Gayatri Mantra" for hours and hours. I was a perfect devotee in those days. Later on I began to live with my father. He is a liberal in as much as the orthodoxy of religions is concerned. It was through his teachings that I aspired to devote my life to the cause of freedom. But he is not an atheist. He is a firm believer. He used to encourage me for offering prayers daily. So, this is how I was brought up. In the Non-Co-operation days I joined the National College. It was there that I began to think liberally and discuss and criticise all the religious problems, even about God. But still I was a devout believer. By that time I had begun to preserve the unshorn and unclipped long hair but I could never believe in the mythology and doctrines of Sikhism or, any other religion. But I had a firm faith in God's existence.

Later on I joined the revolutionary party. The first leader with whom I came in contact, though not convinced, could not dare to deny the existence of God. On my persistent inquiries about God, he used to say, "Pray whenever you want to". Now this is atheism with less courage required for the adoption of that creed. The second leader with whom I came in contact was a firm believer. Let me mention his name – respected comrade Sachindra Nath Sanyal, now undergoing life transportation in connection with the Karachi conspiracy case. From the every first page of his famous and only book, *Bandi Jivan* (or Incarcerated Life), the Glory of God is sung vehemently. In the last page of the second part of that beautiful book his mysticism – because of vedantism – praises showered upon God form a very conspicuous part of his thoughts. "The Revolutionary leaflet" distributed throughout India on January 28th 1925, was according to the prosecution story the result of his intellectual labour. Now, as is inevitable in the secret work the prominent leader expresses his own views which are very dear to his person and the rest of the workers have to acquiesce in them – in spite of differences, which they might have. In that leaflet one full paragraph was devoted to praise the Almighty and His rejoicings and doing. That is all mysticism. What I wanted to point out was that the idea of disbelief had not even germinated in the revolutionary party. The famous Kakori martyrs – all four of them – passed their last day in prayers. Ram Prasad Bismil was an orthodox Arya Samajist. Despite his wide studies in the field of Socialism and Communism, Rajen Lahiri could not suppress his desire, of reciting hymns of the Upanishads and the Gita. I saw only one man amongst them, who never prayed and used to say, "Philosophy is the outcome of human weakness or limitation of knowledge". He is also undergoing a sentence of transportation for life. But he also never dared to deny the existence of God.

Up to that period I was only a romantic idealist revolutionary. Uptil then we were to follow. Now came the time to shoulder the whole responsibility. Due to the inevitable reaction, for some time, the very existence of the Party seemed impossible. Enthusiastic comrades – nay leaders – began to jeer at us. For some time I was afraid that some day I also might be convinced of the futility of our own programme. That was a turning point in my revolutionary career. "Study" was the cry that reverberated in the corridors of my mind. Study to enable yourself to face the arguments advanced by opposition. Study to arm yourself with arguments in favour of your cult. I began to study. My previous faith and convictions underwent a remarkable modification. The romance of the violent methods alone which was so prominent amongst our predecessors, was replaced by serious ideas. No more mysticism, no more blind faith. Realism became our cult. Use of force justifiable when resorted to as a matter of terrible necessity: non-violence as policy indispensable for all mass movements. So much about methods. The most important thing was the clear conception of the ideal for which we were to fight. As there were no important activities in the field of action I got ample opportunity to study various ideals of the world revolution. I studied Bakunin, the anarchist leader, something of Marx, the father of Communism and much of Lenin, Trotsky and others, the men who had successfully carried out a revolution in their country. They were all atheists, Bakunin's "God and State", though only fragmentary, is an interesting study of the subject. Later I came across a book entitled Common Sense by Nirlamba Swami. It was only a sort of mystic atheism. This subject became of utmost interest to me. By the end of 1926 I had been convinced as to the baselessness of the theory of existence of an Almighty Supreme Being who created, guided and controlled the universe. I had given out this disbelief of mine. I begin discussion on the subjects with my friends. I had become a pronounced atheist. But, what it meant will presently be discussed.

In May 1927 I was arrested at Lahore. The arrest was a surprise. I was quite unaware of the fact that the police wanted me. All of a sudden while passing through a garden I found myself surrounded by police. To my own surprise, I was very calm at that time. I did not feel any sensation, neither did I experience any excitement. I was taken into police custody. Next day I was taken to the Railway Police lock-up where I was to pass one full month. After many days conversation with the Police officials I guessed that they had some information regarding my connexion with the Kakori Party and my other activities in connection with the revolutionary movement. They told me that I had been to Lucknow while the trial was going on there, that I had negotiated a certain scheme about their rescue, that after obtaining their approval, we had procured some bombs, that by way of test one of the bombs was thrown in the crowd on the occasion of Dussehra 1926. They further informed me, in my interest, that if I could give any statement throwing some light on the activities of the revolutionary party, I was not to be imprisoned but on the contrary set free and rewarded even without being produced as an approver in the Court. I laughed at the proposal. It was all humbug. People holding ideas like ours do not throw bombs on their own innocent people. One fine morning Mr Newman, the then Senior Superintendent of CID, came to me. And after much sympathetic talk with me imparted the extremely sad news that if I did not give any statement as demanded by them, they would be forced to send me up for trial for conspiracy to wage war in connection with Kakori Case and for brutal murders in connection with Dussehra Bomb outrage. And he further informed me that they had evidence enough to get me convicted and hanged. In those days I believed – though I was quite innocent – the police could do it if they desired. That very day certain police officials began to persuade me to offer my prayers to God regularly both the times. Now I was an atheist. I wanted to settle for myself whether it was in the days of peace and enjoyment alone that I could boast of being an atheist or whether during such hard times as well I could stick to those principles of mine. After great consideration I decided that I could not lead myself to believe in and pray to God. No, I never did. That was the real test and I came out successful. Never for a moment did I desire to save my neck at the cost of certain other things. So I was a staunch disbeliever: and have ever since been. It was not an easy job to stand that test. 'Belief' softens the hardships, even can make them pleasant. In God man can find very strong consolation and support. Without Him, man has to depend upon himself. To stand upon one's own legs amid storms and hurricanes is not a child's play. At such testing moments, vanity – if any – evaporates, and man cannot dare to defy the general beliefs, if he does, then we must conclude that he has got certain other strength than mere vanity. This is exactly the situation now. Judgment is already too well known. Within a week it is to be pronounced. What is the consolation with the exception of the idea that I am going to sacrifice my life for a cause? A God-believing Hindu might be expecting to be reborn as a king, a Muslim or a Christian, might dream of the luxuries to be enjoyed in paradise and the reward he is to get for his sufferings and sacrifices. But what am I to expect? I know the moment the rope is fitted round my neck and rafters removed, from under my feet. That will be the final moment – that will be the last moment. I, or to be more precise, my soul, as interpreted in the metaphysical terminology, shall all be finished there. Nothing further. A short life of struggle with no such magnificent end, shall in itself be the reward if I have the courage to take it in that light. That is all. With no selfish motive, or desire to be awarded here or hereafter, quite disinterestedly have I devoted my life to the cause of independence, because I could not do otherwise. The day we find a great number of men and women with this psychology who cannot devote themselves to anything else than the service of mankind and emancipation of the suffering humanity; that day shall inaugurate the era of liberty. Not to become a king, nor to gain any other rewards here, or in the next birth or after death in paradise, shall they be inspired to challenge the oppressors, exploiters, and tyrants, but to cast off the yoke of serfdom from the neck of humanity and to establish liberty and peace shall they tread this – to their individual selves perilous and to their noble selves the only glorious imaginable – path. Is the pride in their noble cause to be misinterpreted as vanity? Who dares to utter such an abominable epithet? To him, I say either he is a fool or a knave. Let us forgive him for he can not realize the depth, the emotion, the sentiment and the noble feelings that surge in that heart. His heart is dead as a mere lump of flesh, his eyes are weak, the evils of other interests having been cast over them. Self-reliance is always liable to be interpreted as vanity. It is sad and miserable but there is no help.

You go and oppose the prevailing faith, you go and criticise a hero, a great man, who is generally believed to be above criticism because he is thought to be infallible, the strength of your argument shall force the multitude to decry you as vainglorious. This is due to the mental stagnation. Criticism and independent thinking are the two indispensable qualities of a revolutionary. Because Mahatamaji is great, therefore none should criticise him. Because he has risen above, therefore everything he says – may be in the field of Politics or Religion, Economics or Ethics – is right. Whether you are convinced or not you must say, "Yes, that's true". This mentality does not lead towards progress. It is rather too obviously, reactionary.

Because our forefathers had set up a faith in some Supreme Being – the Almighty God – therefore any man who dares to challenge the validity of that faith, or the very existence of that Supreme Being, he shall have to be called an apostate, a renegade. If his arguments are too sound to be refuted by counter arguments and spirit too strong to be cowed down by the threat of misfortunes that may befall him by the wrath of the Almighty – he shall be decried as vainglorious, his spirit to be denominated as vanity. Then why to waste time in this vain discussion? Why try to argue out the whole thing? This question is coming before the public for the first time, and is being handled in this matter of fact way for the first time, hence this lengthy discussion.

As for the first question, I think I have cleared that it is not vanity that has led me to atheism. My way of argument has proved to be convincing or not, that is to be judged by my readers, not me. I know in the present circumstances, my faith in God would have made my life easier, my burden lighter and my disbelief in Him has turned all the circumstances too dry and the situation may assume too harsh a shape. A little bit of mysticism can make it poetical. But I, do not want the help of any intoxication to meet my fate. I am a realist. I have been trying to overpower the instinct in me by the help of reason. I have not always been successful in achieving this end. But man's duty is to try and endeavour, success depends upon chance and environments.

As for the second question that if it was not vanity, then there ought to be some reason to disbelieve the old and still prevailing faith of the existence of God. Yes. I come to that now. Reason there is. According to me, any man who has got some reasoning power at his command always tries to reason out his environments. Where direct proofs are lacking philosophy occupies the important place. As I have already stated, a certain revolutionary friend used to say that Philosophy is the outcome of human weakness. When our ancestors had leisure enough to try to solve out the mystery of this world, its past, present and the future, its whys and wherefores, they having been terribly short of direct proofs, everybody tried to solve the problem in his own way. Hence we find the wide differences in the fundamentals of various religious creeds, which some times assume very antagonistic and conflicting shapes. Not only the Oriental and Occidental philosophies differ, there are differences even amongst various schools of thoughts in each hemisphere. Amongst Oriental religions, the Moslem faith is not at all compatible with Hindu faith. In India alone Buddhism and Jainism are sometimes quite separate from Brahmanism, in which there are again conflicting faiths as Arya Samaj and Sanatan Dharma. Charwak is still another independent thinker of the past ages. He challenged the authority of God in the old times. All these creeds differ from each other on the fundamental question. And everybody considers himself to be on the right. There lies the misfortune. Instead of using the experiments and expressions of the ancient Savants and thinkers as a basis for our future struggle against ignorance and to try to find out a solution to this mysterious problem, we lethargical as we have proved to be raise the hue and cry of faith, unflinching and unwavering faith to their versions and thus are guilty of stagnation in human progress.

Any man who stands for progress has to criticise, disbelieve and challenge every item of the old faith. Item by item he has to reason out every nook and corner of the prevailing faith. If after considerable reasoning one is led to believe in any theory or philosophy, his faith is welcomed. His reasoning can be mistaken, wrong, misled and sometimes fallacious. But he is liable to correction because reason is the guiding star of his life. But mere faith and blind faith is dangerous: it dulls the brain and makes a man reactionary. A man who claims to be a realist has to challenge the whole of the ancient faith. If it does not stand the onslaught of reason it crumbles down. Then the first thing for him is to shatter the whole down and clear a space for the erection of a new philosophy. This is the negative side. After it begins the positive work in which, sometimes, some material of the old faith may be used for the purpose of reconstruction. As far as I am concerned, let me admit at the very outset that I have not been able to study much on this point. I had a great desire to study the Oriental Philosophy but I could not get any chance or opportunity to do the same. But so far as the negative study is under discussion, I think I am convinced to the extent of questioning the soundness of the old faith. I have been convinced as to non-existence of a conscious Supreme Being who is guiding and directing the movements of nature. We believe in nature and the whole progressive movement aims at the domination of man over nature for his service. There is no conscious power behind it to direct. This is what our philosophy is.

As for the negative side, we ask a few questions from the 'believers':

(1) If, as you believe, there is an almighty, omnipresent, omniscient and omnipotent God – who created the earth or world, please let me know why did he create it? This world of woes and miseries, a veritable, eternal combination of numberless tragedies: Not a single soul being perfectly satisfied.

Pray, don't say that it is His Law: If he is bound by any law, he is not omnipotent. He is another slave like ourselves. Please don't say that it is his enjoyment. Nero burnt one Rome. He killed a very limited number of people. He created very few tragedies, all to his perfect enjoyment. And what is his place in history? By what names do the historians mention him? All the venomous epithets are showered upon him. Pages are blackened with invective diatribes condemning Nero, the tyrant, the heartless, the wicked. One Changez Khan sacrificed a few thousand lives to seek pleasure in it and we hate the very name. Then how are you going to justify your almighty, eternal Nero, who has been, and is still causing numberless tragedies every day, every hour and every minute? How do you think to support his misdoings which surpass those of Changez every single moment? I say why did he create this world – a veritable hell, a place of constant and bitter unrest? Why did the Almighty create man when he had the power not to do it? What is the justification for all this? Do you say to award the innocent sufferers hereafter and to punish the wrong-doers as well? Well, well: How far shall you justify a man who may dare to inflict wounds upon your body to apply a very soft and soothing liniment upon it afterwards? How far the supporters and organisers of the Gladiator Institution were justified in throwing men before the half starved furious lions to be cared for and well looked after if they could survive and could manage to escape death by the wild beasts? That is why I ask, Why did the conscious Supreme Being create this world and man in it? To seek pleasure? Where then is the difference between him and Nero?

You Mohammadens and Christians: Hindu Philosophy shall still linger on to offer another argument. I ask you what is your answer to the above-mentioned question? You don't believe in previous birth. Like Hindus you cannot advance the argument of previous misdoings of the apparently quite innocent sufferers? I ask you why did the omnipotent labour for six days to create the world through word and each day to say that all was well. Call him today. Show him the past history. Make him study the present situation. Let us see if he dares to say, "All is well".

From the dungeons of prisons, from the stores of starvation consuming millions upon millions of human beings in slums and huts, from the exploited labourers, patiently or say apathetically watching the procedure of their blood being sucked by the Capitalist vampires, and the wastage of human energy that will make a man with the least common sense shiver with horror, and from the preference of throwing the surplus of production in oceans rather than to distribute amongst the needy producers – to the palaces of kings built upon the foundation laid with human bones....let him see all this and let him say "All is well". Why and wherefore? That is my question. You are silent. All right then, I proceed. Well, you Hindus, you say all the present sufferers belong to the class of sinners of the previous births. Good. You say the present oppressors were saintly people in their previous births, hence they enjoy power. Let me admit that your ancestors were very shrewed people, they tried to find out theories strong enough to hammer down all the efforts of reason and disbelief. But let us analyse how far this argument can really stand.

From the point of view of the most famous jurists punishment can be justified only from three or four ends to meet which it is inflicted upon the wrongdoer. They are retributive, reformative and deterrent. The retributive theory is now being condemned by all the advanced thinkers. Deterrent theory is also following the same fate. Reformative theory is the only one which is essential, and indispensable for human progress. It aims at returning the offender as a most competent and a peace-loving citizen to the society. But what is the nature of punishment inflicted by God upon men even if we suppose them to be offenders. You say he sends them to be born as a cow, a cat, a tree, a herb or a beast. You enumerate these punishments to be 84 lakhs. I ask you what is its reformative effect upon man? How many men have met you who say that they were born as a donkey in previous birth for having committed any sin? None. Don't quote your Puranas. I have no scope to touch your mythologies. Moreover do you know that the greatest sin in this world is to be poor. Poverty is a sin, it is a punishment. I ask you how far would you appreciate a criminologist, a jurist or a legislator who proposes such measures of punishment which shall inevitably force man to commit more offences? Had not your God thought of this or he also had to learn these things by experience, but at the cost of untold sufferings to be borne by humanity? What do you think shall be the fate of a man who has been born in a poor and illiterate family of say a chamar or a sweeper. He is poor, hence he cannot study. He is hated and shunned by his fellow human beings who think themselves to be his superiors having been born in say a higher caste. His ignorance, his poverty and the treatment meted out to him shall harden his heart towards society. Suppose he commits a sin, who shall bear the consequences? God, he or the learned ones of the society? What about the punishment of those people who were deliberately kept ignorant by the haughty and egotist Brahmans and who had to pay the penalty by bearing the stream of being led (not lead) in their ears for having heard a few sentences of your Sacred Books of learning – the Vedas? If they committed any offence – who was to be responsible for them and who was to bear the brunt? My dear friends: These theories are the inventions of the privileged ones: They justify their usurped power, riches and superiority by the help of these theories. Yes: It was perhaps Upton Sinclair, who wrote at some place, that just make a man a believer in immortality and then rob him of all his riches, and possessions. He shall help you even in that ungrudgingly. The coalition amongst the religious preachers and possessors of power brought forth jails, gallows, knouts and these theories.

I ask why your omnipotent God, does not stop every man; when he is committing any sin or offence? He can do it quite easily. Why did he not kill warlords or kill the fury of war in them and thus avoid the catastrophe hurled down on the head of humanity by the Great War? Why does he not just produce a certain sentiment in the mind of the British people to liberate India? Why does he not infuse the altruistic enthusiasm in the hearts of all capitalists to forgo their rights of personal possessions of means of production and thus redeem the whole labouring community – nay the whole human society – from the bondage of Capitalism. You want to reason out the practicability of socialist theory, I leave it for your Almighty to enforce it. People recognize the merits of socialism in as much as the general welfare is concerned. They oppose it under the pretext of its being impracticable. Let the Almighty step in and arrange everything in an orderly fashion. Now don't try to advance round about arguments, they are out of order. Let me tell you, British rule is here not because God wills it but because they possess power and we do not dare to oppose them. Not that it is with the help of God that they are keeping us under their subjection but it is with the help of guns and rifles, bombs and bullets, police and militia and our apathy that they are successfully committing the most deplorable sin against society – the outrageous exploitation of one nation by another. Where is God? What is he doing? Is he enjoying all these woes of human race? A Nero; a Changez: Down with him.

Do you ask me how I explain the origin of this world and origin of man? Alright I tell you. Charles Darwin has tried to throw some light on the subject. Study him. Read Soham Swam's Common Sense. It shall answer your question to some extent. This is a phenomenon of nature. The accidental mixture of different substances in the shape of nebulae produced this earth. When? Consult history. The same process produced animals and in the long run man. Read Darwin's Origin of Species. And all the later progress is due to man's constant conflict with nature and his efforts to override it. This is the briefest possible explanation of this phenomenon.

Your other argument may be just to ask why a child is born blind or lame if not due to his deeds committed in the previous birth? This problem has been explained away by biologists as a mere biological phenomenon. According to them the whole burden rests upon the shoulders of the parents whose deeds, may be conscious or ignorant, previous to the birth of the child, led to its mutilation.

Naturally you may ask another question – though it is quite childish in essence. If no God existed, how did the people come to believe in him? My answer is clear and brief. As they came to believe in ghosts, and evil spirits; the only difference is that belief in God is almost universal and the philosophy well developed. Unlike certain of the radicals I would not attribute its origin to the ingenuity of the exploiters who wanted to keep the people under their subjection by preaching the existence of a Supreme Being and then claiming an authority and sanction from him for their privileged positions. Though I do not differ with them on the essential point that all faiths, religions, creeds and such other institutions became in turn the mere supporters of the tyrannical and exploiting institutions, men and classes. Rebellion against king is always a sin according to every religion.

As regards the origin of God my own idea is that having realised the limitations of man, his weaknesses and shortcomings having been taken into consideration, God was brought into imaginary existence to encourage man to face boldly all the trying circumstances, to meet all dangers manfully and to check and restrain his outbursts in prosperity and affluence. God, both with his private laws and parental generosity was imagined and painted in greater details. He was to serve as a deterrent factor when his fury and private laws were discussed so that man may not become a danger to society. He was to serve as a father, mother, sister and brother, friend and helper when His parental qualifications were to be explained. So that when man be in great distress having been betrayed and deserted by all friends he may find consolation in the idea that an ever true friend was still there to help him, to support him and that He was Almighty and could do anything. Really that was useful to the society in the primitive age. The idea of God is helpful to man in distress.

Society has to fight out this belief as well as the idol worship and the narrow conception of religion. Similarly, when man tries to stand on his own legs, and become a realist he shall have to throw the faith aside, and to face manfully all the distress, trouble, in which the circumstances may throw him. That is exactly my state of affairs. It is not my vanity, my friends. It is my mode of thinking that has made me an atheist. I don't know whether in my case belief in God and offering of daily prayers which I consider to be most selfish and degraded act on the part of man, whether these prayers can prove to be helpful or they shall make my case worse still. I have read of atheists facing all troubles quite boldly, so am I trying to stand like a man with an erect head to the last; even on the gallows.

Let us see how I carry on: one friend asked me to pray. When informed of my atheism, he said, "During your last days you will begin to believe". I said, No, dear Sir, it shall not be. I will think that to be an act of degradation and demoralization on my part. For selfish motives I am not going to pray. Readers and friends, "Is this vanity"? If it is, I stand for it.

Introduction to *The Dreamland*

Bhagat Singh wrote an introduction to a book of an old revolutionary Lala Ram Saran Das, which was a collection of his poems called The Dreamland. This write up reveals Bhagat Singh's intellectual skills and his capability to comprehend complex political and social issues and also his competence to put them across in a lucid manner. Another significant trait of Bhagat Singh that comes out clearly in this piece is his respect and empathy for those who are senior to him and also fundamentally differ from him on matters of faith or religion.

My noble friend, L Ram Saran Das, has asked me to write an introduction to his poetical work, *The Dreamland*. I am neither a poet nor a litterateur, neither am I a journalist nor a critic. Hence, by no stretch of imagination can I find the justification of the demand. But the circumstances in which I am placed do not afford any opportunity of discussing the question with the author arguing back and forth, and thereby do not leave me any alternative but to comply with the desire of my friend.

As I am not a poet I am not going to discuss it from that point of view. I have absolutely no knowledge of meter, and do not even know whether judged from metrical standard it would prove correct. Not being a litteratuer I am not going to discuss it with a view of assigning to it its right place in the national literature.

I, being a political worker, can at the utmost discuss it only from that point of view. But here also one factor is making my work practically impossible or at least very difficult. As a rule the introduction is always written by a man who is at one with the author on the contents of the work. But, here the case is quite different. I do not see eye to eye with my friend on all the matters. He was aware of the fact that I differed from him on many vital points. Therefore, my writing is not going to be an introduction at all. It can at the utmost amount to a criticism, and its place will be at the end and not in the beginning of the book.

In the political field *The Dreamland* occupies a very important place. In the prevailing circumstance it is filling up a very important gap in the movement. As a matter of fact all the political movements of our country that have hitherto played an important role in our modern history, had been lacking the ideal at the achievement of which they aimed. Revolutionary movement is no exception. In spite of all my efforts, I could not find any revolutionary party that had clear ideas as to what they were fighting for, with the exception of the Ghadar Party which, having been inspired by the USA form of government, clearly stated that they wanted to replace the existing government by a Republican form of government. All other parties consisted of men who had but one idea, i.e., to fight against the alien rulers. That idea is quite laudable but cannot be termed a revolutionary idea. We must make it clear that revolution does not merely mean an upheaval or a sanguinary strife. Revolution necessarily implies the programme of systematic reconstruction of society on new and better adapted basis, after complete destruction of the existing state of affairs (i.e., regime).

In the political field the liberals wanted some reform under the present government, while the extremists demanded a bit more and were prepared to employ radical means for the same purpose. Among the revolutionaries, they had always been in favour of extreme methods with one idea, i.e., of overthrowing the foreign domination. No doubt, there had been some who were in favour of extorting some reforms through those means. All these movements cannot rightly be designated as revolutionary movements.

But, L Ram Saran Das is the first revolutionary recruited formally in the Punjab by a Bengali absconder in 1908. Since then he had been in touch with the revolutionary movements and finally joined the Ghadar Party but retaining his old ideas that people held about the ideal of their movement. It has another interesting fact to add to its beauty and value. L Ram Saran Das was sentenced to death in 1915, and the sentence was later on commuted to life transportation. Today, sitting in the condemned cells myself, I can let the readers know as authoritatively that the life imprisonment is comparatively a far harder lot than that of death. L Ram Saran Das had actually to undergo fourteen years of imprisonment. It was in some southern jail that he wrote this poetry. The then psychology and mental struggle of the author has stamped its impressions upon the poetry and makes it all the more beautiful and interesting. He had been struggling hard against some depressing mood before he had decided to write. In the days when many of his comrades had been let off on undertakings and the temptation had been very strong for everyone and for him, too, and when the sweet and painful memories of wife and children had added more to the longing for liberty, he had to struggle hard against the demoralising effect of these things, and had directed attention to this work. Hence, we find the sudden outburst in the opening paragraph:

> "Wife, children, friends that surround me
> Were poisonous snakes all around."

He discusses philosophy in the beginning. This philosophy is the backbone of all the revolutionary movements of Bengal as well as of the Punjab. I differ from him on this point very widely. His interpretation of the universe is teleological and metaphysical; while I am a materialist and my interpretation of the phenomenon would be causal. Nevertheless, it is by no means out of place or out of date. The general ideas that are prevailing in our country, are more in accordance with those expressed by him. To fight that depressing mood he resorted to prayers as is evident that the whole of the beginning of the book is devoted to God, His praise, His definition. Belief in God is the outcome of mysticism which is the natural consequence of depression. That this world is 'Maya' or Mithya', a dream or a fiction, is clear mysticism which has been originated and developed by Hindu sages of old ages, such as Shankaracharya and others. But in the materialist philosophy this mode of thinking has got absolutely no place. But this mysticism of the author is by no means ignoble or deplorable. It has its own beauty and charm. The ideas are encouraging. Just look:

> "Be a foundation-stone obscure,
> And on thy breast cheerfully bear
> The architecture vast and huge,
> In suffering find true refuge.
> Envy not the plastered top-stone,
> On which all worldly praise is thrown." etc., etc.

From my personal experience I can safely assert that in the secret work, when a man constantly leads a risky life, 'without hope and without fear', 'always prepared to die unknown, unhonoured and unsung', then, he cannot but fight the personal temptations and desires by this sort of mysticism which is by no means demoralising. The next thing he deals with is the mentality of a revolutionary. L Ram Saran Das was the member of the revolutionary party, which was held responsible for many a violent deed. But this by no means proves that revolutionaries are blood-thirsty monsters, seeking pleasure in destruction. Read:

> "If need be, outwardly be wild,
> But in thy heart be always mild
> Hiss if need be, but do not bite,
> Love in thy heart and outside fight." etc., etc.

Destruction is not only essential but indispensible for construction. The revolutionaries have to adopt it as a necessary item of their programme, and the philosophy of violence and non-violence is beautifully described in the above lines. Lenin said to Gorky once that he could not hear music, which upset his whole nervous system and used to feel a desire to pat the heads of the artists. "But," added he, "this is not the time to pat the heads. The hands descend now to smash the skulls, though our ultimate aim is the elimination of all sorts of violence." This is truly how the revolutionaries feel when they have to resort to violent means as a terrible necessity.

Next the author deals with the problem concerning the various conflicting religions. He tries to conciliate them just as all the nationalists try to do. His method of dealing with the question is lengthy and round about, though on my part I would have dismissed it with one sentence of Karl Marx that "Religion is opium for the masses."

Lastly comes the most important part of his poetry where he deals with the future society, which we all long to create. But I like to clear one thing at the very outset. The Dreamland is a veritable utopia. The author has very candidly admitted it in the title. He does not pretend to have written a scientific thesis on the subject. The title 'Dreamland' makes it clear enough. But utopias play undoubtedly a very important role in social progress. Without St. Simon, Fourier and Robert Owen and their theories there would have been no scientific Marxian socialism. L Ram Saran Das' utopia occupies the same place. When our work will realise the importance of systematising the philosophy of their movement and of framing a scientific outlook of the movement, then this book will be very useful to them.

I have marked that the mode of expression is a crude one. The ideas of the existing society have in no way left him untouched while dealing with his utopia.

"Giving of alms to those who need."

In the future society, i.e., the Communist society that we want to build, we are not going to establish charitable institutions, but there shall be no needy and poor, and no alms giving and alms taking. In spite of this discrepancy the question has been dealt with in a very beautiful way.

The general outline discussed by him is the very same as that of the scientific socialism. But there are things which one has to oppose or contradict, or to be more precise, to amend. For instance, in a footnote under stanza 427, he writes that public servants have to work in farms, or say, factories for four hours daily to earn their living. But this is again utopian and impracticable. It is rather the outcome of repulsion of the existing order where the public servants are paid unduly very high. As a matter of fact the Bolshevists even had to recognise that mental work is also as productive a labour as the manual labour. And in the future society when the relations of various elements shall be adjusted on the basis of equality, the producers as well as the distributors shall be considered equally important. You cannot expect a sailor to stop his ship and land every twenty-four hours to do his four hours' daily labour to earn his livelihood; or a scientist to leave his laboratory and his experiment (work) to do his quota in the field. Both of them are doing very productive labour. The only difference that the socialist society expects is that the mental workers shall no longer be regarded superior to the manual workers.

L Ram Saran Das' idea about free education is really worth considering, and the socialist government has adopted somewhat the same course in Russia.

His discussion about crime is really the most advanced school of thought. Crime is the most serious social problem which needs a very tactful treatment. He has been in jail for the better part of his life. He has got the practical experience. At one place he employs the typical jail terms, 'the light labour, the medium labour and the hard labour', etc. Like all other socialists he suggests that, instead of retribution, i.e., retaliation, the reformative theory should form the basis of punishment. Not to punish but to reclaim should be the guiding principle of the administration of justice. Jails should be reformatories and not veritable hells. In this connection the readers should study the Russian prison system.

While dealing with militia he discusses war as well. In my opinion war as an institution shall only occupy a few pages in the Encyclopaedia then, and war materials shall adorn no conflicting or diverse interests that cause war.

At the utmost we can say that war shall have to be retained as an institution for the transitional period. We can easily understand if we take the example of the present-day Russia. There is the dictatorship of the proletariat at present. They want to establish a socialist society. Meanwhile they have to maintain an army to defend themselves against the capitalist society. But the war-aims would be different. Imperialist designs shall no more actuate our dreamland people to wage wars. There shall be no more war trophies. The revolutionary armies shall march to other lands not to rule or loot the people, but to pull the parasitic rulers down from their thrones and stop their blood sucking exploitation and thus to liberate the toiling masses. But, there shall not be the primitive national or racial hatred to goad our men to fight.

World-federation is the most popular and immediate object of all the free thinking people, and the author has well dilated on the subject, and his criticism of the so-called League of Nations is beautiful.

In a footnote under stanza 571 (572) the author touches, though briefly, the question of methods. He says: "Such a kingdom cannot be brought about by physical violent revolutions. It cannot be forced upon society from without. It must grow from within….This can be brought about by the gradual process of Evolution, by educating the masses on the lines mentioned above", etc. This statement does not in itself contain any discrepancy. It is quite correct, but having not been fully explained, is liable to create some misunderstanding, or worse still, a confusion. Does it mean that L Ram Saran Das has realised the futility of the cult of force? Has he become an orthodox believer in non-violence? No, it does not mean that.

Let me explain what the above quoted statement amounts to. The revolutionaries know better than anybody else that the socialist society cannot be brought about by violent means, but that it should grow and evolve from within. The author suggests education as the only weapon to be employed. But, everybody can easily realise that the present Government here, or, as a matter of fact, all the capitalist governments are not only not going to help any such effort, but on the contrary, suppress it mercilessly. Then, what will his 'evolution' achieve? We the revolutionaries are striving to capture power in our hands and to organize a revolutionary government which should employ all its resources for mass education, as is being done in Russia today. After capturing power, peaceful methods shall be employed for constructive work, force shall be employed to crush the obstacles. If that is what the author means, then we are at one. And I am confident that it is exactly this what he means.

I have discussed the book at great length. I have rather criticised it. But, I am not going to ask any alteration in it, because this has got its historical value. These were the ideas of 1914-15 revolutionaries.

I strongly recommend this book to young men in particular, but with a warning. Please do not read it to follow blindly and take for granted what is written in it. Read it, criticize it, think over it, try to formulate your own ideas with its help.

To the Young Political Workers

This document was written by Bhagat Singh on February 2, 1931, a little more than a month before he was hanged by the British. It clearly reflects his commitment to mass politics and also his maturity as a Marxist political thinker and activist.

Dear Comrades,

Our movement is passing through a very important phase at present. After a year's fierce struggle some definite proposals regarding the constitutional reforms have been formulated by the Round Table Conference and the Congress leaders have been invited to give this [...] think it desirable in the present circumstances to call off their movement. Whether they decide in favour or against is a matter of little importance to us. The present movement is bound to end in some sort of compromise. The compromise may be effected sooner or later. And compromise is not such ignoble and deplorable a thing as we generally think. It is rather an indispensable factor in the political strategy. Any nation that rises against the oppressors is bound to fail in the beginning, and to gain partial reforms during the medieval period of its struggle through compromises. And it is only at the last stage – having fully organized all the forces and resources of the nation – that it can possibly strike the final blow in which it might succeed to shatter the ruler's government. But even then it might fail, which makes some sort of compromise inevitable. This can be best illustrated by the Russian example.

In 1905 a revolutionary movement broke out in Russia. All the leaders were very hopeful. Lenin had returned from the foreign countries where he had taken refuge. He was conducting the struggle. People came to tell him that a dozen landlords were killed and a score of their mansions were burnt. Lenin responded by telling them to return and to kill twelve hundred landlords and burn as many of their palaces. In his opinion that would have meant something if revolution failed. Duma was introduced. The same Lenin advocated the view of participating in the Duma. This is what happened in 1907. In 1906 he was opposed to the participation in this first Duma which had granted more scope of work than this second one whose rights had been curtailed. This was due to the changed circumstances. Reaction was gaining the upper hand and Lenin wanted to use the floor of the Duma as a platform to discuss socialist ideas.

Again after the 1917 revolution, when the Bolsheviks were forced to sign the Brest Litovsk Treaty, everyone except Lenin was opposed to it. But Lenin said: "Peace". "Peace and again peace: peace at any cost – even at the cost of many of the Russian provinces to be yielded to German War Lord". When some anti-Bolshevik people condemned Lenin for this treaty, he declared frankly that the Bolsheviks were not in a position to face the German onslaught and they preferred the treaty to the complete annihilation of the Bolshevik Government.

The thing that I wanted to point out was that compromise is an essential weapon which has to be wielded every now and then as the struggle develops. But the thing that we must keep always before us is the idea of the movement. We must always maintain a clear notion as to the aim for the achievement of which we are fighting. That helps us to verify the success and failures of our movements and we can easily formulate the future programme. Tilak's policy, quite apart from the ideal i.e. his strategy, was the best. You are fighting to get sixteen annas from your enemy, you get only one anna. Pocket it and fight for the rest. What we note in the moderates is of their ideal. They start to achieve one anna and they can't get it. The revolutionaries must always keep in mind that they are striving for a complete revolution. Complete mastery of power in their hands. Compromises are dreaded because the conservatives try to disband the revolutionary forces after the compromise from such pitfalls. We must be very careful at such junctures to avoid any sort of confusion of the real issues especially the goal. The British Labour leaders betrayed their real struggle and have been reduced to mere hypocrite imperialists. In my opinion the diehard conservatives are better to us than these polished imperialist Labour leaders. About the tactics and strategy one should study life-work of Lenin. His definite views on the subject of compromise will be found in "Left Wing" Communism.

I have said that the present movement, i.e. the present struggle, is bound to end in some sort of compromise or complete failure.

I said that, because in my opinion, this time the real revolutionary forces have not been invited into the arena. This is a struggle dependent upon the middle class shopkeepers and a few capitalists. Both these, and particularly the latter, can never dare to risk its property or possessions in any struggle. The real revolutionary armies are in the villages and in factories, the peasantry and the labourers. But our bourgeois leaders do not and cannot dare to tackle them. The sleeping lion once awakened from its slumber shall become irresistible even after the achievement of what our leaders aim at. After his first experience with the Ahmedabad labourers in 1920 Mahatma Gandhi declared: "We must not tamper with the labourers. It is dangerous to make political use of the factory proletariat" (*The Times*, May 1921). Since then, they never dared to approach them. There remains the peasantry. The Bardoli resolution of 1922 clearly defines the horror the leaders felt when they saw the gigantic peasant class rising to shake off not only the domination of an alien nation but also the yoke of the landlords.

It is there that our leaders prefer a surrender to the British than to the peasantry. Leave alone Pt. Jawaharlal. Can you point out any effort to organize the peasants or the labourers? No, they will not run the risk. There they lack. That is why I say they never meant a complete revolution. Through economic and administrative pressure they hoped to get a few more reforms, a few more concessions for the Indian capitalists. That is why I say that this movement is doomed to die, may be after some sort of compromise or even without. The young workers who in all sincerity raise the cry "Long Live Revolution", are not well organized and strong enough to carry the movement themselves. As a matter of fact, even our great leaders, with the exception of perhaps Pt. Motilal Nehru, do not dare to take any responsibility on their shoulders, that is why every now and then they surrender unconditionally before Gandhi. In spite of their differences, they never oppose him seriously and the resolutions have to be carried for the Mahatma.

In these circumstances, let me warn the sincere young workers who seriously mean a revolution that harder times are coming. Let them beware lest they should get confused or disheartened. After the experience made through two struggles of the Great Gandhi, we are in a better position to form a clear idea of our present position and the future programme.

Now allow me to state the case in the simplest manner. You cry "Long Live Revolution." Let me assume that you really mean it. According to our definition of the term, as stated in our statement in the Assembly Bomb Case, revolution means the complete overthrow of the existing social order and its replacement with the socialist order. For that purpose our immediate aim is the achievement of power. As a matter of fact, the state, the Government machinery is just a weapon in the hands of the ruling class to further and safeguard its interest. We want to snatch and handle it to utilise it for the consummation of our ideal, i.e., social reconstruction on new, i.e., Marxist, basis. For this purpose we are fighting to handle the Government machinery. All along we have to educate the masses and to create a favourable atmosphere for our social programme. In the struggles we can best train and educate them.

With these things clear before us, i.e., our immediate and ultimate object having been clearly put, we can now proceed with the examination of the present situation. We must always be very candid and quite business-like while analysing any situation.

We know that since a hue and cry was raised about the Indians' participation in and share in the responsibility of the Indian Government, the Minto–Morley Reforms were introduced, which formed the Viceroy's council with consultation rights only. During the Great War, when the Indian help was needed the most, promises about self-government were made and the existing reforms were introduced. Limited legislative powers have been entrusted to the Assembly but subject to the goodwill of the Viceroy. Now is the third stage.

Now reforms are being discussed and are to be introduced in the near future. How can our young men judge them? This is a question; I do not know by what standard are the Congress leaders going to judge them. But for us, the revolutionaries, we can have the following criteria:

1. Extent of responsibility transferred to the shoulders of the Indians.

2. Form of the Government institutions that are going to be introduced and the extent of the right of participation given to the masses.

3. Future prospects and the safeguards.

These might require a little further elucidation. In the first place, we can easily judge the extent of responsibility given to our people by the control our representatives will have on the executive. Up till now, the executive was never made responsible to the Legislative Assembly and the Viceroy had the veto power, which rendered all the efforts of the elected members futile. Thanks to the efforts of the Swaraj Party, the Viceroy was forced every now and then to use these extraordinary powers to shamelessly trample the solemn decisions of the national representatives under foot. It is already too well known to need further discussion.

Now in the first place we must see the method of the executive formation: Whether the executive is to be elected by the members of a popular assembly or is to be imposed from above as before, and further, whether it shall be responsible to the house or shall absolutely affront it as in the past?

As regards the second item, we can judge it through the scope of franchise. The property qualifications making a man eligible to vote should be altogether abolished and universal suffrage be introduced instead. Every adult, both male and female, should have the right to vote. At present we can simply see how far the franchise has been extended.

I may here make a mention about provincial autonomy. But from whatever I have heard, I can only say that the Governor imposed from above, equipped with extraordinary powers, higher and above the legislative, shall prove to be no less than a despot. Let us better call it the "provincial tyranny" instead of "autonomy." This is a strange type of democratisation of the state institutions.

The third item is quite clear. During the last two years the British politicians have been trying to undo Montague's promise for another dole of reforms to be bestowed every ten years till the British Treasury exhausts.

We can see what they have decided about the future.

Let me make it clear that we do not analyse these things to rejoice over the achievement, but to form a clear idea about our situation, so that we may enlighten the masses and prepare them for further struggle. For us, compromise never means surrender, but a step forward and some rest. That is all and nothing else.

Having discussed the present situation, let us proceed to discuss the future programme and the line of action we ought to adopt. As I have already stated, for any revolutionary party a definite programme is very essential. For, you must know that revolution means action. It means a change brought about deliberately by an organized and systematic work, as opposed to sudden and unorganised or spontaneous change or breakdown. And for the formulation of a programme, one must necessarily study:

1. The goal.

2. The premises from where were to start, i.e., the existing conditions.

3. The course of action, i.e., the means and methods.

Unless one has a clear notion about these three factors, one cannot discuss anything about programme.

We have discussed the present situation to some extent. The goal also has been slightly touched. We want a socialist revolution, the indispensable preliminary to which is the political revolution. That is what we want. The political revolution does not mean the transfer of state (or more crudely, the power) from the hands of the British to the Indian, but to those Indians who are at one with us as to the final goal, or to be more precise, the power to be transferred to the revolutionary party through popular support. After that, to proceed in right earnest is to organize the reconstruction of the whole society on the socialist basis. If you do not mean this revolution, then please have mercy. Stop shouting "Long Live Revolution." The term revolution is too sacred, at least to us, to be so lightly used or misused. But if you say you are for the national revolution and the aims of your struggle is an Indian republic of the type of the United State of America, then I ask you to please let me know on what forces you rely that will help you bring about that revolution. The only forces on which you can rely to bring about any revolution, whether national or the socialist, are the peasantry and the labour. Congress leaders do not dare to organize those forces. You have seen it in this movement. They know it better than anybody else that without these forces they are absolutely helpless. When they passed the resolution of complete independence – that really meant a revolution – they did not mean it. They had to do it under pressure of the younger element, and then they wanted to use it as a threat to achieve their hearts' desire – Dominion Status. You can easily judge it by studying the resolutions of the last three sessions of the Congress. I mean Madras, Calcutta and Lahore. At Calcutta, they passed a resolution asking for Dominion Status within twelve months, otherwise they would be forced to adopt complete independence as their object, and in all solemnity waited for some such gift till midnight after the 31st December, 1929. Then they found themselves "honour bound" to adopt the Independence resolution, otherwise they did not mean it. But even then Mahatmaji made no secret of the fact that the door (for compromise) was open. That was the real spirit. At the very outset they knew that their movement could not but end in some compromise. It is this half-heartedness that we hate, not the compromise at a particular stage in the struggle. Anyway, we were discussing the forces on which you can depend for a revolution. But if you say that you will approach the peasants and labourers to enlist their active support, let me tell you that they are not going to be fooled by any sentimental talk. They ask you quite candidly: what are they going to gain by your revolution for which you demand their sacrifices, what difference does it make to them whether Lord Reading is the head of the Indian Government or Sir Purshotamdas Thakordas? What difference for a peasant if Sir Tej Bahadur Sapru replaces Lord Irwin! It is useless to appeal to his national sentiment. You can't "use" him for your purpose; you shall have to mean seriously and to make him understand that the revolution is going to be his and for his good. The revolution of the proletariat and for the proletariat.

When you have formulated this clear-cut idea about your goals you can proceed in right earnest to organize your forces for such an action. Now there are two different phases through which you shall have to pass. First, the preparation; second, the action.

After the present movement ends, you will find disgust and some disappointment amongst the sincere revolutionary workers.

But you need not worry. Leave sentimentalism aside. Be prepared to face the facts. Revolution is a very difficult task. It is beyond the power of any man to make a revolution. Neither can it be brought about on any appointed date. It is brought about by special environments, social and economic. The function of an organized party is to utilise any such opportunity offered by these circumstances. And to prepare the masses and organize the forces for the revolution is a very difficult task. And that required a very great sacrifice on the part of the revolutionary workers. Let me make it clear that if you are a businessman or an established worldly or family man, please don't play with fire. As a leader you are of no use to the party. We have already very many such leaders who spare some evening hours for delivering speeches. They are useless. We require – to use the term so dear to Lenin – the "professional revolutionaries". The whole-time workers who have no other ambitions or life-work except the revolution. The greater the number of such workers organized into a party, the great the chances of your success.

To proceed systematically, what you need the most is a party with workers of the type discussed above with clear-cut ideas and keen perception and ability of initiative and quick decisions. The party shall have iron discipline and it need not necessarily be an underground party, rather the contrary. Though the policy of voluntarily going to jail should altogether be abandoned. That will create a number of workers who shall be forced to lead an underground life. They should carry on the work with the same zeal. And it is this group of workers that shall produce worthy leaders for the real opportunity.

The party requires workers which can be recruited only through the youth movement. Hence we find the youth movement as the starting point of our programme. The youth movement should organize study circles, class lectures and publication of leaflets, pamphlets, books and periodicals. This is the best recruiting and training ground for political workers.

Those young men who may have matured their ideas and may find themselves ready to devote their life to the cause, may be transferred to the party. The party workers shall always guide and control the work of the youth movement as well. The party should start with the work of mass propaganda. It is very essential. One of the fundamental causes of the failure of the efforts of the Ghadar Party (1914-15) was the ignorance, apathy and sometimes active opposition of the masses. And apart from that, it is essential for gaining the active sympathy of and organising the peasants and workers. The name of party or rather, [...] a communist party. This party of political workers, bound by strict discipline, should handle all other movements. It shall have to organize the peasants' and workers' parties, labour unions, and may even venture to capture the Congress and kindred political bodies. And in order to create political consciousness, not only of national politics but class politics as well, the party should organize a big publishing campaign. Subjects on all proletens (original transcription not clear) enlightening the masses of the socialist theory shall be within easy reach and distributed widely. The writings should be simple and clear.

There are certain people in the labour movement who enlist some absurd ideas about the economic liberty of the peasants and workers without political freedom. They are demagogues or muddle-headed people. Such ideas are unimaginable and preposterous. We mean the economic liberty of the masses, and for that very purpose we are striving to win the political power. No doubt in the beginning, we shall have to fight for little economic demands and privileges of these classes. But these struggles are the best means for educating them for a final struggle to conquer political power.

Apart from these, there shall necessarily be organized a military department. This is very important. At times its need is felt very badly. But at that time you cannot start and formulate such a group with substantial means to act effectively. Perhaps this is the topic that needs a careful explanation. There is very great probability of my being misunderstood on this subject. Apparently I have acted like a terrorist. But I am not a terrorist. I am a revolutionary who has got such definite ideas of a lengthy programme as is being discussed here. My "comrades in arms" might accuse me, like Ram Prasad Bismil, for having been subjected to certain sort of reaction in the condemned cell, which is not true. I have got the same ideas, same convictions, same zeal and same spirit as I used to have outside, perhaps – nay, decidedly – better. Hence I warn my readers to be careful while reading my words. They should not try to read anything between the lines. Let me announce with all the strength at my command, that I am not a terrorist and I never was, except perhaps in the beginning of my revolutionary career. And I am convinced that we cannot gain anything through those methods. One can easily judge it from the history of the Hindustan Socialist Republican Association. All our activities were directed towards an aim, i.e., identifying ourselves with the great movement as its military wing. If anybody has misunderstood me, let him amend his ideas. I do not mean that bombs and pistols are useless, rather the contrary. But I mean to say that mere bomb-throwing is not only useless but sometimes harmful. The military department of the party should always keep ready all the war-material it can command for any emergency. It should back the political work of the party. It cannot and should not work independently.

On these lines indicated above, the party should proceed with its work. Through periodical meetings and conferences they should go on educating and enlightening their workers on all topics.

If you start the work on these lines, you shall have to be very sober. The programme requires at least twenty years for its fulfillment. Cast aside the youthful dreams of a revolution within ten years of Gandhi's utopian promises of Swaraj in One Year. It requires neither the emotion nor the death, but the life of constant struggle, suffering and sacrifice. Crush your individuality first. Shake off the dreams of personal comfort. Then start to work. Inch by inch you shall have to proceed. It needs courage, perseverance and very strong determination. No difficulties and no hardships shall discourage you. No failure and betrayals shall dishearten you. No travails (!) imposed upon you shall snuff out the revolutionary will in you. Through the ordeal of sufferings and sacrifice you shall come out victorious. And these individual victories shall be the valuable assets of the revolution.

LONG LIVE REVOLUTION

2nd February, 1931

APPENDIX C: 1

Manifesto of the Hindustan Republican Association

It was drafted by Sachindra Nath Sanyal in 1924. It gives an outline of the social, political and economic problems that confronted India at that time. The HRA, as will be reflected in the manifesto, did not completely dissociate itself from the romantic revolutionary ideals of the early revolutionaries, but it surely talked about transcending them by raising the issue of ending the exploitation of man by man.

An organ of the Revolutionary Party of India, January 1, 1925, Vol.1, No.1.

(Every honest Indian should read the whole of it and circulate it among his friends.)

Manifesto of the Revolutionary Party of India

"Chaos is necessary to the birth of a new star." And the birth of life is accompanied by agony and pain. India is also taking a new birth, and is passing through that inevitable chaos and agony. Indians shall play their destined role, when all calculations shall prove futile, when the wise and the mighty shall be bewildered by the simple and the weak, when great empires shall crumble down and new nations shall arise and surprise humanity with the splendour and glory which shall be all its own.

This new power, which is shaking the world from its very depths, this new spirit which is working miracles behind the scene, is also manifesting itself in the young blood of India and is taking the shape of a movement which is despised and ignored by the wise and the learned, and is being described as the wild dreams of a few mad men. This remarkable movement is the revolutionary movement in young India. The revolutionary movement has unnerved the weak, has inspired the robust and healthy, and has confounded the worldly wise and the learned. This movement can never be crushed just as much as the coming of the spring can never be thwarted. It will never die out until it has fulfilled the mission for which it has taken its birth. Tyrants will oppress it, the faithless will taunt at it, and the confounded will denounce it, but thoughts and ideas can never be crushed by the sword, and the noble impulse that has taken birth in the very depths of our being can never be ignored, nor taunted.

This revolutionary movement is the manifestation of the new life that has taken birth in the Nation. To denounce this life is to denounce one's own understanding.

Twenty years of ruthless repression has not been able to crush it. Scathing denunciation by the renowned public leaders has not been able to arrest its steady growth. The movement stands mightier today than what it was before. The prospects of this revolutionary party were never so bright as they are today. The future is assured.

Let no Indian deny the existence of this revolutionary party in order to denounce the repressive measures of the foreign rulers. The foreigners have no right to rule over India and therefore they must be denounced and driven out. Not that they have committed any particular act of violence or crime. There are the natural consequences of a foreign rule. This foreign rule must be abolished. They have no justification to rule over India except the justification of sword and therefore the revolutionary party had taken to the sword. But the sword of the revolutionary party bears ideas at its edge.

The immediate object of the revolutionary party in the domain of politics is to establish a Federal Republic of United State of India by an organised and armed revolution. The final constitution of this Republic shall be framed and declared at a time when the representatives of India shall have the power to carry out their decision. But the basic principles of this Republic will be universal suffrage and abolition of all systems which make the exploitation of man by man possible, e.g. the railways and other means of transportation and communication, the mines and other kinds of very great industries such as the manufacture of steel and ships all these shall be nationalised. In this Republic the electors shall have the right to recall their representatives, if so desired, otherwise the democracy shall become a mockery. In this Republic, the legislature shall have the power to control the executives and replace them whenever necessity will arise.

The revolutionary party is not national but international in the sense that its ultimate object is to bring harmony in the world by respecting and guaranteeing the diverse interests of the different nations. It aims not at competition but at cooperation between the different nations and states and in this respect it follows the footsteps of great Indian Rishis of the glorious past and of Bolshevik Russia in the modern age. Good for humanity is no vain and empty word with the Indian revolutionaries. But the weak, the coward and the powerless can do no good either to themselves or to humanity.

With regard to the communal question, the revolutionary party contemplates to grant whatever rights the different communities may demand, provided they do not clash with the interests of other communities and they lead ultimately to hearty and organic union in different communities in the near future.

In the domain of economic and social welfare the party will foster the spirit of cooperation on as large a scale as possible. Instead of private and unorganised business enterprises, the party prefers cooperative union.

In the spiritual domain the party aims at establishing the truth and preaching it that the world is not Maya, an illusion to be ignored and despised at, but that it is the manifestation of the one individual soul, the supreme source of all power, all knowledge and all beauty. The revolutionary party has its own policy and its own programme.

It cannot for obvious reasons divulge all its secrets. But when it will become quite sure that the Govt. happens to know more than our own people, then the public will also be informed of its plan and methods without any hesitation at all. This revolutionary party pursues the policy of cooperation when possible and dissociation where necessary with the Congress and its different parties. But this party views all constitutional agitation in this country with contempt and ridicule. It is a mockery to say that India's salvation can be achieved through constitutional means, where no constitution exists. It is a self-deception to say that India's political liberty can be attained through peaceful and legitimate means. When the enemy is determined to break the peace at his own convenience, the fine phrase "legitimate" loses all its charm and significance when one pledges himself to maintain peace at all costs.

Our public leaders hesitate to speak in plain terms that India wants complete autonomy free from foreign control. They perhaps are ignorant of the fact that nations are born through the inspiration of great ideals. The spiritual ideal which hesitates to accept the spirit of complete autonomy can hardly be called spiritual, though it may seemingly appear the most sublime. The time has come to speak the truth in the most unmistakable terms and to place before the nation an ideal worth the name.

The ideal before us is to serve humanity in an organised way. The ideal can never be realised by India so long as she remains in bondage or slavery, so long as India remains British India. In order that India may realise her ideal she must have a separate and independent existence. This independence can never be achieved through peaceful and constitutional means. Even a child can understand that the laws that govern British India are not made by Indians, nor can they have any control over them. British India can never be transformed into a federal republic of the United States of India through the British laws and constitution. Young Indians, shake off your illusion, face realities with a stout heart, and do not avoid struggle, difficulties and sacrifices. The inevitable is to come.

Do not be misguided any more. Peace and tranquility you cannot achieve by peaceful and legitimate means. The following memorable words of a great English author Mr Robertson may serve to make the wise men of India wiser still:

> The movement and programme of reform was mainly the achievement of Irish and Protestant leaders, to whom British statement had revealed the fatal secret that England could be bullied but not argued into justice and generosity. (*English Under Hanoverians*, p.197).

Indian public leaders are still ignorant of this fatal secret, or else they are foolishly wise to remain ignorants.

The wise men of India say that it is absurd to cherish the hope that India can be reconquered by force of arms, though they forget that it is equally or more absurd to believe that a handful of Englishmen have kept under subjugation by the force of arms one-fifth of the whole human race. Posterity may well doubt the authenticity of this fact that a handful of Englishmen even ruled over India for a century; it is so inconceivable.

A few words more about terrorism and anarchism. These two words are playing the most mischievous part in India today. They are being invariably misapplied whenever any reference to revolution arises to be made, because it is so very convenient to denounce the revolutionary under that name. The Indian revolutionaries are neither terrorists nor anarchists. They never aim at spreading anarchy in the land and therefore they can never properly be called anarchists. Terrorism is never their object and they cannot be called terrorists. They do not believe that terrorism alone can bring independence and they do not want terrorism for terrorism's sake although they may at times resort to this method as a very effective means of retaliation. The present Govt. exists simply because the foreigners have successfully been able to terrorise the Indian people. The Indian people do not love their English masters, they do not want them to be here; but they do help the Britishers simply because they are terribly afraid of them and this very fear resists the Indians from extending their helping hands to the revolutionaries, not that they do not love them.

The official terrorism is surely to be met by counter terrorism. A spirit of utter helplessness pervades every strata of our society and terrorism is an effective means of restoring the proper spirits in the society without which progress will be difficult. Moreover, the English masters and their hired lackeys can never be allowed to do whatever they like, uninterrupted, unmodested. Every possible difficulty and resistance must be thrown in their way. Terrorism has an international bearing also, because the ardent enemies of England are at once drawn towards India through terrorism and revolutionary demonstrations, and the revolutionary party has deliberately abstained itself from entering into this terroristic campaign at the present movement even at the greatest of provocations in the form of outrages committed on their sisters and mothers by the agents of a foreign government, simply because the party is waiting to deliver the final blow. But when expediency will demand it, the party will unhesitatingly enter into a desperate campaign of terrorism, when the life of every official and individual who will be helping the foreign ruler in any way will be made intolerable, be he Indian or European, high or low. But even then the party will never forget that terrorism is not the object, and they will try incessantly to organise a band of selfless and devoted workers who will devote their best energies towards the political and social emancipation of their country.

They will always remember that the making of nations requires the self-sacrifice of thousands of obscure men and women who care more for the idea of their country than for their own comfort or interest, their own lives or the lives of those whom they love.

Sd/- V.K.

President, Central Council,

R.P. of India.

Manifesto of the Naujawan Bharat Sabha, Punjab

Naujawan Bharat Sabha was founded by Bhagat Singh in 1926 in Lahore as an open organization of the revolutionary party (HSRA). It soon spread its network in most of the towns of Punjab as well as United Provinces and Rajasthan. The Sabha remained a politically vibrant organization of the youth for 5/6 years till most of its leaders were implicated in various cases.

Young Comrades,

Our country is passing through a chaos. There is mutual distrust and despair prevailing everywhere. The great leaders have lost faith in the cause and most of them no more enjoy the confidence of the masses. There is no programme and no enthusiasm among the 'champions' of Indian independence. There is chaos everywhere. But chaos is inevitable and a necessary phase in the course of making of a nation. It is during such critical periods that the sincerity of the workers is tested, their character built, real programme formed, and then, with a new spirit, new hopes, new faith and enthusiasm, the work is started. Hence there is nothing to be disgusted of.

We are, however, very fortunate to find ourselves on the threshold of a new era. We no more hear the news of reaching chaos that used to be sung vastly in praise of the British bureaucracy. The historic question "Would you be governed by sword or pen", no more lies unanswered. Those who put that question to us have themselves answered it. In the words of Lord Birkenhead, "With the sword we won India and with the sword we shall retain it." Thanks to this candour everything is clear now. After remembering Jallianwala and Manawala outrages it looks absurd to quote that "A good government cannot be a substitute for self-government." It is self-evident.

A word about the blessings of the British rule in India. Is it necessary to quote the whole volumes of Romesh Chandra Dutt, William Digby and Dadabhai Naoroji in evidence to prove the decline and ruin of Indian industries? Does it require any authorities to prove that India, with the richest soil and mines, is today one of the poorest, that India which could be proud of so glorious a civilisation, is today the most backward country with only 5% literacy? Do not the people know that India has to pay the largest toll of human life with the highest child death rate in the world? The epidemics like plague, cholera, influenza and such other diseases are becoming common day by day. Is it not disgraceful for us to hear again and again that we are not fit for self-government? Is it not really degrading for us, with Guru Govind Singh, Shivaji and Hari Singh as our heroes, to be told that we are incapable of defending ourselves? Alas, we have done little to prove the contrary. Did we not see our trade and commerce being crushed in its very infancy in the first effort of Guru Nanak Steamship Company started by Baba Gurdit Singh in 1914; the inhuman treatment meted out to them, far away in Canada, on the way, and, finally, the bloody reception of those despairing, broken-hearted passengers with volleys of shots at Bajbaj, and what not? Did we not see all this? In India, where for the honour of one Dropadi, the great Mahabharat was fought, dozens of them were ravaged in 1919. They were spit at, in their naked faces. Did we not see all this? Yet, we are content with the existing order of affairs. Is this life worth living?

Does it require any revelation now to make us realise that we are enslaved and must be free? Shall we wait for an uncertain sage to make us feel that we are an oppressed people? Shall we expectantly wait for divine help or some miracle to deliver us from bondage? Do we not know the fundamental principles of liberty? "Those who want to be free, must themselves strike the blow." Young men, awake, arise; we have slept too long!

We have appealed to the young only. Because the young bear the most inhuman tortures smilingly and face death without hesitation. Because the whole history of human progress is written with the blood of young men and young women. And because the reforms are ever made by the vigour, courage, self-sacrifice and emotional conviction of the young men who do not know enough to be afraid and who feel much more than they think.

Were it not the young men of Japan who come forth in hundreds to throw themselves in the ditches to make a dry path to Port Arthur? And Japan is today one of the foremost nations in the world. Were it not the young Polish people who fought again and again and failed, but fought again heroically throughout the last century? And today we see a free Poland. Who freed Italy from the Austrian yoke? Young Italy.

Do you know the wonders worked by the Young Turks? Do you not daily read what the young Chinese are doing? Were it not the young Russians who sacrificed their lives for Russia's emancipation? Throughout the last century hundreds and thousands of them were exiled to Siberia for the mere distribution of socialist pamphlets or, like Dostoyevsky, for merely belonging to socialist debating society. Again and again they faced the storm of oppression. But they did not lose the courage. It were they, the young only, who fought. And everywhere the young can fight without hope, without fear and without hesitation. And we find today in the great Russia, the emancipation of the world.

While, we Indians, what are we doing? A branch of peepal tree is cut and religious feelings of the Hindus are injured. A corner of a paper idol, tazia, of the idol-breaker Mohammedans is broken, and 'Allah' gets enraged, who cannot be satisfied with anything less than the blood of the infidel Hindus. Man ought to be attached more importance than the animals and, yet, here in India, they break each other's heads in the name of 'sacred animals'. Our vision is circumscribed by.. .. * thinks in terms of internationalism.

There are many others among us who hide their lethargy under the garb of internationalism. Asked to serve their country they reply: "Oh Sirs, we are cosmopolitans and believe in universal brotherhood. Let us not quarrel with the British. They are our brothers." A good idea, a beautiful phrase. But they miss its implication. The doctrine of universal brotherhood demands that the exploitation of man by man and nation by nation must be rendered impossible. Equal opportunity to all without any sort of distinction. But British rule in India is a direct negation of all these, and we shall have nothing to do with it.

A word about social service here. Many good men think that social service (in the narrow sense, as it is used and understood in our country) is the panacea to all our ills and the best method of serving the country. Thus we find many ardent youth contending themselves with distributing grain among the poor and nursing the sick all their life. These men are noble and self-denying but they cannot understand that charity cannot solve the problem of hunger and disease in India and, for that matter, in any other country.

Religious superstitions and bigotry are a great hindrance in our progress. They have proved an obstacle in our way and we must do away with them. "The thing that cannot bear free thought must perish." There are many other such weaknesses which we are to overcome. The conservativeness and orthodoxy of the Hindus, extra-territorialism and fanaticism of the Mohammedans and narrow-mindedness of all the communities in general are always exploited by the foreign enemy. Young men with revolutionary zeal from all communities are required for the task.

Having achieved nothing, we are not prepared to sacrifice anything for any achievement; our leaders are fighting amongst themselves to decide what will be the share of each community in the hoped achievement. Simply to conceal their cowardice and lack of spirit of self-sacrifice, they are creating a false issue and screening the real one. These arm-chair politicians have their eyes set on the handful of bones that may be thrown to them, as they hope, by the mighty rulers. That is extremely humiliating. Those who come forth to fight the battle of liberty cannot sit and decide first that after so much sacrifices, so much achievement must be sure and so much share to be divided. Such people never make any sort of sacrifice. We want people who may be prepared to fight without hope, without fear and without hesitation, and who may be willing to die unhonoured, unwept and unsung. Without that spirit we will not be able to fight the great two-fold battle that lies before us – two-fold because of the internal foe, on the one hand, and a foreign enemy, on the other. Our real battle is against our own disabilities which are exploited by the enemy and some of our own people for their selfish motives.

Young Punjabis, the youth of other provinces are working tremendously in their respective spheres. The organisation and awakening displayed by young Bengal on February 3, should serve as an example to us. Our Punjab, despite the greatest amount of sacrifice and suffering to its credit, is described as a politically backward province. Why? Because, although it belongs to the martial race, we are lacking in organisation and discipline; we who are proud of the ancient University of Taxila, today stand badly in need of culture. And culture requires fine literature which cannot be prepared without a common and well developed language. Alas, we have got none.

While trying to solve the above problem that faces our country, we will also have to prepare the masses to fight the greater battle that lies before us. Our political struggle began just after the great War of Independence of 1857. It has passed through different phases. Along with the advent of the 20th century the British bureaucracy has adopted quite a new policy towards India. They are drawing our bourgeoisie and petty bourgeoisie into their fold by adopting the policy of concessions. Their cause is being made common. The progressive investment of British capital in India will inevitably lead to that end. In the very near future we will find that class and their great leaders having thrown their lot with the foreign rulers. Some round-table conference or any such body will end in a compromise between the two. They will no more be lions and cubs. Even without any conciliation the expected Great War of the entire people will surely thin the ranks of the so-called champions of Indian independence.

The future programme of preparing the country will begin with the motto: "Revolution by the masses and for the masses." In other words, Swaraj for the 90%; Swaraj not only attained by the masses but also for the masses. This is a very difficult task. Though our leaders have offered many suggestions, none had the courage to put forward and carry out successfully any concrete scheme of awakening the masses. Without going into details, we can safely assert that to achieve our object, thousands of our most brilliant young men, like Russian youth, will have to pass their precious lives in villages and make the people understand what the Indian revolution would really mean. They must be made to realise that the revolution which is to come will mean more than a change of masters. It will, above all, mean the birth of new order of things, a new state. This is not the work of a day or a year. Decades of matchless self-sacrifice will prepare the masses for the accomplishment of that great work and only the revolutionary young men will be able to do that. A revolutionary does not necessarily mean a man of bombs and revolvers.

The task before the young is hard and their resources are scanty. A great many obstacles are likely to block their way. But the earnestness of the few but sincere can overcome them all. The young must come forth. They must see the hard and difficult path that lies before them, the great tasks they have to perform. They must remember in the heart of hearts that "success is but a chance; sacrifice a law". Their lives might be the lives of constant failures, even more wretched than those which Guru Govind Singh had to face throughout his life. Even then they must not repent and say, "Oh, it was all an illusion."

Young men, do not get disheartened when you find such a great battle to fight single-handed, with none to help you. You must realise your own latent strength. Rely on yourselves and success is yours. Remember the words of the great mother of James Garfield which she spoke to her son while sending him away, penniless, helpless and resourceless, to seek his fortune: "Nine times out of ten the best thing that can happen to a young man is to be thrown overboard to swim or sink for himself." Glory to the mother who said these words and glory to those who will rely on them.

Mazzini, that oracle of Italian regeneration, once said: "All great national movements begin with unknown men of the people without influence, except for the faith and the will that counts neither time nor difficulties." Let the boat of life weigh another time. Let it set sail in the Great Ocean, and then:

> Anchor is in no stagnant shallow.
> Trust the wide and wonderous sea,
> Where the tides are fresh for ever,
> And the mighty currents free.
> There perchance, O young Columbus,
> Your new world of truth may be.

Do not hesitate, let not the theory of incarnation haunt your mind and break your courage. Everybody can become great if he strives. Do not forget your own martyrs. Kartar Singh was a young man. Yet, in his teens, when he came forth to serve his country, he ascended the scaffold smiling and echoing "Bande Mataram". Bhai Balmukund and Awadh Bihari were both quite young when they gave their lives for the cause. They were from amongst you. You must try to become as sincere patriots and as ardent lovers of liberty as they were. Do not lose patience and sense at one time, and hope at another. Try to make stability and determination a second nature to yourselves.

Let then young men think independently, calmly, serenely and patiently. Let them adopt the cause of Indian independence as the sole aim of their lives. Let them stand on their own feet. They must organise themselves free from any influence and refuse to be exploited any more by the hypocrites and insincere people who have nothing in common with them and who always desert the cause at the critical juncture. In all seriousness and sincerity, let them make the triple motto of "service, suffering, sacrifice" their sole guide. Let them remember that "the making of a nation requires self-sacrifice of thousands of obscure men and women who care more for the idea of their country than for their own comfort and interest, than own lives and the lives of those who they love".

6-4-1928

Bande Mataram

Printed & published by BC.Vohra, BA, Propaganda Secretary, Naujawan Bharat Sabha, Lahore.

THE PHILOSOPHY OF THE BOMB

'The Philosophy of the Bomb' was written by Bhagwati Charan Vohra in response to Gandhi's 'The Cult of the Bomb', which Gandhi wrote condemning the attempt to blow up Viceroy Lord Irwin's train in December 1929. The manifesto was seriously discussed and commented upon by all the revolutionaries, including Bhagat Singh, who managed to receive a copy inside the prison.

Introductory

Recent events, particularly the Congress resolution on the attempt to blow up the Viceregal Special on the 23 December, 1929, and Gandhi's subsequent writings in *Young India*, clearly show that the Indian National Congress, in conjunction with Gandhi, has launched a crusade against the revolutionaries. A great amount of public criticism, both from the press and the platform, has been made against them. It is a pity that they have all along been, either deliberately or due to sheer ignorance, misrepresented and misunderstood. The revolutionaries do not shun criticism and public scrutiny of their ideals or actions. They rather welcome these as chances of making those understand, who have a genuine desire to do so, the basic principles of the revolutionary movement and the high and noble ideals that are a perennial source of inspiration and strength to it. It is hoped that this article will help the general public to know the revolutionaries as they are and will prevent it from taking them for what interested and ignorant persons would have it believe them to be.

Violence or Non-violence

Let us, first of all, take up the question of violence and non-violence. We think that the use of these terms in itself, is a grave injustice to either party, for they express the ideals of neither of them correctly. Violence is physical force applied for committing injustice, and that is certainly not what the revolutionaries stand for. On the other hand, what generally goes by the name of non-violence is in reality the theory of soul-force, as applied to the attainment of personal and national rights through courting suffering and hoping thus to finally convert your opponent to your point of view. When a revolutionary believes certain things to be his right he asks for them, pleads for them, argues for them, wills to attain them with all the soul-force at his command, stands the greatest amount of suffering for them, is always prepared to make the highest sacrifice for their attainment, and also backs his efforts with all the physical force he is capable of. You may coin what other word you like to describe his methods but you cannot call it violence, because that would constitute an outrage on the dictionary meaning of that word. Satyagraha is insistence upon truth. Why press, for the acceptance of truth, by soul-force alone? Why not add physical force also to it? While the revolutionaries stand for winning independence by all forces, physical as well as moral, at their command, the advocates of soul-force would like to ban the use of physical force. The question really, therefore, is not whether you will have violence, but whether you will have soul-force plus physical force or soul force alone.

Our Ideal

The revolutionaries believe that the deliverance of their country will come through revolution. The revolution, they are constantly working and hoping for, will not only express itself in the form of an armed conflict between the foreign government and its supporters and the people, it will also usher in a new social order. The revolution will ring the death knell of capitalism and class distinctions and privileges. It will bring joy and prosperity to the starving millions who are seething today under the terrible yoke of both foreign and Indian exploitation. It will bring the nation into its own. It will give birth to a new state a new social order. Above all, it will establish the dictatorship of the proletariat and will for ever banish social parasites from the seat of political power.

Terrorism

The revolutionaries already see the advent of the revolution in the restlessness of youth, in its desire to break free from the mental bondage and religious superstition that hold them. As the youth will get more and more saturated with the psychology of revolution, it will come to have a clearer realisation of national bondage and a growing, intense, unquenchable thirst for freedom. It will grow, this feeling of bondage, this insatiable desire for freedom, till, in their righteous anger, the infuriated youth will begin to kill the oppressors. Thus has terrorism been born in the country. It is a phase, a necessary, an inevitable phase of the revolution. Terrorism is not the complete revolution and the revolution is not complete without terrorism. This thesis can be supported by an analysis of any and every revolution in history. Terrorism instils fear in the hearts of the oppressors, it brings hopes of revenge and redemption to the oppressed masses, it gives courage and self-confidence to the wavering, it shatters the spell of the superiority of the ruling class and raises the status of the subject race in the eyes of the world, because it is the most convincing proof of a nation's hunger for freedom. Here in India, as in other countries in the past, terrorism will develop into the revolution and the revolution into independence, social, political and economic.

Revolutionary Methods

This then is what the revolutionaries believe in, that is what they hope to accomplish for their country. They are doing it both openly and secretly, and in their own way. The experience of a century long and world-wide struggle, between the masses and the governing class, is their guide to their goal, and the methods they are following have never been known to have failed.

The Congress and the Revolutionaries

Meanwhile, what has the Congress been doing? It has changed its creed from Swaraj to Complete Independence. As a logical sequence to this, one would expect it to declare a war on the British government. Instead, we find, it has declared war against the revolutionaries. The first offensive of the Congress came in the form of a resolution deploring the attempt made on the 23 December, 1929, to blow up the Viceroy's Special. It was drafted by Gandhi and he fought tooth and nail for it, with the result that is was passed by a trifling majority of 81 in a house of 1,713. Was even this bare majority a result of honest political convictions? Let us quote the opinion of Sarla Devi Chaudhrani who has been a devotee of the Congress all her life, in reply. She says: "I discovered in the course of my conversations with a good many of the Mahatma's followers that it was only their sense of personal loyalty to him that was keeping them back from an expression of the independent views and preventing them from voting against any resolution whatsoever that was fathered by Mahatmaji." As to Gandhi's arguments in favour of the proposition, we will deal with them later, when we discuss his article "The Cult of the Bomb" which is more or less an amplification of his speech in the Congress. There is one fact about this deplorable resolution which we must not lose sight of, and that is this. In spite of the fact, that the Congress is pledged to non~violence and has been actively engaged in carrying on propaganda in its favour for the last ten years, and in spite of the fact also that the supporters of the resolution indulged in abuse, called the revolutionaries 'cowards' and described their actions as 'dastardly' – and one of them even threateningly remarked that if they wanted to be led by Gandhi, they should pass this resolution without any opposition – in spite of all this, the resolution could only be adopted by a dangerously narrow majority. That demonstrates, beyond the shadow of a doubt, how solidly the country is backing the revolutionaries. In a way Gandhi deserved our thanks for having brought the question up for discussion and thus having shown to the world at large that even the Congress – that stronghold of non-violence – is at least as much, if not more, with the revolutionaries as with him.

Gandhi on War Path

Having achieved a victory which cost him more than a defeat, Gandhi has returned to the attack in his article "The Cult of the Bomb". We will give it our closest attention before proceeding further. That article consists of three things – his faith, his opinion and his arguments. We will not discuss what is a matter of faith with him because reason has little in common with faith. Let us then take such of his opinions as are backed by arguments and his arguments proper, against what he calls violence and discuss them one by one.

Do the Masses Believe in Non-violence

He thinks that on the basis of his experience during his latest tour in the country, he is right in believing that the large masses of Indian humanity are yet untouched by the spirit of violence and that non-violence has come to stay as a political weapon. Let him not delude himself on the experiences of his latest tour in the country. Though it is true that the average leader confines his tours to places where only the mail train can conveniently land him while Gandhi has extended his tour limit to where a motorcar can take him, the practice of staying only with the richest people in the places visited, of spending most of his time on being complimented by his devotees in private and public, and of granting Darshan now and then to the illiterate masses whom he claims to understand so well, disqualifies him from claiming to know the mind of the masses. No man can claim to know a people's mind by seeing them from the public platform and giving them Darshan and Updesh. He can at the most claim to have told the masses what he thinks about things. Has Gandhi, during recent years, mixed in the social life of the masses? Has he sat with the peasant round the evening fire and tried to know what he thinks? Has he passed a single evening in the company of a factory labourer and shared with him his vows? We have, and therefore we claim to know what the masses think. We assure Gandhi that the average Indian, like the average human being, understands little of the fine theological niceties about Ahimsa and loving one's enemy. The way of the world is like this. You have a friend: you love him, sometimes so much that you even die for him. You have an enemy: you shun him, you fight against him and, if possible, kill him. The gospel of the revolutionaries is simple and straight. It is what has been since the days of Adam and Eve, and no man has any difficulty about understanding it. We affirm that the masses of India are solidly with us because we know it from personal experience. The day is not far off when they will flock in their thousands to work the will of the Revolution.

The Gospel of Love

Gandhi declares that his faith in the efficacy of non-violence has increased. That is to say, he believes more and more, that through his gospel of love and self-imposed suffering, he hopes someday to convert the foreign rulers to his way of thinking. Now, he has devoted his whole life to the preaching of his wonderful gospel and has practised it with unwavering constance, as few others have done. Will he let the world know how many enemies of India he has been able to turn into friends? How many O'Dwyers, Readings and Irwins has he been able to convert into friends of India? If none, how can India be expected to share his 'growing faith' that he will be able to persuade or compel England to agree to Indian Independence through the practice of non-violence?

What would have Happened?

If the bomb, that burst under the Viceroy's Special, had exploded properly, one of the two things suggested by Gandhi would have surely happened. The Viceroy would have either been badly injured or killed. Under such circumstances there certainly would have been no meeting between the leaders of political parties and the Viceroy. The uncalled for and undignified attempt on the part of these individuals, to lower the national prestige by knocking at the gates of the Government house with the beggar's bowl in their hands and dominion status on their lips, in spite of the clear terms of the Calcutta Ultimatum, would have been checkmated and the nation would have been the better off for that. If, fortunately, the explosion had been powerful enough to kill the Viceroy, one more enemy of India would have met a well deserved doom. The author of the Meerut prosecution and the Lahore and Bhusawal persecutions can appear a friend of India only to the enemies of her freedom. In spite of Gandhi and Nehru and their claims to political sagacity and statesmanship, Irwin has succeeded in shattering the unity between different political parties in the country that had resulted from the boycott of the Simon Commission. Even the Congress today is a house divided against itself. Who else, except the Viceroy and his olive tongue, have we to thank for our grave misfortunes? And yet, there exist people in our country who proclaim him a Friend of India!

The Future of the Congress

There might be those who have no regard for the Congress and hope nothing from it. If Gandhi thinks that the revolutionaries belong to the category, he wrongs them grievously. They fully realise the part played by Congress in awakening among the ignorant masses a keen desire for freedom. They expect great things of it in the future.

Though they hold firmly to their opinion, that so long as person like Sen Gupta whose wonderful intelligence compels him to discern the hand of the CID in the late attempt to blow up the Viceroy's Special, and persons like Ansari, who think abuse the better part of argument and know so little of politics as to make the ridiculous and fallacious assertion that no nation had achieved freedom by the bomb, have a determining voice in the affairs of the Congress, the country can hope little from it; they are hopefully looking forward to the day, when the mania of non-violence would have passed away from the Congress, and it would march arm in arm with the revolutionaries to their common goal of Complete Independence. This year it has accepted the ideal which the revolutionaries have preached and lived up to more than a quarter of a century. Let us hope the next year will see it endorse their methods also.

Violence and Military Expenditure

Gandhi is of opinion that as often as violence has been practised in the country, it has resulted in an increase of military expenditure. If his reference is to revolutionary activities during the last twenty-five years we dispute the accuracy of his statement and challenge him to prove his statement with facts and figures. If, on the other hand, he had the wars that have taken place in India since the British came here in mind, our reply is that even his modest experiment in Ahimsa and Satyagraha which had little to compare in it with the wars for independence produced its effect on the finances of the bureaucracy. Mass action, whether violent or non-violent, whether successful or unsuccessful, is bound to produce the same kind of repercussion on the finances of a state.

The Reforms

Why should Gandhi mix up the revolutionaries with the various constitutional reforms granted by the Government? They never cared or worked for the Morley–Minto Reforms, Montague Reforms and the like. These the British government threw before the constitutionalist agitators to lure them away from the right path. This was the bribe paid to them for their support to the Government in its policy of crushing and uprooting the revolutionaries. These toys – as Gandhi calls them – were sent to India for the benefit of those, who, from time to time, raised the cry of 'Home Rule', 'Self-Government', 'Responsible', 'Full Responsible Government', 'Dominion Status' and such other constitutional names for slavery. The revolutionaries never claim the Reforms as their achievements. They raised the standard of independence long ago. They have lived for it. They have ungrudgingly laid their lives down for the sake of this ideal. They claim that their sacrifices have produced a tremendous change in the mentality of the people. That their efforts have advanced the country a long way on the road to independence is granted by even those who do not see eye to eye with them in politics.

The Way of Progress

As to Gandhi's contention that violence impedes the march of progress and thus directly postpones the day of freedom, we can refer him to so many contemporary instances where violence has led to the social progress and political freedom of the people who practised it. Take the case of Russia and Turkey for example. In both countries the party of progress took over the state organisation through an armed revolution. Yet social progress and political freedom have not been impeded. Legislation, backed by force, has made the masses go 'double march' on the road of progress. The solitary example of Afghanistan cannot establish a political formula. It is rather the exception that proves the rule.

Failure of Non-cooperation

Gandhi is of opinion that the great awakening in the people, during the days of non-cooperation, was a result of the preaching of non-violence. It is wrong to assigm to non-violence the widespread awakening of the masses which, in fact, is manifested wherever a programme of direct action is adopted. In Russia, for instance, there came about widespread awakening in the peasants and workers when the communists launched forth their great programme of Militant Mass Action, though nobody preached non-violence to them. We will even go further and state that it was mainly the mania for non-violence and Gandhi's compromise mentality that brought about the disruption of the forces that had come together at the call of Mass Action. It is claimed that non-violence can be used as a weapon for righting political wrongs. To say the least, it is novel idea, yet untried. It failed to achieve what were considered to be the just rights of Indians in South Africa. It failed to bring 'Swaraj within a year' to the Indian masses in spite of the untiring labours of an army of national workers and one and a quarter crores of rupees. More recently, it failed to win for the Bardoli peasants what the leaders of the Satyagraha movement had promised them – the famous irreducible minimum of Gandhi and Patel. We know of no other trials non-violence has had on a country-wide scale. Up to this time non-violence has been blessed with one result – Failure. Little wonder, then, that the country refuses to give it another trial. In fact Satyagraha as preached by Gandhi is a form of agitation – a protest, leading up invariably, as has already been seen, to a compromise. It can hardly be of any use to a nation striving for national independence which can never come as the result of a compromise. The sooner we recognise that there can be no compromise between independence and slavery, the better.

Is it a New Era

'We are entering upon a new era', thinks Gandhi. The mere act of defining Swaraj as Complete Independence, this technical change in the Congress constitution, can hardly constitute a new era. It will be a great day indeed when the Congress will decide upon a country-wide programme of Mass Action, based on well recognised revolutionary principles. Till then the unfurling of the flag of Independence is a mockery and we concur with the following remarks of Sarla Devi Chaudhrani which she recently made in a press interview.

"The unfurling of the Flag of Independence", she says, "at just one minute after midnight of the 31 December, 1929, was too stagy for words – just as the GOC and the assistant GOC and others in gaudy uniforms were card board Grand Officers Commanding.

"The fact that the unfurling of the flag of Independence lay hanging in the balance till midnight of that date, and that the scales might have been turned at even the eleventh hour fifty-ninth minute had a message from the Viceroy or the Secretary of State come to the Congress granting Dominion Status, proves that Independence is not a heart hunger of the leaders but that the declaration of it is only like a petulant child's retort. It would have been a worthy action of the Indian National Congress if Independence was achieved first and declared afterwards."

It is true that the Congress orators will henceforth harangue the masses on Complete Independence instead of Dominion Status. They will call upon the people to prepare for a struggle in which one party is to deliver blows and the other is simply to receive them, till beaten and demoralised beyond hope of recovery. Can such a thing be named a struggle and can it ever lead the country to Complete Independence? It is all very well to hold fast to the highest ideal worthy of a nation, but it is nonetheless necessary to adopt the best, the most efficacious and tried means to achieve it, ere you became the laughing stock of the whole world.

No Bullying Please

Gandhi has called upon all those who are not past reason to withdraw their support from the revolutionaries and condemn their actions so that "our deluded patriots may, for want of nourishment to their violent spirit, realise the futility of violence and the great harm that violent activities have every time done". How easy and convenient it is to call people deluded, to declare them to be past reason, to call upon the public to withdraw its support and condemn them so that they may get isolated and be forced to suspend their activities, specially when a man holds the confidence of an influential section of the public! It is a pity that Gandhi does not and will not understand revolutionary psychology in spite of the life-long experience of public life. Life is a precious thing. It is dear to everyone. If a man becomes a revolutionary, if he goes about with his life in the hollow of his hand ready to sacrifice it at any moment, he does not do so merely for the fun of it. He does not risk his life merely because sometimes, when the crowd is in a sympathetic mood, it cries 'Bravo' in appreciation. He does it because his reason forces him to take that course, because his conscience dictates it. A revolutionary believes in reason more than anything. It is to reason, and reason alone, that he bows. No amount of abuse and condemnation, even if it emanates from the highest of the high can turn him from his set purpose. To think that a revolutionary will give up his ideas if public support and appreciation is withdrawn from him, is the highest folly. Many a revolutionary has, ere now, stepped on the scaffold and laid his life down for the cause, regardless of the curses that the constitutionalist agitators rained plentifully upon him. If you will have the revolutionaries suspend their activities, reason with them squarely. That is the one and the only way. For the rest let there be no doubt in anybody's mind. A revolutionary is the last person on earth to submit to bullying.

An Appeal

We take this opportunity to appeal to our countrymen – to the youth, to the workers and peasants, to the revolutionary intelligentsia – to come forward and join us in carrying aloft the banner of freedom. Let us establish a new order of society in which political and economic exploitation will be an impossibility. In the name of those gallant men and women who willingly accepted death so that we, their descendants, may lead a happier life, who toiled ceaselessly and perished for the poor, the famished, and exploited millions of India, we call upon every patriot to take up the fight in all seriousness. Let nobody toy with nation's freedom which is her very life, by making psychological experiments in non-violence and such other novelties. Our slavery is our shame. When shall we have courage and wisdom enough to be able to shake ourselves free of it? What is our great heritage of civilisation and culture worth if we have not enough self-respect left in us to prevent us from bowing surveillance to the commands of foreigners and paying homage to their flag and king?

Victory or Death

There is no crime that Britain has not committed in India. Deliberate misrule has reduced us to paupers, has 'bled us white'. As a race and a people we stand dishonoured and outraged. Do people still expect us to forget and to forgive? We shall have our revenge – a people's righteous revenge on the tyrant. Let cowards fall back and cringe for compromise and peace. We ask not for mercy and we give no quarter. Ours is a war to the end – to Victory or Death.

LONG LIVE THE REVOLUTION

Kartar Singh
President
Hindustan Socialist Republican Association

APPENDIX C: 4

This is the poem **Chhabil Das** recited to Sukhdeoraj in the 1960s.
It gives us an idea of his satirical talent, which he used effectively
in his tracts for the Naujawan Bharat Sabha.

राम और सीता छः पैसे में !
कृष्ण और राधा छः पैसे में !!
मैंने पुकारा रावण दे दो !
बोला तीन आने में ले लो !!
मैंने कहा ऐ मूरतवाले !
भोली भाली सूरत वाले !!
राम और सीता छः पैसे में !
कृष्ण और राधा छः पैसे में !!
लछमन सस्ता, शिवजी सस्ता !
रावण है क्यों इतना महँगा !!
बोला वे हैं छोटे-छोटे !
बनते हैं थोड़ी मिट्टी से !!
उफ रे ! रावण का मुँह काला !
लम्बा मोटा दस सिर वाला !!
जब भी हूं इसे मैं बनाता !
माल मसाला सब चुक जाता !!
बोला 'इसे बनाते क्यों हो !'
इतना माल लगाते क्यों हो ?'
राम को बेचो सीता बेचो !
लक्ष्मन बेचो शिवजी बेचो !!
बोला, इसकी माँग बहुत है !
घर घर इसकी धाक बहुत है !!
हर घर हर मन इसका मन्दर !
मुँह में राम तो रावण अन्दर !!
सीताराम के गए पुजारी !
अब है रावण की मुख्तारी !!
रावण का है राज जगत में !
खेत को खाये बाढ़ जगत में !!

GLOSSARY

Ahimsa	non-violence
Allah-o-Akbar	God is great
Bagh	Garden
Balidan Divas	day of sacrifice/martyrdom
Bande Mataram	Hail Mother
Bandi Jivan	Prison life
Desh	nation, place, environment
Desi	country-made, indigenous
Durga	Goddess of power
Ghadar	Mutiny
Ghat	a bathing place by the river side
Gita	a Hindu religious book
Halal	an Islamic way of animal slaughter
Hartal	strike
Hindustan Zindabad	Long Live India
Inquilab Zindabad	Long Live Revolution
Jhatka	a Sikh way of animal slaughter
Kal	time
Khaddar	cloth made of hand-spun cotton
Kharif	summer crop
Kirti	name of a newspaper, *lit.* fame
Kisan	peasant
Kolis	a backward caste in India

Naujawan	youth
Nawab	a title of rank conferred on Muslim nobles
Pandal	canopy
Panchayat Raj	republican state
Patra	recipient, deserving person
Purana Qila	Old Fort
Raj	rule, kingdom
Rishis	sages
Sabha	assembly, conference, organization
Sadhana	spiritual practice
Sadhu	sage
Sahukar	moneylender
Sat Sri Akal	a Sikh way of greeting
Shaheed	martyr
Shakti	power, force
Swadeshi	indigenous
Taluka	an administrative unit
Tapasya	penance
Tehsil	an administrative unit
Thana	police station
Utsav	festival
Veda	earliest Hindu religious scriptures
Vinashaya cha dushkritam	destruction of the wicked
Zindabad	Long live

Bibliography and Sources

A. Primary Sources

a. *Proceedings of the Home Political Department and the Fortnightly Reports on the political situation in India from 1908 to 1932. National Archives of India, New Delhi.*

b. *Proceedings of the annual sessions of the Indian National Congress from 1924 to 1931. Nehru Memorial Museum and Library, New Delhi.*

c. *AICC files 1925–32. Nehru Memorial Museum and Library, New Delhi.*

d. *Private Papers*

    i. Meerut Conspiracy Case Papers, NMML
    ii. Lahore Conspiracy Case Papers,NMML
    iii. Delhi Conspiracy Case Papers, NAI
    iv. MN Roy Papers, NMML
    v. Gopi Chand Bhargava Papers, NMML
    vi. Thakurdas Papers, NMML
    vii. Halifax Papers, NMML.

e. *Diaries*

    i. Diary of Sardar Bhagat Singh, available with the author.

    ii. Bhagat Singh, *The Jail Notebook and Other Writings*, compiled, with an Introduction by Chaman Lal, New Delhi, 2007.

f.   Interviews, conversations and correspondence

   i.   Shri Manmathnath Gupta
   ii.   Shri Shiv Verma
   iii.   Shri Kultar Singh
   iv.   Shri Jaidev Kapoor
   v.   Comrade Ramchandra
   vi.   Smt Durga Devi Vohra
   vii.   Shri Rajendra Pal Singh 'Warrior'
   viii. Shri Vishnu Sharan Dublish

B.   Secondary Sources

a.   Newspapers

The Tribune, Lahore, 1924 to 1932.
The Bombay Chronicle, Bombay, 1924 to 1931.
The People, Lahore, 1929 to 1931.
The Pioneer, Lucknow, 1925 to 1931.
Young India, Ahmedabad, 1924 to 1931.
The Times of India, Bombay, 1926 to 1932.
The Amrita Bazar Patrika,Calcutta, 1925 to 1931.
The Leader, Allahabad, 1928 to 1931.
The Searchlight, Patna, 1926 to 1931.
The Punjabee, Lahore, 1908.
Abhyudaya, Allahabad, 1930 to 1931.

b.   Journals, magazines and periodicals

The Modern Review, Calcutta, 1909 to 1931.
Chand, Allahabad, 1927 to 1931.
Mukti, New Delhi, July 1972.
Yuvakranti, New Delhi, 1972.
Souvenir on the occasion of Chandrashekhar Azad's Balidan Diwas,
    New Delhi, February 26-27, 1979.
Souvenir on the occasion of Jatin Das's 50th Balidan Diwas, New
Delhi, September 13, 1979.

c.   Books

Argov, D, *Moderates and Extremists in the Indian Nationalist Movement*,
Bombay, 1967.

Azad, Abul Kalam, *India Wins Freedom*, Bombay, 1959.

Azad, Chaman Lal, *Revolutionary Movement in India*, New Delhi.

Bipan Chandra, *The Rise and Growth of Economic Nationalism in India*, New Delhi, 1966.

Bose, SC, *The Indian Struggle, 1920–42*, Calcutta, 1967.

Brown, EC, *Har Dayal: Hindu Revolutionary and Rationalist*, Delhi, 1975.

Chatterjee, JC, *In Search of Freedom*, Calcutta, 1967.

Chatterjee, NL, *India's Freedom Struggle*, Allahabad, 1958.

Chattopadhayaya, Debiprasad (ed.), *History and Society*, Calcutta, 1978.

Chaturvedi, BD (ed.), *Yash ka Dharohar*, Delhi, n.d.

Chauhan, Shivdan Singh (ed.), *Prithvi Singh Azad in Lenin's Land*, New Delhi, 1980.

Chirol, Valentine, *Indian Unrest*, New Delhi, 1979.

Coatman, J, *Years of Destiny*, London, 1932.

Collected Works of Mahatma Gandhi, New Delhi, Vol.XXII to XLVIII.

Deol, GS, *Shaheed Bhagat Singh*, Patiala, 1985.

Deol, GS, *Shaheed-e-Azam Bhagat Singh: The Man and His Ideology*, New Delhi, 1978.

Desai, AR, *Social Background of Indian Nationalism*, Bombay, 1959.

Dutt RC, *The Economic History of India*, New Delhi, 1963.

Dutt, RP, *India Today*, Bombay, 1949.

Ghosh, Ajoy, *Articles and Speeches*,Moscow, 1962.

Gopal, Ram, *Lokmanya Tilak*, Bombay, 1965.

Gopal, S, *Viceroyalty of Lord Irwin*, Oxford, 1957.

Grewal, PMS, *Bhagat Singh: Liberation's Blazing Star*, New Delhi, 2007.

Gupta, AC (ed.), *Studies in Bengal Renaissance*, Calcutta, 1958.

Gupta, DN (ed.), *Bhagat Singh: Select Speeches & Writings*, New Delhi, 2007.

Gupta, Maya and Gupta, Amit Kumar, *Defying Death, Struggles against Imperialism and Feudalism*, New Delhi, 2001.

Gupta, MN, *The History of the Indian Revolutionary Movement*, Bombay, 1972.

Gupta, MN, *Bhagat Singh and his Times*, New Delhi, 1977.

Gupta, MN, *They Lived Dangerously*, Delhi, 1969.

Haithcox, JP, *Communism and Nationalism in India*, Bombay, 1971.

Hale, HW, *Political Trouble in India 1917–1937*, Allahabad, 1974.

Iyer, G Subramania, *Some Economic Aspects of the British Rule in India*, Madras, 1903.

Jayakar, MR, *The Story of My Life*, Vol.II, Bombay, 1959.

Josh, Sohan Singh, *My Meetings with Bhagat Singh and on Other Early Revolutionaries*, New Delhi, 1976.

Josh, Sohan Singh, *Hindustan Ghadr Party: A Short History*, New Delhi, 1977.

Kamlesh Mohan, *Militant Nationalism in the Punjab 1919–1935*, New Delhi, 1985.

Keer, Dhananjay, *Veer Savarkar*, Bombay, 1966.

Keer, Dhananjay, *Mahatma Gandhi: Political Saint and Unarmed Prophet*, Bombay, 1973.

Kerr, JC, *Political Trouble in India*, Delhi, 1973.

Khullar, KK, *Shaheed Bhagat Singh*, New Delhi, 1981.

Kumar, Kapil, *Peasant Movement in Oudh, 1918–22*, New Delhi, 1984.

Laushey, David M, *Bengal Renaissance and Marxist Left*, Calcutta, 1975.

Majumdar BB, *Indian Political Associations and Reform of Legislatures, 1818–1917*, Calcutta, 1965.

Majumdar, RC, *Three Phases of India's Struggle for Freedom*, Bombay, 1961.

Mazumdar, BB, *Militant Nationalism in India and Its Socio-Religious Background 1897–1917*, Calcutta, 1966.

Mathur, LP, *The Indian Revolutionary Movement in the USA*, New Delhi, 1970.

Mazumdar, SN, *In Search of a Revolutionary Ideology and a Revolutionary Programme*, New Delhi, 1979.

Mitra, KK, *The Indian Annual Register*, Calcutta.

Mukherjee, Hiren, *India's Struggle for Freedom*, Bombay, 1948.

Naoroji, Dadabhai, *Poverty and Un-British Rule in India*, London, 1901.

Nayar, Kuldip, *The Martyr-Bhagat Singh: Experiments in Revolution*, New Delhi, 2000.

Nehru, Jawaharlal, *An Autobiography*, New Delhi, 1962.

Nigam, NK, *Balidan: Chandrashekhar Azad ki Romanchkari Jeewani*, Delhi, n.d.

Noorani AG , *The Trial of Bhagat Singh, Politics of Justice*, OUP, New Delhi, 1996.

Pal, BC, *Birth of Our New Nationalism, Memoirs of My Life and Times*, Vol.I, Calcutta.

Raghuvanshi, VPS, *Indian Nationalist Movement and Thought*, Agra, 1951.

Rai, Lajpat, *Unhappy India*, Calcutta, 1928.

Reisler, IM and Goldberg, NM (ed.), *Tilak and the Struggle for Indian Freedom*, New Delhi, 1966.

Roy, MN, *India in Transition*, Bombay, 1971.

Sandhu, Virendra, *Amar Shaheed Bhagat Singh*, New Delhi, 1974.

Sandhu Virendra, *Yugdrishta Bhagat Singh, Delhi*, 1968.

Sanyal, Jatindra Nath, *Amar Shaheed Sardar Bhagat Singh*, Mirzapur, 1970.

Sanyal, Sachindranath, *Bandi Jivan*, in two volumes, Allahabad.

Sarkar, Sumit, *The Swadeshi Movement in Bengal, 1903–1908*, New Delhi, 1973.

Selected Works of Jawaharlal Nehru, Vols. 3&4.

Sen, SP (ed.), *Dictionary of National Biography*, 4 volumes, Calcutta,

Sharma, RS and Jha, V (eds.), *Indian Society: Historical Probings* , New Delhi, 1974.

Singh, Jagmohan and Lal, Chaman (eds.), *Bhagat Singh Aur unke Sathiyon ke Dastavez*, Delhi, 1987.

Sitaramayya, Pattabhi, *The History of the Indian National Congress*, Bombay, 1946.

Sukhdeoraj, *Jab Jyoti Jagi*, Mirzapur, 1971.

Thakur, Gopal, *Bhagat Singh – The Man and His Ideas*, New Delhi, 1976.

Thapar, Mathradas, *Amar Shaheed Sukhdev*, New Delhi, 1980.

Vaishampayan, *Amar Shaheed Chandrashekhar Azad*, Vol.II, Varanasi, 1967.

Verma, Shiv, *Memoirs*, Kanpur, 1974.

Watson, Miss Blanche (ed.), *Gandhi and Non-violent Resistance*, Madras, 1923.

Yashpal, *Sinhavalocan*, 3 volumes, Lucknow, 1951.

INDEX